Children's
Atlas
of the
United
States

Maps created by
MapQuest.com. Inc.

MAPQUEST.

Gareth Stevens Publishing
A WORLD ALMANAC EDUCATION GROUP COMPANY

Please visit our web site at: www.garethstevens.com
For a free color catalog describing Gareth Stevens' list
of high-quality books and multimedia programs, call
1-800-542-2595 (USA) or 1-800-387-3178 (Canada).
Gareth Stevens Publishing's fax: (414) 332-3567.

This edition published in 2004 by
Gareth Stevens Publishing
A World Almanac Education Group Company
330 West Olive Street, Suite 100
Milwaukee, Wisconsin 53212 USA

Copyright © 2003

Library of Congress Cataloging-in-Publication Data

MapQuest.com, Inc.
    Children's atlas of the United States.
        p. cm.
    Maps copyrighted by MapQuest.
    Includes index.
    Summary: Maps, illustrations, photographs, and text
present information about the United States as a whole,
as well as each of the fifty states, Washington, D.C.,
Puerto Rico, and other outlying areas.
    ISBN 0-8368-3778-9 (lib. bdg.)
    1. Children's atlases. 2. United States—Maps for
children. [1. Atlases. 2. United States—Maps.] I. Title.
G1200.M25   2003
912.73—dc21   2003055012

Cover images: © CORBIS

Photographs on pages 10–11 (from Nature, Landscapes,
Hawaii, Caribbean disks), 14–15 (from Arctic disk) Copyright
© 2002 Corel Corp. and their suppliers.

Photographs on pages 10–11 (from Vols. 16, 44), pages 14–15
(from Vols. 16, 44) Copyright © 2002 PhotoDisc, Inc.

Photograph on page 10 (Tundra) Copyright © Tom Dew,
National Park Service; Alaska Division of Tourism.

Gareth Stevens editorial direction:
    Mark J. Sachner
Gareth Stevens art direction/cover design:
    Tammy Gruenewald

Using the index and grid to find information quickly

All of the political maps in the *World Almanac Children's Atlas of the United States* use a grid system to help you locate specific cities or points of interest. There are numbers across the top and bottom of each map and letters along both sides. These numbers and letter are used in the index to give you directions to find what you are looking for. For example, to find out where Cleveland, Ohio, is located, you would look up Cleveland in the index. The index entry for Cleveland shows the page number of the map in bold and the grid location next to it: Cleveland…**104** B4. To find Cleveland, go to page 104, draw an imaginary line across from B and down from 4, and you'll find Cleveland.

About This Atlas

The Children's Atlas of the United States is the perfect introduction to our country and the states that make it unique.

Begin with the United States political and physical maps that detail state and international boundaries, capitals, mountain ranges, bodies of water, and other geographical features of the country.

Follow that with the thematic maps that give you insight into the country's diverse characteristics and history. Landforms, weather, climate, and vegetation maps highlight the country's natural resources. A series of historical maps shows you how the land that is now the United States evolved from the times of the first Americans. You'll see how exploration, colonization and territorial growth formed the country. Historical maps help you visualize the great changes that have shaped American history.

With this picture in mind, you can explore the states in each of the country's six regions: New England, Middle Atlantic, Southeast, Midwest, Southwest, and West.

Arranged alphabetically, each two-page state entry contains a political, physical and economic map. You'll see cities, counties, parks, mountains, rivers, and major industries. An "almanac" fact box and a brief description of the state's history, people, way of life, and tourist attractions help you discover what's fun and unique about each state. For instance, did you know that the highest and lowest points in the contiguous U.S. are both in California?

Colorful and up-to-date, this atlas is a wonderful way to discover the many diverse states that make up the U.S.A. It will help make basic geography and social studies concepts interesting and easy to understand.

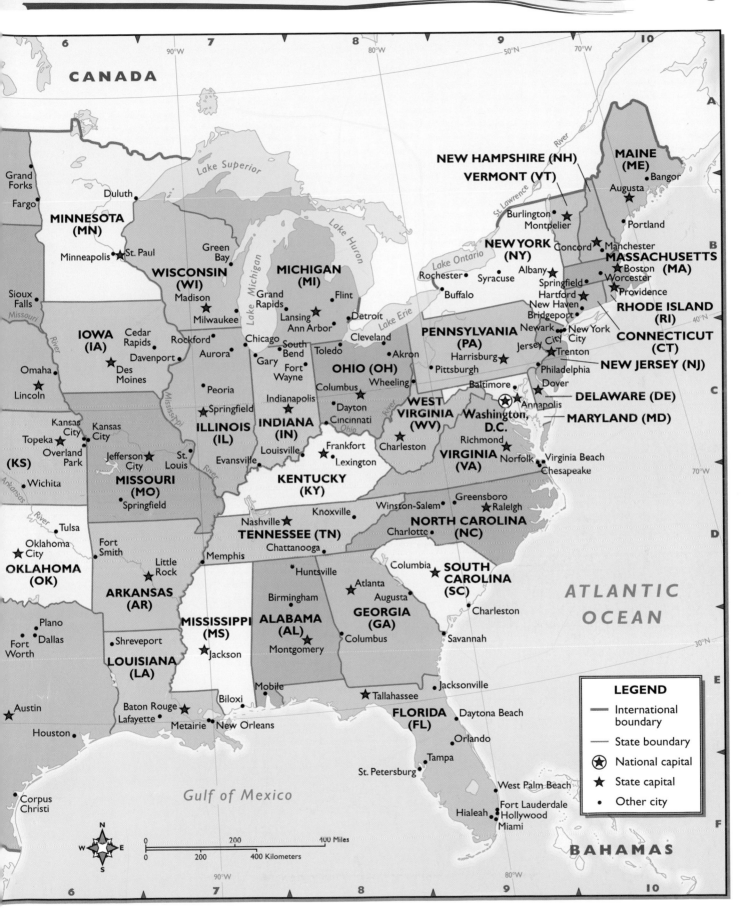

CANADA

Lake Superior

MINNESOTA (MN)
Grand Forks
Fargo
Duluth
Minneapolis ★ St. Paul
Sioux Falls

Missouri River

IOWA (IA)
Cedar Rapids
Davenport
Omaha
Lincoln
Des Moines ★

MISSOURI (MO)
Kansas City
Topeka ★ Kansas City
Overland Park
Jefferson City ★ St. Louis
(KS)
Wichita
Springfield

OKLAHOMA (OK)
Tulsa
Oklahoma City ★
Fort Smith

ARKANSAS (AR)
Little Rock ★

LOUISIANA (LA)
Plano
Fort Worth • Dallas
Shreveport
Austin ★
Houston
Baton Rouge ★
Lafayette
Metairie • New Orleans

Corpus Christi

WISCONSIN (WI)
Green Bay
Madison ★
Milwaukee
Rockford

MICHIGAN (MI)
Grand Rapids
Flint
Lansing ★
Ann Arbor
Detroit

Lake Michigan
Lake Huron

Chicago
Aurora
South Bend
Gary
Fort Wayne
Peoria

ILLINOIS (IL)
Springfield ★

INDIANA (IN)
Indianapolis ★
Dayton
Cincinnati
Evansville
Louisville

KENTUCKY (KY)
Frankfort ★
Lexington

Ohio River

TENNESSEE (TN)
Nashville ★
Knoxville
Memphis
Chattanooga

MISSISSIPPI (MS)
Jackson ★

ALABAMA (AL)
Huntsville
Birmingham
Montgomery ★

Mobile
Biloxi

GEORGIA (GA)
Atlanta ★
Augusta
Columbus

FLORIDA (FL)
Tallahassee ★
Jacksonville
Daytona Beach
Orlando
Tampa
St. Petersburg
West Palm Beach
Fort Lauderdale
Hialeah • Hollywood
Miami

Columbia

SOUTH CAROLINA (SC)
Charleston
Savannah

NORTH CAROLINA (NC)
Greensboro
Winston-Salem • Raleigh ★
Charlotte

Columbus ★
Toledo
Akron
Cleveland
Wheeling

OHIO (OH)

Lake Erie
Lake Ontario

WEST VIRGINIA (WV)
Charleston ★

VIRGINIA (VA)
Richmond ★
Norfolk
Virginia Beach
Chesapeake

PENNSYLVANIA (PA)
Harrisburg ★
Pittsburgh

Washington, D.C. ✪
Annapolis ★
Baltimore
Dover ★
DELAWARE (DE)
MARYLAND (MD)

NEW YORK (NY)
Rochester
Syracuse
Buffalo
Albany ★

St. Lawrence River

NEW HAMPSHIRE (NH)
VERMONT (VT)
Burlington
Montpelier ★
Concord ★
Manchester

MAINE (ME)
Augusta ★
Bangor
Portland

MASSACHUSETTS (MA)
Springfield
Boston ★
Worcester
Providence ★
RHODE ISLAND (RI)
Hartford ★
New Haven
Bridgeport
Newark • New York City
Jersey City
Trenton ★
CONNECTICUT (CT)
NEW JERSEY (NJ)
Philadelphia

ATLANTIC OCEAN

Gulf of Mexico

BAHAMAS

90°W   80°W   50°N   70°W
40°N
70°W
30°N
80°W
90°W

N
W E
S

0   200   400 Miles
0   200   400 Kilometers

LEGEND
— International boundary
— State boundary
✪ National capital
★ State capital
• Other city

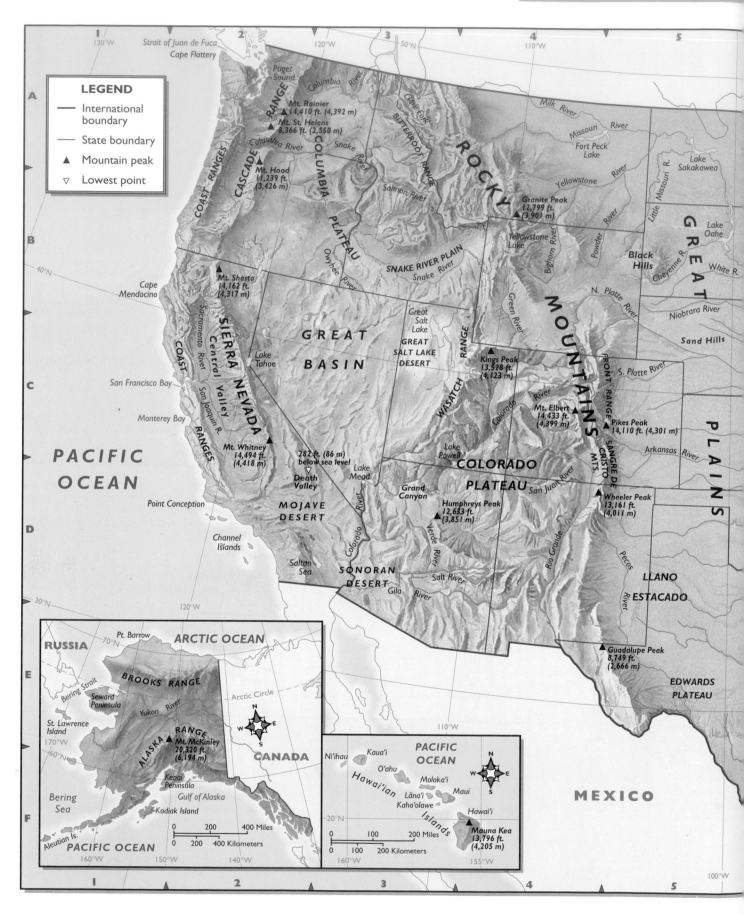

LEGEND
International boundary
State boundary
▲ Mountain peak
▽ Lowest point

Strait of Juan de Fuca
Cape Flattery
Puget Sound
Columbia River
COAST RANGES
CASCADE RANGE
Mt. Rainier 14,410 ft. (4,392 m)
Mt. St. Helens 8,366 ft. (2,550 m)
Columbia River
Mt. Hood 11,239 ft. (3,426 m)
COLUMBIA PLATEAU
Snake River
Owyhee River
Clark Fork
BITTERROOT RANGE
Salmon River
SNAKE RIVER PLAIN
Snake River
ROCKY
Milk River
Missouri River
Fort Peck Lake
Yellowstone River
Granite Peak 12,799 ft. (3,901 m)
Yellowstone Lake
Bighorn River
Powder River
GREAT
Lake Sakakawea
Lake Oahe
Black Hills
Cheyenne R.
White R.
Cape Mendocino
Mt. Shasta 14,162 ft. (4,317 m)
Sacramento River
SIERRA NEVADA
Central Valley
GREAT BASIN
Lake Tahoe
Great Salt Lake
GREAT SALT LAKE DESERT
WASATCH RANGE
Kings Peak 13,528 ft. (4,123 m)
Green River
N. Platte River
Niobrara River
Sand Hills
MOUNTAINS
COAST RANGES
San Francisco Bay
San Joaquin R.
Monterey Bay
Mt. Whitney 14,494 ft. (4,418 m)
282 ft. (86 m) below sea level
▽ Death Valley
Lake Mead
Colorado River
Lake Powell
COLORADO PLATEAU
Mt. Elbert 14,433 ft. (4,399 m)
FRONT RANGE
Pikes Peak 14,110 ft. (4,301 m)
S. Platte River
Arkansas River
PLAINS
PACIFIC OCEAN
Point Conception
MOJAVE DESERT
Grand Canyon
Humphreys Peak 12,633 ft. (3,851 m)
Verde River
San Juan River
Rio Grande
SANGRE DE CRISTO MTS.
Wheeler Peak 13,161 ft. (4,011 m)
Pecos River
Channel Islands
Salton Sea
Colorado River
SONORAN DESERT
Salt River
Gila River
LLANO ESTACADO
Guadalupe Peak 8,749 ft. (2,666 m)
EDWARDS PLATEAU
MEXICO

RUSSIA
Pt. Barrow
ARCTIC OCEAN
70°N
BROOKS RANGE
Bering Strait
Seward Peninsula
Yukon River
Arctic Circle
St. Lawrence Island
170°W
ALASKA RANGE
Mt. McKinley 20,320 ft. (6,194 m)
60°N
CANADA
Kenai Peninsula
Bering Sea
Gulf of Alaska
Kodiak Island
Aleutian Is.
PACIFIC OCEAN
160°W   150°W   140°W

0   200   400 Miles
0   200   400 Kilometers

Ni'ihau
Kaua'i
PACIFIC OCEAN
O'ahu
Moloka'i
Hawai'ian
Lāna'i   Maui
Kaho'olawe
Islands
20°N
Hawai'i
Mauna Kea 13,796 ft. (4,205 m)

0   100   200 Miles
0   100   200 Kilometers
160°W   155°W

100°W

130°W   120°W   50°N   110°W   40°N   30°N   120°W   110°W   100°W

CANADA

Lake of the Woods

MESABI RANGE

Isle Royale

Lake Superior

Upper Peninsula

Lake Michigan

Lower Peninsula

Grand River

Lake Huron

Lake St. Clair

Lake Erie

Lake Ontario

Red River of the North

St. Croix R.

Minnesota River

Mississippi

Wisconsin River

River

Rock River

Illinois River

Kaskaskia River

Wabash

White River

River

Green River

Cumberland River

Ohio

Kentucky R.

Scioto River

River

James River

Des Moines River

Cedar River

Iowa River

Loup R.

Platte River

Missouri

Republican R.

Kansas River

River

Smoky Hill R

Flint Hills

CENTRAL LOWLAND

OZARK PLATEAU

BOSTON MTS.

White

Cimarron River

Canadian

River

OUACHITA MOUNTAINS

Arkansas River

Ouachita

Red

River

River

Mississippi

Tombigbee

Yazoo River

River

Pearl River

Sabine River

River

Brazos River

Trinity River

Colorado River

Nueces River

Rio Grande

Padre Island

Galveston Bay

GULF COASTAL PLAIN

Lake Pontchartrain

Mississippi Delta

Mobile Bay

Alabama River

Apalachicola

Chattahoochee River

Flint River

St. Lawrence River

WHITE MTS.

Mt. Washington 6,288 ft. (1,917 m)

Lake Champlain

GREEN MTS.

Merrimack R.

ADIRONDACK MTS.

Hudson River

Connecticut River

Genesee R.

Allegheny

ALLEGHENY PLATEAU

APPALACHIAN MOUNTAINS

ALLEGHENY MOUNTAINS

Susquehanna River

Delaware

River

Potomac R.

BLUE RIDGE MTS.

James River

Roanoke River

CUMBERLAND PLATEAU

Tennessee River

Mt. Mitchell 6,684 ft. (2,037 m)

PIEDMONT

Pee Dee R.

Savannah River

Oconee River

Ocmulgee River

Altamaha River

ATLANTIC COASTAL PLAIN

St. Johns River

Saint John River

Penobscot River

Quoddy Head

Gulf of Maine

Cape Cod

Long Island Sound

Long Island

Delaware Bay

Chesapeake Bay

Cape Hatteras

Cape Fear

ATLANTIC OCEAN

Cape Canaveral

Tampa Bay

Lake Okeechobee

Florida Keys

Straits of Florida

BAHAMAS

Gulf of Mexico

N
W E
S

0   200   400 Miles

0   200   400 Kilometers

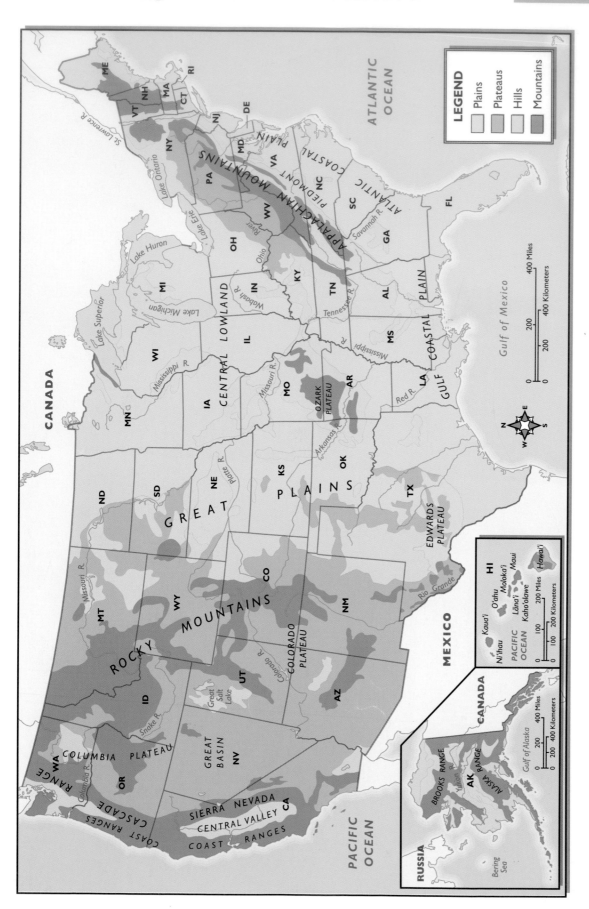

Landform Regions

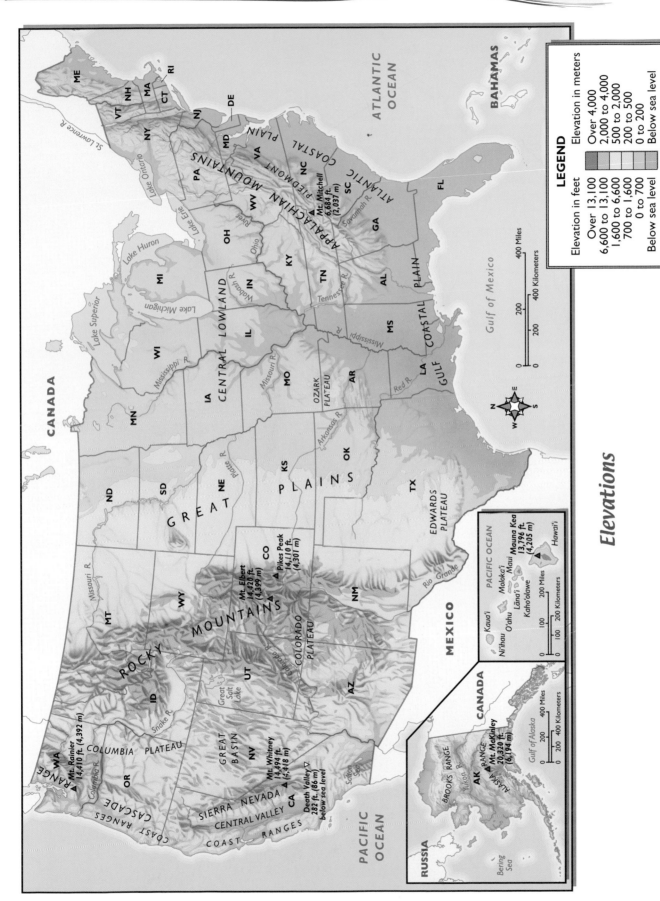

Elevations

Highland

Marine

Mediterranean

Tundra

Semiarid

Arid

Subarctic

WASHINGTON
Seattle
Olympia
Spokane

OREGON
Portland
Salem
Eugene

Great Falls
Helena
MONTANA
Billings

NORTH DAKOTA
Bismarck

IDAHO
Boise

SOUTH DAKOTA
Pierre

Pocatello
WYOMING
Casper

Reno
NEVADA
Sacramento
Carson City
Oakland
San Francisco
San Jose

Ogden
Salt Lake City
Provo
UTAH

Cheyenne

NEBRASKA

Denver
COLORADO
Colorado Springs
Pueblo

KANSAS

CALIFORNIA

Las Vegas

Wichita

Los Angeles
Long Beach

San Diego

ARIZONA
Phoenix

Tucson

Santa Fe
Albuquerque

NEW MEXICO

OKLAHOMA
Oklahoma City

PACIFIC OCEAN

40°N

120°W

30°N

El Paso

Fort Worth

TEXAS
Austin
San Antonio

Corpus Christi
Laredo

MEXICO

RUSSIA
70°N
Arctic Circle
Nome
Fairbanks
ALASKA
CANADA
Anchorage
Juneau
60°N
Bering Sea
170°W
Gulf of Alaska
0   200   400 Miles
0   200   400 Kilometers
160°W   150°W   140°W
110°W

HAWAII
Honolulu
PACIFIC OCEAN
Hilo
20°N
0   100   200 Miles
0   100   200 Kilometers
160°W   155°W

Humid continental

CANADA

Lake Superior

MINNESOTA
Grand Forks
Fargo
Duluth

WISCONSIN
St. Paul
Minneapolis
Madison
Milwaukee
Green Bay

Sioux Falls

IOWA
Cedar Rapids
Davenport
Rockford
Omaha
Des Moines
Lincoln

MICHIGAN
Lake Michigan
Lake Huron
Grand Rapids
Lansing
Detroit

Lake Ontario
Lake Erie
Buffalo

VERMONT
Burlington
Montpelier

MAINE
Augusta
Portland
Concord

NEW HAMPSHIRE
MASSACHUSETTS
Boston
Providence

NEW YORK
Albany

RHODE ISLAND
CONNECTICUT
Hartford

ATLANTIC OCEAN

50°N
60°W
40°N
70°W

ILLINOIS
Chicago
Gary
Peoria
Springfield

INDIANA
Fort Wayne
Indianapolis

OHIO
Toledo
Cleveland
Columbus
Wheeling

PENNSYLVANIA
Harrisburg
Pittsburgh

Newark
New York City
Trenton
NEW JERSEY
Philadelphia
Dover
DELAWARE
Baltimore
Annapolis
MARYLAND
Washington, D.C.

Kansas City
Kansas City
Topeka

MISSOURI
Jefferson City
St. Louis

Evansville
Cincinnati
WEST VIRGINIA
Frankfort
Charleston

Richmond
Norfolk
VIRGINIA

Humid subtropical

KENTUCKY
Louisville

Tulsa

TENNESSEE
Nashville
Knoxville
Memphis

Raleigh
NORTH CAROLINA
Charlotte

Fort Smith

ARKANSAS
Little Rock

Columbia
SOUTH CAROLINA
Charleston

Dallas

MISSISSIPPI
ALABAMA
Birmingham
Montgomery
Jackson
Shreveport

Atlanta
Columbus
GEORGIA
Savannah

LOUISIANA
Baton Rouge
New Orleans
Biloxi
Mobile

Jacksonville
Tallahassee
FLORIDA
Orlando
Tampa
St. Petersburg
Fort Lauderdale
Miami

30°N
80°W

Houston

Gulf of Mexico

N W E S

0   200   400 Miles
0   200   400 Kilometers

90°W
Tropic of Cancer

Tropical wet

Tropical wet and dry

LEGEND

Tropical wet
Hot and wet all year

Tropical wet and dry
Hot all year; wet with one dry season

Arid
Very dry; hot or cold depending on elevation

Semiarid
Little precipitation; hot or cold depending on elevation

Mediterranean
Mild, wet winter; hot, dry summer

Humid subtropical
Mild to warm winter; hot summer; wet all year

Marine
Mild winter; cool summer; wet all year

Humid continental
Cold winter; hot summer; medium precipitation

Subarctic
Very cold winter; cool summer; wet

Tundra
Very cold winter; cold summer; dry

Highland
High mountains; climate varies with elevation

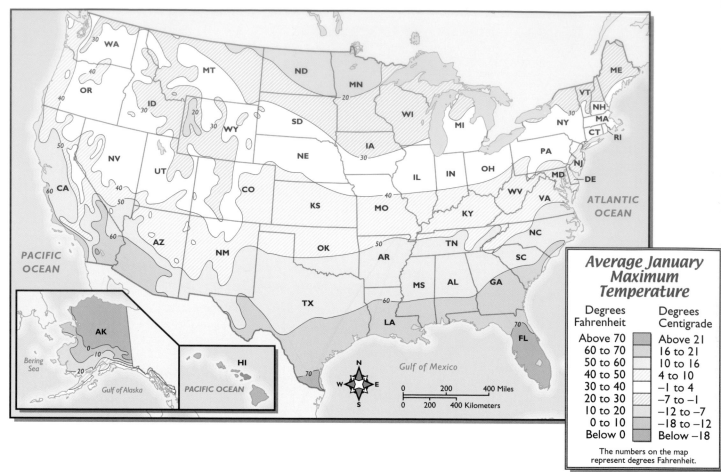

Average January Maximum Temperature

Degrees Fahrenheit	Degrees Centigrade
Above 70	Above 21
60 to 70	16 to 21
50 to 60	10 to 16
40 to 50	4 to 10
30 to 40	−1 to 4
20 to 30	−7 to −1
10 to 20	−12 to −7
0 to 10	−18 to −12
Below 0	Below −18

The numbers on the map represent degrees Fahrenheit.

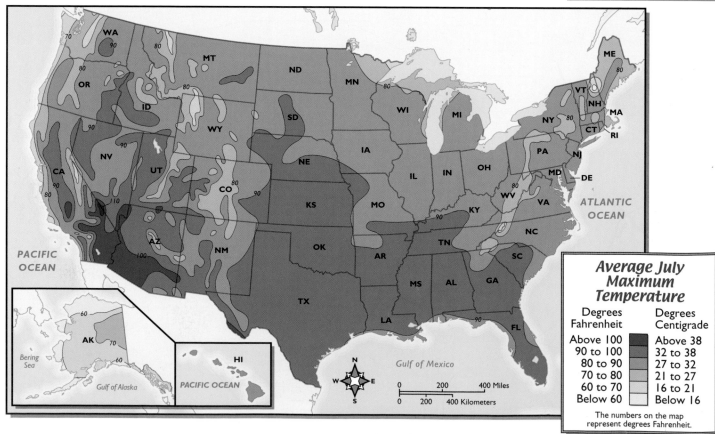

Average July Maximum Temperature

Degrees Fahrenheit	Degrees Centigrade
Above 100	Above 38
90 to 100	32 to 38
80 to 90	27 to 32
70 to 80	21 to 27
60 to 70	16 to 21
Below 60	Below 16

The numbers on the map represent degrees Fahrenheit.

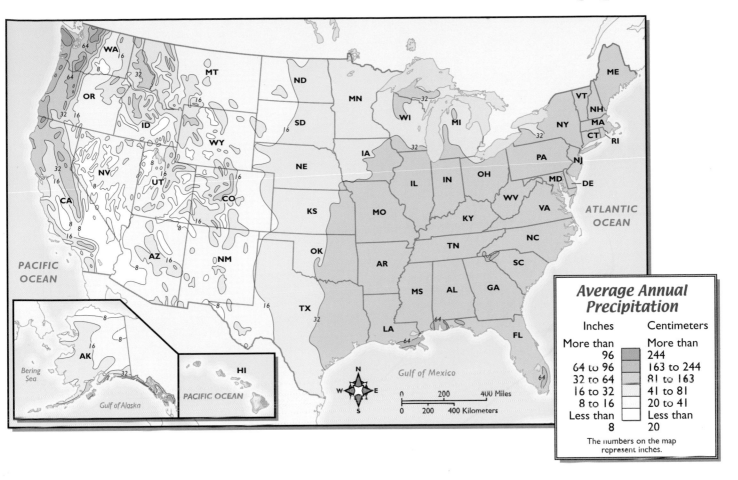

Average Annual Precipitation

Inches	Centimeters
More than 96	More than 244
64 to 96	163 to 244
32 to 64	81 to 163
16 to 32	41 to 81
8 to 16	20 to 41
Less than 8	Less than 20

The numbers on the map represent inches.

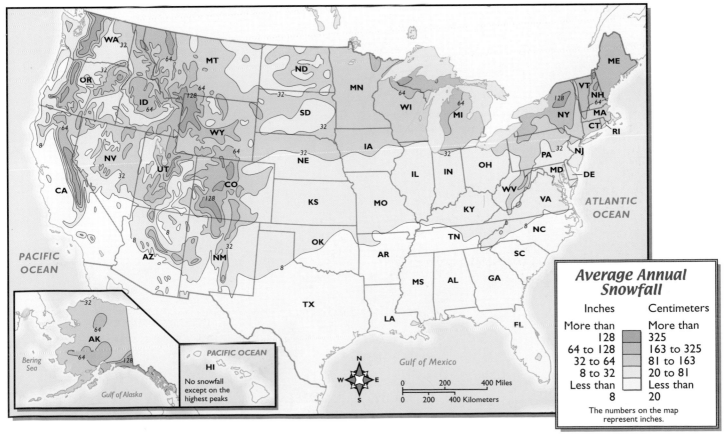

Average Annual Snowfall

Inches	Centimeters
More than 128	More than 325
64 to 128	163 to 325
32 to 64	81 to 163
8 to 32	20 to 81
Less than 8	Less than 20

The numbers on the map represent inches.

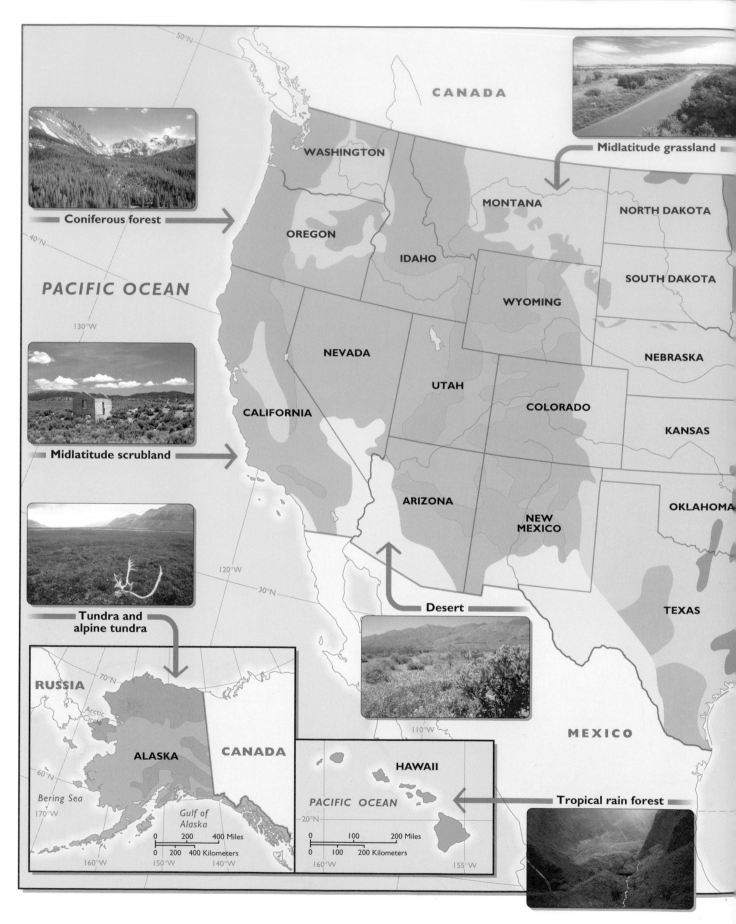

CANADA

Midlatitude grassland

WASHINGTON

MONTANA

NORTH DAKOTA

OREGON

IDAHO

SOUTH DAKOTA

WYOMING

Coniferous forest

PACIFIC OCEAN

50°N

130°W

40°N

NEVADA

UTAH

COLORADO

NEBRASKA

CALIFORNIA

KANSAS

Midlatitude scrubland

ARIZONA

NEW
MEXICO

OKLAHOMA

TEXAS

120°W

30°N

Tundra and
alpine tundra

Desert

110°W

MEXICO

RUSSIA

70°N

Arctic
Circle

ALASKA

CANADA

HAWAII

60°N

Bering Sea

PACIFIC OCEAN

Tropical rain forest

170°W

Gulf of
Alaska

20°N

0   200   400 Miles

0   100   200 Miles

0   200   400 Kilometers

0   100   200 Kilometers

160°W   150°W   140°W

160°W   155°W

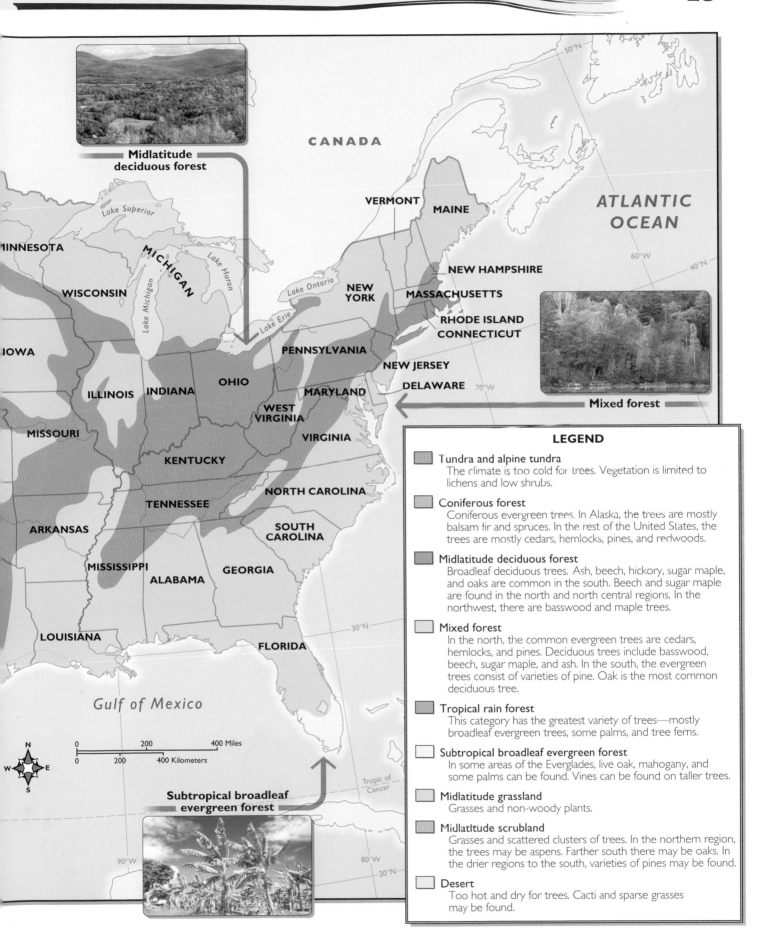

Midlatitude
deciduous forest

CANADA

VERMONT

MAINE

NEW HAMPSHIRE

NEW YORK

MASSACHUSETTS

RHODE ISLAND
CONNECTICUT

NEW JERSEY

DELAWARE

ATLANTIC
OCEAN

Mixed forest

MINNESOTA

Lake Superior

MICHIGAN

Lake Huron

WISCONSIN

Lake Michigan

Lake Ontario

Lake Erie

PENNSYLVANIA

OHIO

MARYLAND

IOWA

ILLINOIS   INDIANA

WEST
VIRGINIA

VIRGINIA

MISSOURI

KENTUCKY

NORTH CAROLINA

TENNESSEE

ARKANSAS

SOUTH
CAROLINA

MISSISSIPPI   GEORGIA

ALABAMA

LOUISIANA

FLORIDA

Gulf of Mexico

Subtropical broadleaf
evergreen forest

Tropic of
Cancer

0   200   400 Miles
0   200   400 Kilometers

LEGEND

Tundra and alpine tundra
The climate is too cold for trees. Vegetation is limited to lichens and low shrubs.

Coniferous forest
Coniferous evergreen trees. In Alaska, the trees are mostly balsam fir and spruces. In the rest of the United States, the trees are mostly cedars, hemlocks, pines, and redwoods.

Midlatitude deciduous forest
Broadleaf deciduous trees. Ash, beech, hickory, sugar maple, and oaks are common in the south. Beech and sugar maple are found in the north and north central regions. In the northwest, there are basswood and maple trees.

Mixed forest
In the north, the common evergreen trees are cedars, hemlocks, and pines. Deciduous trees include basswood, beech, sugar maple, and ash. In the south, the evergreen trees consist of varieties of pine. Oak is the most common deciduous tree.

Tropical rain forest
This category has the greatest variety of trees—mostly broadleaf evergreen trees, some palms, and tree ferns.

Subtropical broadleaf evergreen forest
In some areas of the Everglades, live oak, mahogany, and some palms can be found. Vines can be found on taller trees.

Midlatitude grassland
Grasses and non-woody plants.

Midlatitude scrubland
Grasses and scattered clusters of trees. In the northern region, the trees may be aspens. Farther south there may be oaks. In the drier regions to the south, varieties of pines may be found.

Desert
Too hot and dry for trees. Cacti and sparse grasses may be found.

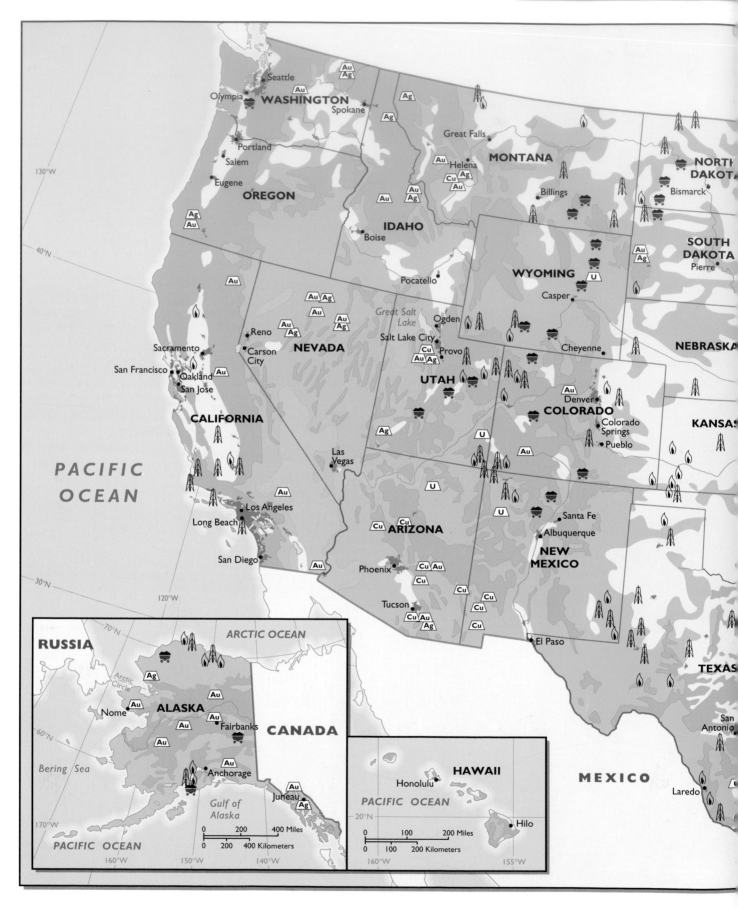

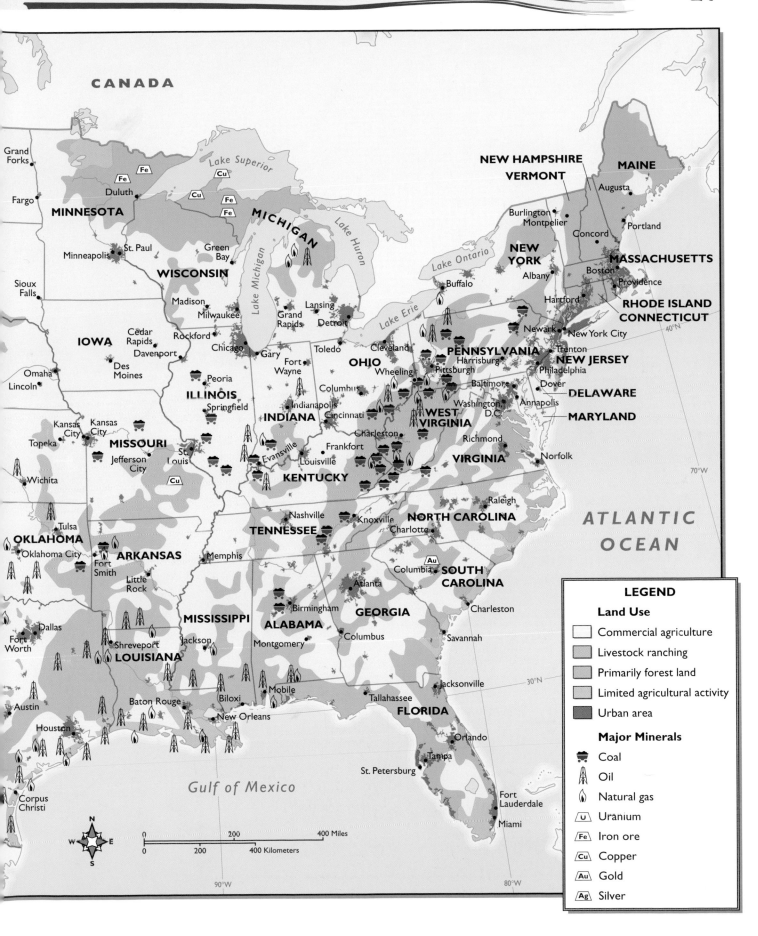

CANADA

Grand Forks
Fargo
MINNESOTA
Fe Fe
Duluth
Cu
Lake Superior
Minneapolis St. Paul
Sioux Falls
Cu
Fe
Fe
MICHIGAN
Lake Huron
Green Bay
Lake Michigan
WISCONSIN
Madison
Milwaukee
Lansing
Grand Rapids
Detroit
IOWA
Cedar Rapids
Rockford
Chicago
Gary
Fort Wayne
Toledo
Lake Erie
Davenport
Des Moines
Omaha
Lincoln
Peoria
ILLINOIS
Springfield
Indianapolis
INDIANA
Columbus
OHIO
Cincinnati
Cleveland
Wheeling
Pittsburgh

NEW HAMPSHIRE
VERMONT
MAINE
Augusta
Burlington
Montpelier
Concord
Portland
NEW YORK
Albany
MASSACHUSETTS
Boston
Providence
Lake Ontario
Buffalo
Hartford
RHODE ISLAND
CONNECTICUT
Newark
New York City
40°N
Trenton
Harrisburg
PENNSYLVANIA
NEW JERSEY
Philadelphia
Dover
DELAWARE
Baltimore
Annapolis
MARYLAND
Washington, D.C.

Kansas City Kansas City
Topeka
MISSOURI
Jefferson City
St. Louis
Cu
Wichita
Evansville
Louisville
Frankfort
KENTUCKY
WEST VIRGINIA
Charleston
Richmond
VIRGINIA
Norfolk
70°W

OKLAHOMA
Tulsa
Oklahoma City
ARKANSAS
Fort Smith
Little Rock
Memphis
Nashville
TENNESSEE
Knoxville
Charlotte
NORTH CAROLINA
Raleigh
Columbia
Au
SOUTH CAROLINA
Atlanta
Charleston

Dallas
Fort Worth
Shreveport
LOUISIANA
Jackson
MISSISSIPPI
Montgomery
Birmingham
ALABAMA
Columbus
GEORGIA
Savannah

Austin
Baton Rouge
New Orleans
Biloxi
Mobile
Tallahassee
Jacksonville
30°N

Houston
Gulf of Mexico
FLORIDA
Orlando
Tampa
St. Petersburg
Corpus Christi
Fort Lauderdale
Miami

ATLANTIC OCEAN

N
W E
S

0   200   400 Miles
0   200   400 Kilometers

90°W   80°W

LEGEND

Land Use

- ☐ Commercial agriculture
- ◻ Livestock ranching
- ◻ Primarily forest land
- ◻ Limited agricultural activity
- ◼ Urban area

Major Minerals

- Coal
- Oil
- Natural gas
- U Uranium
- Fe Iron ore
- Cu Copper
- Au Gold
- Ag Silver

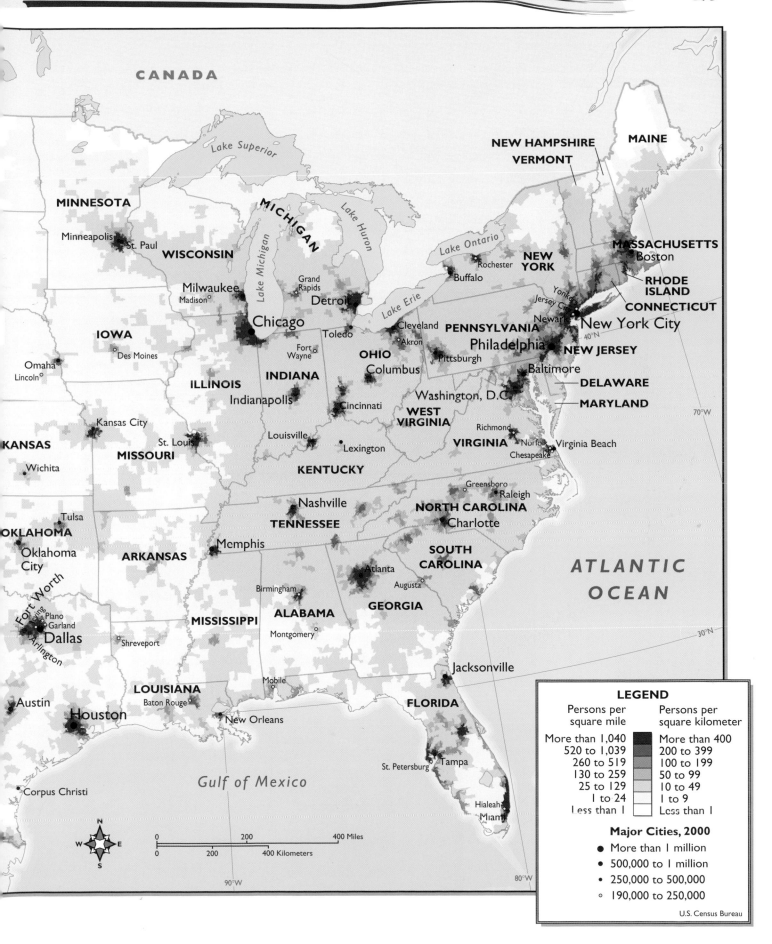

CANADA

MINNESOTA

Minneapolis
St. Paul

WISCONSIN

MICHIGAN

Lake Superior

Lake Michigan

Lake Huron

Milwaukee
Madison

Grand
Rapids

Detroit

IOWA

Des Moines

Chicago

Toledo

Fort
Wayne

Lake Erie

Cleveland
Akron

Lake Ontario

Rochester

Buffalo

NEW
YORK

NEW HAMPSHIRE
VERMONT

MAINE

MASSACHUSETTS
Boston

RHODE
ISLAND

CONNECTICUT

Yonkers
Jersey City
Newark

New York City

Omaha
Lincoln

ILLINOIS

INDIANA

Indianapolis

Cincinnati

OHIO

Columbus

PENNSYLVANIA

Pittsburgh

Philadelphia

NEW JERSEY

Baltimore

DELAWARE

40°N

KANSAS

Wichita

Kansas City

MISSOURI

St. Louis

Louisville

Lexington

KENTUCKY

Washington, D.C.

WEST
VIRGINIA

Richmond

VIRGINIA

MARYLAND

Norfolk
Chesapeake

Virginia Beach

70°W

Tulsa

OKLAHOMA

Oklahoma
City

ARKANSAS

Nashville

TENNESSEE

Memphis

Greensboro
Raleigh

NORTH CAROLINA

Charlotte

SOUTH
CAROLINA

ATLANTIC
OCEAN

Fort Worth

Irving
Plano
Garland

Dallas

Arlington

MISSISSIPPI

Shreveport

Birmingham

ALABAMA

Montgomery

Atlanta

GEORGIA

Augusta

Austin

Houston

LOUISIANA

Baton Rouge

Mobile

New Orleans

Jacksonville

FLORIDA

30°N

Corpus Christi

Gulf of Mexico

St. Petersburg

Tampa

Hialeah
Miami

N
W   E
S

0   200   400 Miles

0   200   400 Kilometers

90°W

80°W

LEGEND

Persons per square mile	Persons per square kilometer
More than 1,040	More than 400
520 to 1,039	200 to 399
260 to 519	100 to 199
130 to 259	50 to 99
25 to 129	10 to 49
1 to 24	1 to 9
Less than 1	Less than 1

Major Cities, 2000

● More than 1 million
● 500,000 to 1 million
• 250,000 to 500,000
○ 190,000 to 250,000

U.S. Census Bureau

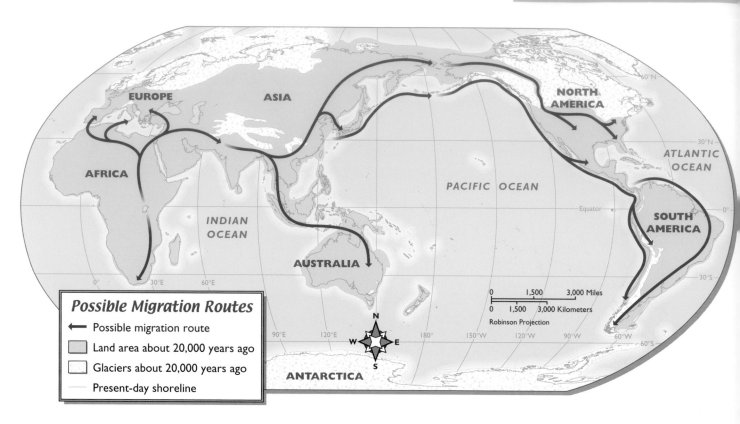

Possible Migration Routes

← Possible migration route

Land area about 20,000 years ago

Glaciers about 20,000 years ago

Present-day shoreline

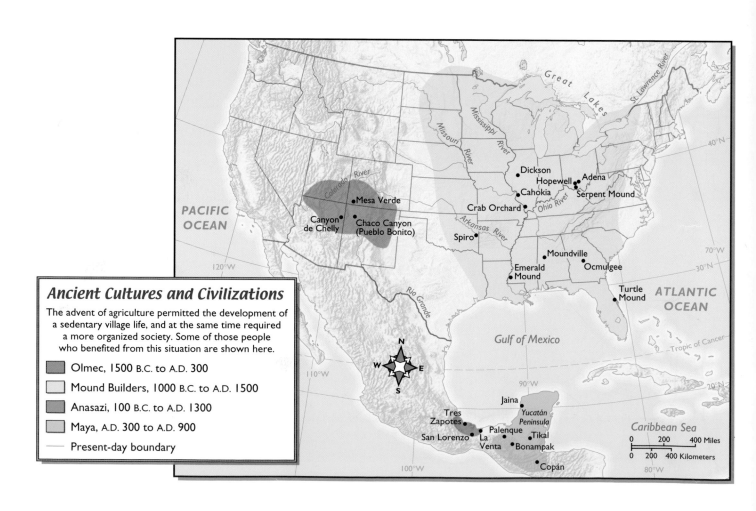

Ancient Cultures and Civilizations

The advent of agriculture permitted the development of a sedentary village life, and at the same time required a more organized society. Some of those people who benefited from this situation are shown here.

Olmec, 1500 B.C. to A.D. 300

Mound Builders, 1000 B.C. to A.D. 1500

Anasazi, 100 B.C. to A.D. 1300

Maya, A.D. 300 to A.D. 900

Present-day boundary

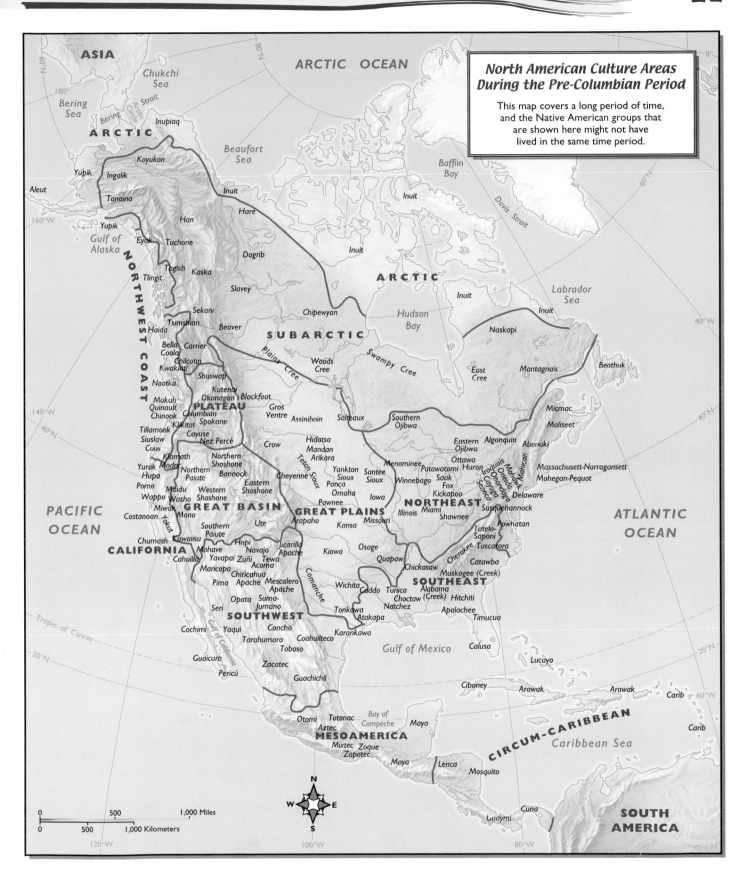

North American Culture Areas During the Pre-Columbian Period

This map covers a long period of time, and the Native American groups that are shown here might not have lived in the same time period.

ASIA
Chukchi Sea
Bering Sea
ARCTIC OCEAN
ARCTIC
Inupiaq
Yupik
Aleut
Ingalik
Tanaina
Yupik
Eyak
Koyukon
Beaufort Sea
Inuit
Hare
Han
Tuchone
Dogrib
Gulf of Alaska
Tlingit
Tagish
Kaska
Slavey
Sekani
Tsimshian
Beaver
Haida
Bella Coola
Carrier
Chilcotin
Kwakiutl
Nootka
Shuswap
Kutenai
Okanagan
Blackfoot
Mukah
Quinault
Columbian
Spokane
Chinook
Klikitat
Cayuse
Tillamook
Siuslaw
Coos
Nez Percé
Klamath
Modoc
Northern Shoshone
Yurok
Hupa
Northern Paiute
Bannock
Pomo
Maidu
Washo
Western Shoshone
Eastern Shoshone
Wappo
Miwok
Mono
Costanoan
Yokut
Southern Paiute
Ute
Chumash
Kawaiisu
Hopi
Mohave
Navajo
Yavapai
Zuñi
Tewa
Acoma
Jicarilla Apache
Cahuilla
Maricopa
Chiricahua
Pima
Apache
Mescalero Apache
Seri
Opata
Suma-Jumano
Concho
Cochimi
Yaqui
Tarahumara
Coahuilteco
Toboso
Guaicura
Zacatec
Pericú
Guachichil
Otomi
Totonac
Aztec
Mixtec
Zoque
Zapotec
Maya
Lenca
Mosquito
Guaymí
Cuna

PACIFIC OCEAN
NORTHWEST COAST
PLATEAU
GREAT BASIN
CALIFORNIA
SOUTHWEST
Gulf of California
Tropic of Cancer

Plains Cree
Chipewyan
SUBARCTIC
Woods Cree
Swampy Cree
Hudson Bay
Baffin Bay
Inuit
ARCTIC
Inuit
Labrador Sea
Naskapi
East Cree
Montagnais
Beothuk
Davis Strait
Inuit

Gros Ventre
Assiniboin
Saulteaux
Southern Ojibwa
Eastern Ojibwa
Algonquin
Abenaki
Micmac
Maliseet
Crow
Hidatsa
Mandan
Arikara
Teton Sioux
Yankton Sioux
Santee Sioux
Menominee
Winnebago
Ottawa
Potawatomi
Sauk
Fox
Huron
Iroquois
Mohawk
Mahican
Oneida
Onondaga
Cayuga
Seneca
Massachusett-Narragansett
Mohegan-Pequot
Cheyenne
Ponca
Omaha
Iowa
Kickapoo
Delaware
Pawnee
Illinois
Miami
Shawnee
Susquehannock
Powhatan
Arapaho
Kansa
Missouri
NORTHEAST
Lutelo-Saponi
Tuscatora
GREAT PLAINS
Kiowa
Osage
Quapaw
Catawba
Cherokee
Comanche
Wichita
Caddo
Tunica
Chickasaw
Muskogee (Creek)
Tonkawa
Natchez
Alabama
Choctaw (Creek)
Hitchiti
Apalachee
SOUTHEAST
Atakapa
Karankawa
Timucua
Calusa
Gulf of Mexico
Bay of Campeche
MESOAMERICA
Maya

ATLANTIC OCEAN
Lucayo
Ciboney
Arawak
Arawak
Carib
Carib
CIRCUM-CARIBBEAN
Caribbean Sea
SOUTH AMERICA

0   500   1,000 Miles
0   500   1,000 Kilometers

N W E S

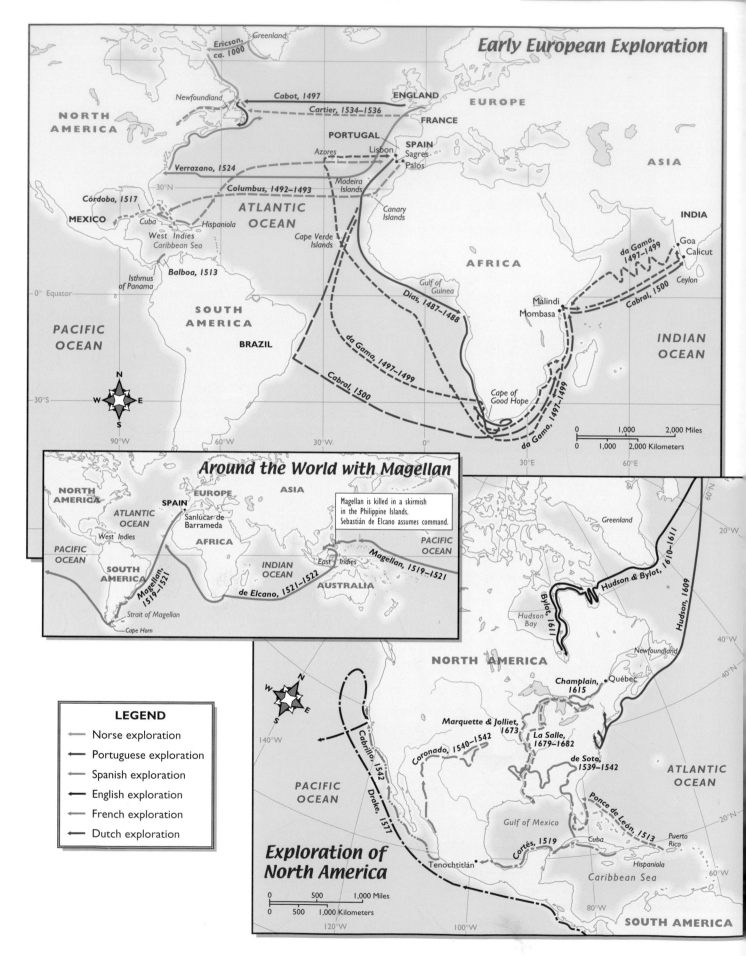

Early European Exploration

Ericson, ca. 1000
Greenland
NORTH AMERICA
Newfoundland
Cabot, 1497
ENGLAND
EUROPE
Cartier, 1534–1536
FRANCE
PORTUGAL
SPAIN
Azores
Lisbon
Sagres
Palos
Verrazano, 1524
Madeira Islands
Columbus, 1492–1493
Córdoba, 1517
MEXICO
Cuba
Hispaniola
West Indies
Caribbean Sea
ATLANTIC OCEAN
Canary Islands
Cape Verde Islands
ASIA
INDIA
da Gama, 1497–1499
Goa
Calicut
Ceylon
Cabral, 1500
AFRICA
Dias, 1487–1488
Gulf of Guinea
Malindi
Mombasa
INDIAN OCEAN
Isthmus of Panama
Balboa, 1513
0° Equator
SOUTH AMERICA
BRAZIL
PACIFIC OCEAN
da Gama, 1497–1499
Cabral, 1500
Cape of Good Hope
da Gama, 1497–1499
30°S
30°N
90°W
60°W
30°W
0°
30°E
60°E

0   1,000   2,000 Miles
0   1,000   2,000 Kilometers

Around the World with Magellan

NORTH AMERICA
EUROPE
ASIA
SPAIN
Sanlúcar de Barrameda
ATLANTIC OCEAN
West Indies
PACIFIC OCEAN
AFRICA
SOUTH AMERICA
INDIAN OCEAN
East Indies
Magellan, 1519–1521
de Elcano, 1521–1522
AUSTRALIA
PACIFIC OCEAN
Magellan, 1519–1521
Strait of Magellan
Cape Horn

Magellan is killed in a skirmish in the Philippine Islands. Sebastián de Elcano assumes command.

Exploration of North America

Greenland
Hudson & Bylot, 1610–1611
Bylot, 1611
Hudson Bay
Hudson, 1609
NORTH AMERICA
Newfoundland
Champlain, 1615
Québec
Marquette & Jolliet, 1673
La Salle, 1679–1682
Cabrillo, 1542
Drake, 1577
Coronado, 1540–1542
de Soto, 1539–1542
ATLANTIC OCEAN
PACIFIC OCEAN
Ponce de León, 1513
Gulf of Mexico
Cortés, 1519
Cuba
Puerto Rico
Hispaniola
Caribbean Sea
Tenochtitlán
SOUTH AMERICA
140°W
120°W
100°W
80°W
60°W
20°W
20°N
40°N
60°N

0   500   1,000 Miles
0   500   1,000 Kilometers

LEGEND
- Norse exploration
- Portuguese exploration
- Spanish exploration
- English exploration
- French exploration
- Dutch exploration

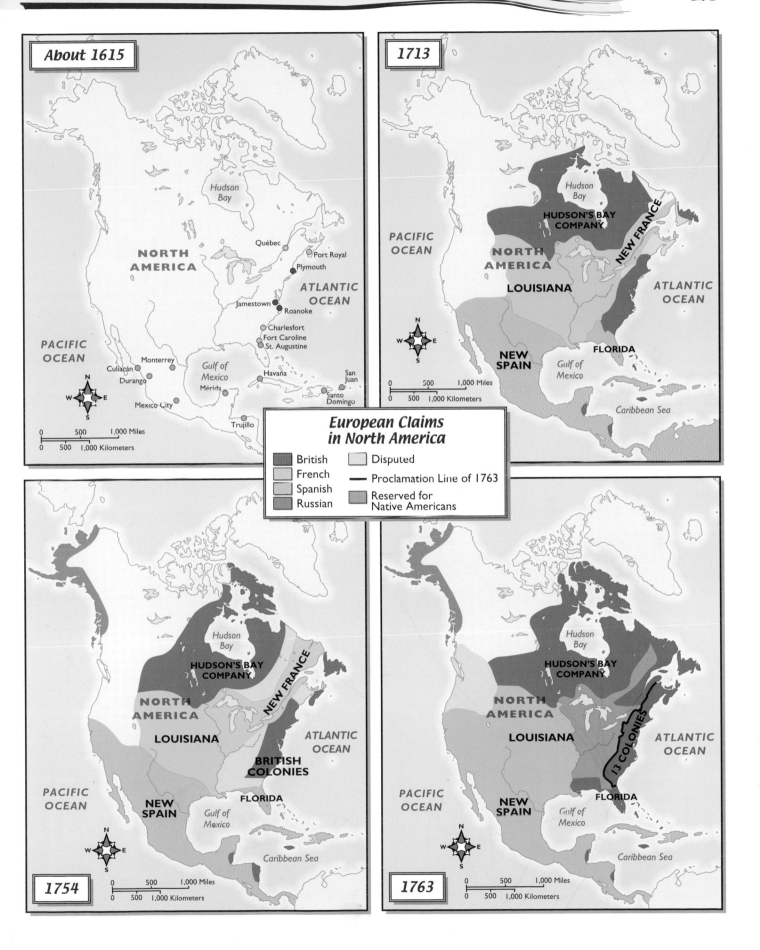

About 1615

Hudson Bay

NORTH AMERICA

Québec
Port Royal
Plymouth

ATLANTIC OCEAN

Jamestown
Roanoke

Charlesfort
Fort Caroline
St. Augustine

PACIFIC OCEAN

Monterrey
Culiacán
Durango

Gulf of Mexico
Havana
Mérida

San Juan

Santo Domingo

Mexico City

Trujillo

0   500   1,000 Miles
0   500   1,000 Kilometers

1713

PACIFIC OCEAN

Hudson Bay

HUDSON'S BAY COMPANY

NEW FRANCE

NORTH AMERICA

LOUISIANA

ATLANTIC OCEAN

NEW SPAIN

FLORIDA

Gulf of Mexico

Caribbean Sea

0   500   1,000 Miles
0   500   1,000 Kilometers

European Claims in North America

- British
- French
- Spanish
- Russian
- Disputed
- Proclamation Line of 1763
- Reserved for Native Americans

1754

Hudson Bay

HUDSON'S BAY COMPANY

NEW FRANCE

NORTH AMERICA

LOUISIANA

BRITISH COLONIES

ATLANTIC OCEAN

PACIFIC OCEAN

NEW SPAIN

FLORIDA

Gulf of Mexico

Caribbean Sea

0   500   1,000 Miles
0   500   1,000 Kilometers

1763

Hudson Bay

HUDSON'S BAY COMPANY

NORTH AMERICA

LOUISIANA

13 COLONIES

ATLANTIC OCEAN

PACIFIC OCEAN

NEW SPAIN

FLORIDA

Gulf of Mexico

Caribbean Sea

0   500   1,000 Miles
0   500   1,000 Kilometers

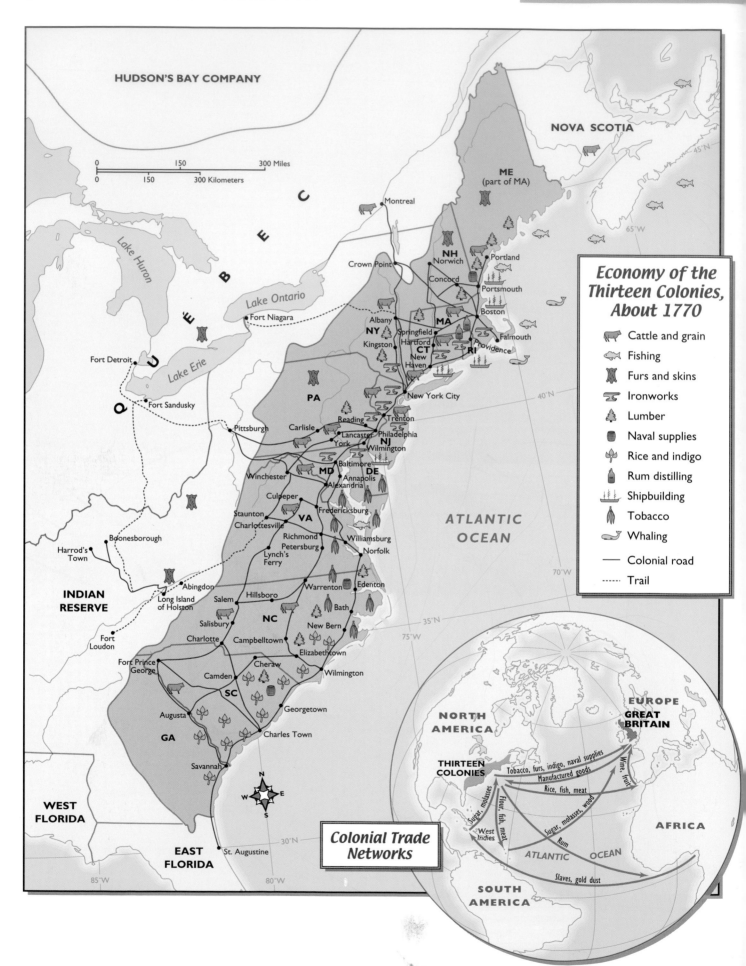

HUDSON'S BAY COMPANY

NOVA SCOTIA

ME
(part of MA)

150 / 300 Miles
150 / 300 Kilometers

Economy of the Thirteen Colonies, About 1770

Cattle and grain
Fishing
Furs and skins
Ironworks
Lumber
Naval supplies
Rice and indigo
Rum distilling
Shipbuilding
Tobacco
Whaling
— Colonial road
······ Trail

Montreal

QUEBEC

Lake Huron

Lake Ontario

Fort Niagara

Crown Point

NH
Norwich
Portland
Concord
Portsmouth
Boston

Fort Detroit

Lake Erie

Albany
NY
Springfield
MA
Kingston
Hartford
Falmouth
CT
New Haven
RI
Providence

Fort Sandusky

PA

New York City

Pittsburgh

Reading
Trenton
Carlisle
Lancaster
Philadelphia
York
NJ
Wilmington

Winchester
Baltimore
MD
DE
Annapolis
Alexandria

Culpeper

ATLANTIC
OCEAN

Staunton
VA
Fredericksburg
Charlottesville
Richmond
Williamsburg
Petersburg
Norfolk
Lynch's Ferry

Boonesborough

Harrod's Town

Abingdon
Warrenton
Edenton

INDIAN RESERVE

Long Island of Holston
Salem
Hillsboro
Bath

Salisbury
NC
New Bern

Fort Loudon
Charlotte
Campbelltown
Elizabethtown

Fort Prince George
Cheraw
Wilmington
Camden

SC
Georgetown
Augusta

GA
Charles Town

Savannah

WEST FLORIDA

N
W E
S

EUROPE
GREAT BRITAIN

NORTH AMERICA

THIRTEEN COLONIES

AFRICA

EAST FLORIDA
St. Augustine

Tobacco, furs, indigo, naval supplies
Manufactured goods
Rice, fish, meat
Wine, fruit

West Indies
Sugar, molasses
Flour, fish, meat
Sugar, molasses, wood
Rum
ATLANTIC OCEAN

Slaves, gold dust

SOUTH AMERICA

Colonial Trade Networks

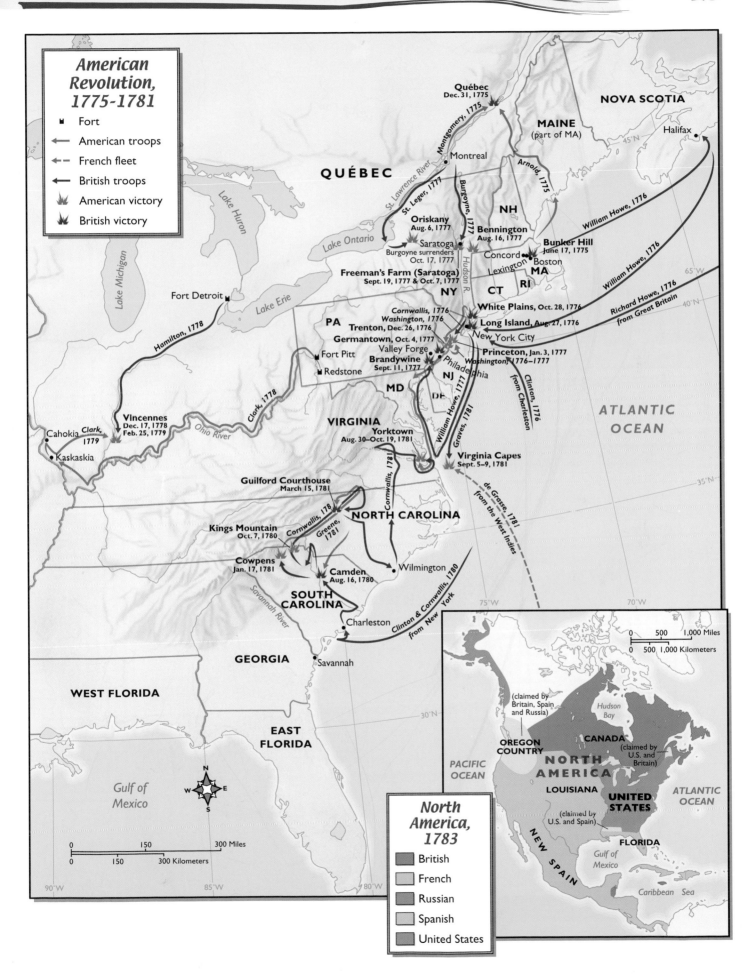

American Revolution, 1775-1781

- ■ Fort
- ← American troops
- ◄-- French fleet
- ← British troops
- ✹ American victory
- ✹ British victory

Québec Dec. 31, 1775

NOVA SCOTIA

Halifax

MAINE (part of MA)

QUÉBEC

Montreal

St. Lawrence River

Arnold, 1775

Montgomery, 1775

Lake Huron

Lake Michigan

Lake Ontario

Lake Erie

St. Leger, 1777

Burgoyne, 1777

Oriskany Aug. 6, 1777

Saratoga Burgoyne surrenders Oct. 17, 1777

NH

Bennington Aug. 16, 1777

Bunker Hill June 17, 1775

Concord

Boston

Lexington

MA

William Howe, 1776

William Howe, 1776

Richard Howe, 1776

from Great Britain

Freeman's Farm (Saratoga) Sept. 19, 1777 & Oct. 7, 1777

NY

CT **RI**

Fort Detroit

Hamilton, 1778

PA

Cornwallis, 1776

Washington, 1776

Trenton, Dec. 26, 1776

Germantown, Oct. 4, 1777

Valley Forge

Brandywine Sept. 11, 1777

Fort Pitt

Redstone

Hudson R.

White Plains, Oct. 28, 1776

Long Island, Aug. 27, 1776

New York City

Princeton, Jan. 3, 1777

Washington, 1776-1777

Clinton, 1776 from Charleston

William Howe, 1777

Philadelphia

NJ

DE

MD

Clark 1778

Vincennes Dec. 17, 1778 Feb. 25, 1779

Ohio River

Cahokia *Clark, 1779*

Kaskaskia

VIRGINIA

Yorktown Aug. 30–Oct. 19, 1781

Cornwallis, 1781

Graves, 1781

Virginia Capes Sept. 5–9, 1781

de Grasse, 1781 from the West Indies

ATLANTIC OCEAN

Guilford Courthouse March 15, 1781

Kings Mountain Oct. 7, 1780

Cornwallis, 178

Greene, 1781

NORTH CAROLINA

Wilmington

Cowpens Jan. 17, 1781

Camden Aug. 16, 1780

SOUTH CAROLINA

Clinton & Cornwallis, 1780 from New York

Charleston

Savannah River

GEORGIA

Savannah

WEST FLORIDA

EAST FLORIDA

Gulf of Mexico

N W E S

| 0 | 150 | 300 Miles |
| 0 | 150 | 300 Kilometers |

North America, 1783

- British
- French
- Russian
- Spanish
- United States

(claimed by Britain, Spain and Russia)

OREGON COUNTRY

PACIFIC OCEAN

Hudson Bay

CANADA

(claimed by U.S. and Britain)

NORTH AMERICA

LOUISIANA

UNITED STATES

ATLANTIC OCEAN

(claimed by U.S. and Spain)

NEW SPAIN

FLORIDA

Gulf of Mexico

Caribbean Sea

| 0 | 500 | 1,000 Miles |
| 0 | 500 | 1,000 Kilometers |

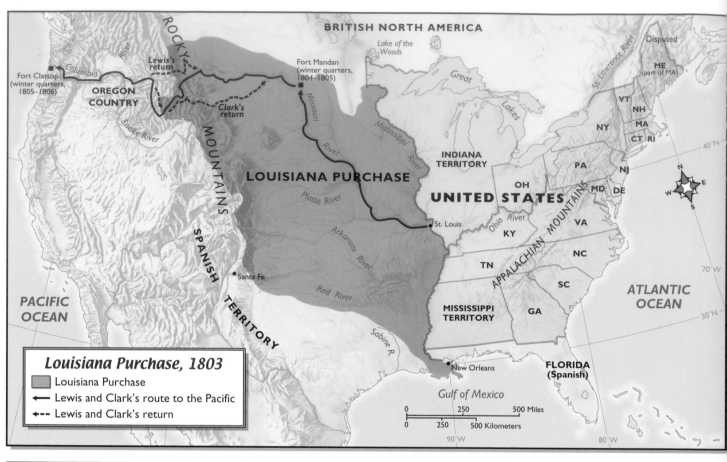

Louisiana Purchase, 1803

- Louisiana Purchase
- ← Lewis and Clark's route to the Pacific
- ←--- Lewis and Clark's return

BRITISH NORTH AMERICA

Lake of the Woods

Disputed

ME (part of MA)

Fort Clatsop (winter quarters, 1805–1806)

Lewis's return

ROCKY

Columbia River

Fort Mandan (winter quarters, 1804–1805)

Clark's return

OREGON COUNTRY

Snake River

MOUNTAINS

Missouri River

Mississippi River

Great Lakes

INDIANA TERRITORY

VT
NH
NY
MA
CT RI
PA
NJ
OH
MD DE

UNITED STATES

LOUISIANA PURCHASE

Platte River

St. Louis

KY

Ohio River

APPALACHIAN MOUNTAINS

VA
NC

SPANISH TERRITORY

Arkansas River

Santa Fe

Red River

TN
SC

MISSISSIPPI TERRITORY

GA

ATLANTIC OCEAN

PACIFIC OCEAN

Sabine R.

New Orleans

FLORIDA (Spanish)

Gulf of Mexico

0   250   500 Miles
0   250   500 Kilometers

40°N
70°W
30°N
90°W
80°W

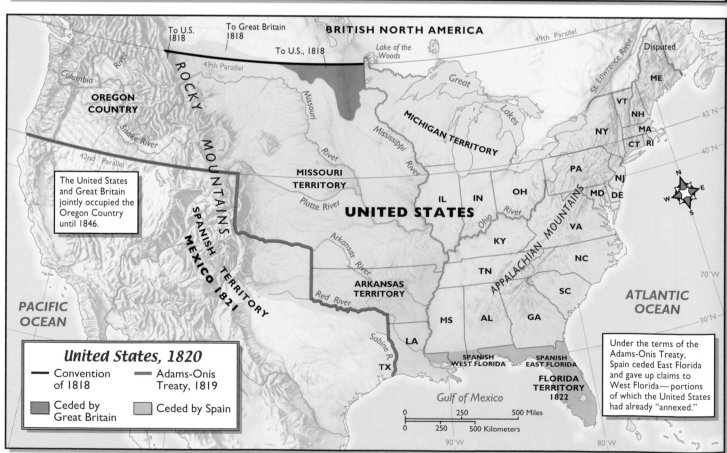

United States, 1820

- Convention of 1818
- Adams-Onís Treaty, 1819
- Ceded by Great Britain
- Ceded by Spain

To U.S. 1818

To Great Britain 1818

BRITISH NORTH AMERICA

49th Parallel

To U.S., 1818

Lake of the Woods

Disputed

ROCKY

Columbia River

49th Parallel

OREGON COUNTRY

Snake River

42nd Parallel

MOUNTAINS

Missouri River

Great Lakes

MICHIGAN TERRITORY

ME
VT
NH
NY
MA
CT RI

The United States and Great Britain jointly occupied the Oregon Country until 1846.

SPANISH TERRITORY
MEXICO 1821

MISSOURI TERRITORY

Platte River

UNITED STATES

IL
IN
OH
PA
NJ
MD DE

KY

Ohio River

VA

Arkansas River

ARKANSAS TERRITORY

TN

APPALACHIAN MOUNTAINS

NC

PACIFIC OCEAN

Red River

Sabine R.

MS
AL
GA
SC

ATLANTIC OCEAN

LA

TX

SPANISH WEST FLORIDA

SPANISH EAST FLORIDA

FLORIDA TERRITORY 1822

Gulf of Mexico

Under the terms of the Adams-Onís Treaty, Spain ceded East Florida and gave up claims to West Florida—portions of which the United States had already "annexed."

0   250   500 Miles
0   250   500 Kilometers

42°N
40°N
70°W
30°N
90°W
80°W

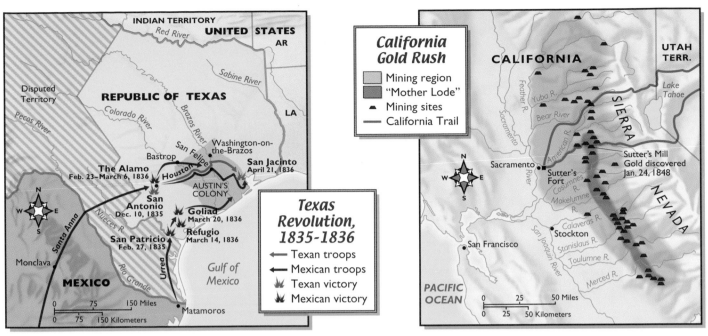

Texas Revolution, 1835-1836

The Alamo Feb. 23–March 6, 1836
San Jacinto April 21, 1836
Goliad March 20, 1836
Refugio March 14, 1836
San Patricio Feb. 27, 1835
San Antonio Dec. 10, 1835

→ Texan troops
← Mexican troops
🔥 Texan victory
🔥 Mexican victory

INDIAN TERRITORY
UNITED STATES
Red River
AR
Sabine River
REPUBLIC OF TEXAS
LA
Disputed Territory
Pecos River
Colorado River
Brazos River
San Felipe
Washington-on-the-Brazos
Bastrop
Houston
AUSTIN'S COLONY
Santa Anna
Nueces R.
San Antonio
Urrea
Rio Grande
MEXICO
Monclava
Gulf of Mexico
Matamoros

0 75 150 Miles
0 75 150 Kilometers

California Gold Rush

- Mining region
- "Mother Lode"
- ▲ Mining sites
- California Trail

CALIFORNIA
UTAH TERR.
Feather R.
Yuba R.
Bear River
Sacramento
American R.
SIERRA
Lake Tahoe
Sutter's Mill Gold discovered Jan. 24, 1848
Sutter's Fort
Cosumnes R.
Mokelumne R.
NEVADA
Calaveras R.
Stockton
Stanislaus R.
San Joaquin River
Toulumne R.
San Francisco
Merced R.
PACIFIC OCEAN

0 25 50 Miles
0 25 50 Kilometers

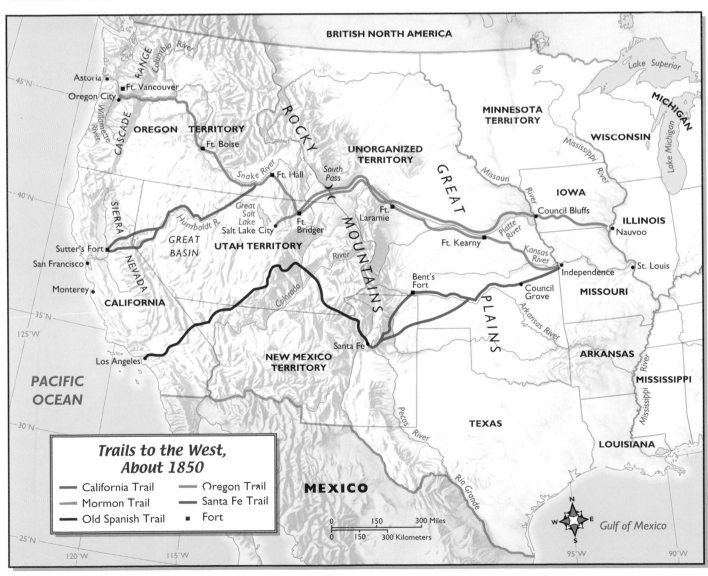

Trails to the West, About 1850

— California Trail
— Mormon Trail
— Old Spanish Trail
— Oregon Trail
— Santa Fe Trail
■ Fort

BRITISH NORTH AMERICA
Lake Superior
MICHIGAN
Lake Michigan
Astoria
Ft. Vancouver
Columbia River
CASCADE RANGE
Oregon City
Willamette River
OREGON TERRITORY
Ft. Boise
Snake River
ROCKY
South Pass
Ft. Hall
UNORGANIZED TERRITORY
MINNESOTA TERRITORY
WISCONSIN
Missouri
GREAT
IOWA
Council Bluffs
ILLINOIS
Nauvoo
Mississippi River
SIERRA
Humboldt R.
Great Salt Lake
Salt Lake City
Ft. Bridger
MOUNTAINS
Ft. Laramie
Platte River
Ft. Kearny
Kansas River
St. Louis
GREAT BASIN
UTAH TERRITORY
Independence
Sutter's Fort
NEVADA
Colorado
River
MISSOURI
San Francisco
Bent's Fort
Council Grove
PLAINS
Monterey
CALIFORNIA
Santa Fe
Arkansas River
ARKANSAS
Los Angeles
NEW MEXICO TERRITORY
MISSISSIPPI
PACIFIC OCEAN
Pecos River
TEXAS
LOUISIANA
MEXICO
Rio Grande
Gulf of Mexico

0 150 300 Miles
0 150 300 Kilometers

45°N
40°N
35°N
30°N
25°N
125°W 120°W 115°W 95°W 90°W

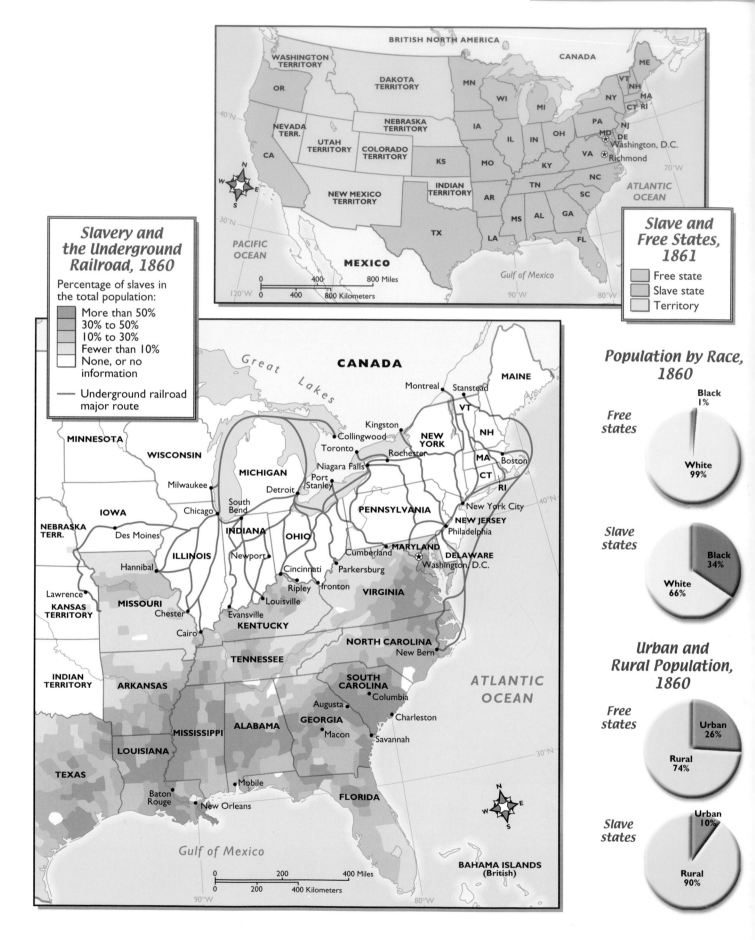

Slavery and the Underground Railroad, 1860

Percentage of slaves in the total population:
- More than 50%
- 30% to 50%
- 10% to 30%
- Fewer than 10%
- None, or no information

— Underground railroad major route

Slave and Free States, 1861
- Free state
- Slave state
- Territory

Population by Race, 1860

Free states
- Black 1%
- White 99%

Slave states
- Black 34%
- White 66%

Urban and Rural Population, 1860

Free states
- Urban 26%
- Rural 74%

Slave states
- Urban 10%
- Rural 90%

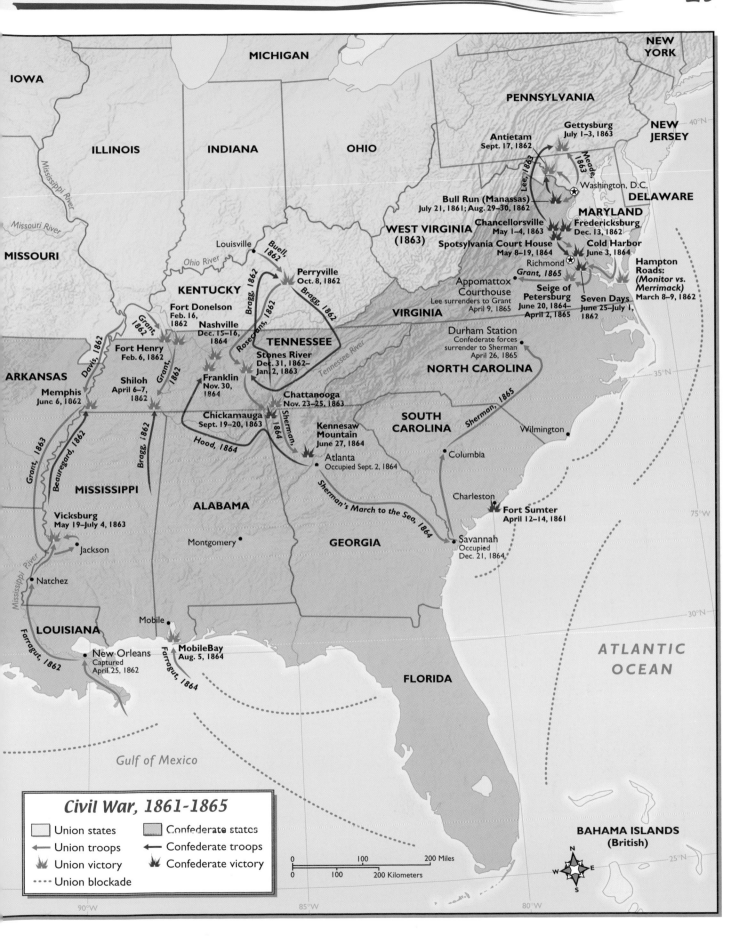

IOWA
MICHIGAN
NEW YORK
ILLINOIS
INDIANA
OHIO
PENNSYLVANIA
NEW JERSEY

MISSOURI

Mississippi River
Missouri River
Ohio River

Louisville

KENTUCKY

Buell, 1862
Perryville
Oct. 8, 1862

Antietam
Sept. 17, 1862

Gettysburg
July 1–3, 1863

Washington, D.C.

DELAWARE

MARYLAND

WEST VIRGINIA
(1863)

Bull Run (Manassas)
July 21, 1861; Aug. 29–30, 1862

Chancellorsville
May 1–4, 1863

Fredericksburg
Dec. 13, 1862

Spotsylvania Court House
May 8–19, 1864

Cold Harbor
June 3, 1864

Richmond
Grant, 1865

Hampton
Roads:
(Monitor vs.
Merrimack)
March 8–9, 1862

VIRGINIA

Appomattox
Courthouse
Lee surrenders to Grant
April 9, 1865

Seige of
Petersburg
June 20, 1864–
April 2, 1865

Seven Days
June 25–July 1,
1862

Fort Donelson
Feb. 16, 1862

Nashville
Dec. 15–16, 1864

TENNESSEE

Tennessee River

Durham Station
Confederate forces
surrender to Sherman
April 26, 1865

NORTH CAROLINA

Fort Henry
Feb. 6, 1862

Stones River
Dec. 31, 1862–
Jan. 2, 1863

ARKANSAS

Memphis
June 6, 1862

Shiloh
April 6–7, 1862

Franklin
Nov. 30, 1864

Chattanooga
Nov. 23–25, 1863

Chickamauga
Sept. 19–20, 1863

SOUTH CAROLINA

Sherman, 1865

Wilmington

Kennesaw
Mountain
June 27, 1864

Columbia

Hood, 1864

MISSISSIPPI

ALABAMA

Atlanta
Occupied Sept. 2, 1864

GEORGIA

Charleston

Fort Sumter
April 12–14, 1861

Vicksburg
May 19–July 4, 1863

Jackson

Montgomery

Sherman's March to the Sea, 1864

Savannah
Occupied
Dec. 21, 1864

Natchez

LOUISIANA

Mobile

New Orleans
Captured
April 25, 1862

MobileBay
Aug. 5, 1864

Farragut, 1862
Farragut, 1864

FLORIDA

ATLANTIC OCEAN

Gulf of Mexico

BAHAMA ISLANDS
(British)

Grant, 1862
Davis, 1862
Bragg, 1862
Rosecrans, 1862
Grant, 1862
Beauregard, 1862
Grant, 1863
Bragg, 1862
Sherman, 1864
Lee, 1863
Meade, 1863

Civil War, 1861–1865

- ☐ Union states
- ☐ Confederate states
- ← Union troops
- ← Confederate troops
- 🔥 Union victory
- 🔥 Confederate victory
- ····· Union blockade

0   100   200 Miles
0   100   200 Kilometers

N E S W

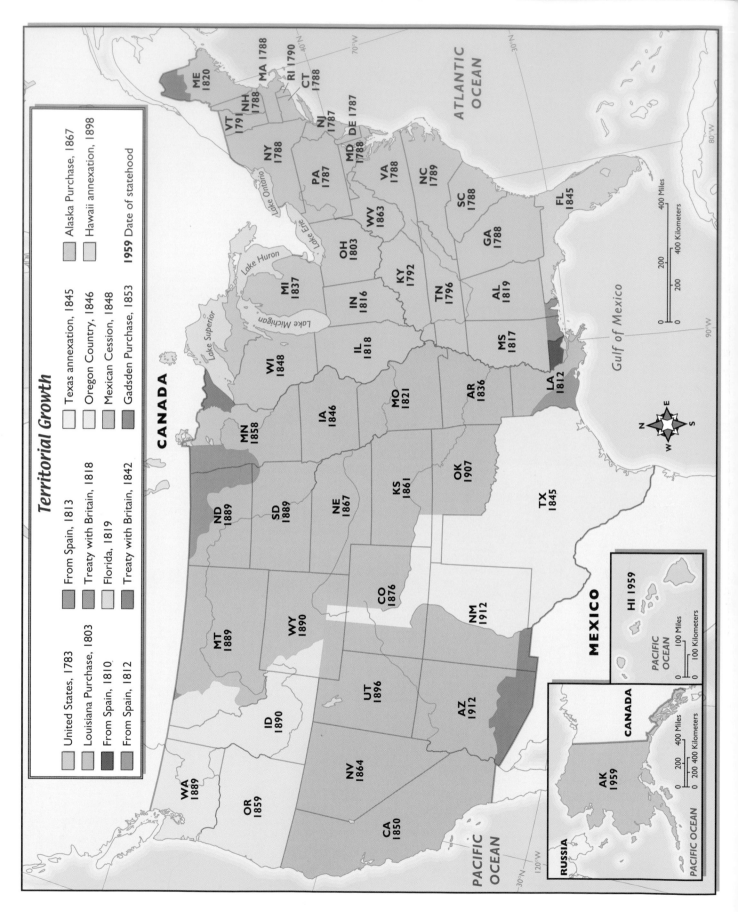

Territorial Growth

Territorial Growth

- United States, 1783
- Louisiana Purchase, 1803
- From Spain, 1810
- From Spain, 1812
- From Spain, 1813
- Treaty with Britain, 1818
- Florida, 1819
- Treaty with Britain, 1842
- Texas annexation, 1845
- Oregon Country, 1846
- Mexican Cession, 1848
- Gadsden Purchase, 1853
- Alaska Purchase, 1867
- Hawaii annexation, 1898
- **1959** Date of statehood

ME 1820
MA 1788
RI 1790
CT 1788
NH 1788
VT 1791
NJ 1787
DE 1787
NY 1788
PA 1787
MD 1788
VA 1788
NC 1789
WV 1863
OH 1803
KY 1792
TN 1796
SC 1788
GA 1788
FL 1845
MI 1837
IN 1816
IL 1818
MO 1821
AL 1819
MS 1817
AR 1836
LA 1812
WI 1848
IA 1846
MN 1858
OK 1907
KS 1861
NE 1867
ND 1889
SD 1889
TX 1845
CO 1876
NM 1912
MT 1889
WY 1890
UT 1896
AZ 1912
ID 1890
NV 1864
WA 1889
OR 1859
CA 1850

HI 1959
AK 1959

ATLANTIC OCEAN
PACIFIC OCEAN
Gulf of Mexico
CANADA
MEXICO
RUSSIA

Lake Ontario
Lake Erie
Lake Huron
Lake Superior
Lake Michigan

400 Miles
400 Kilometers
200
200

100 Miles
100 Kilometers

200 400 Miles
200 400 Kilometers

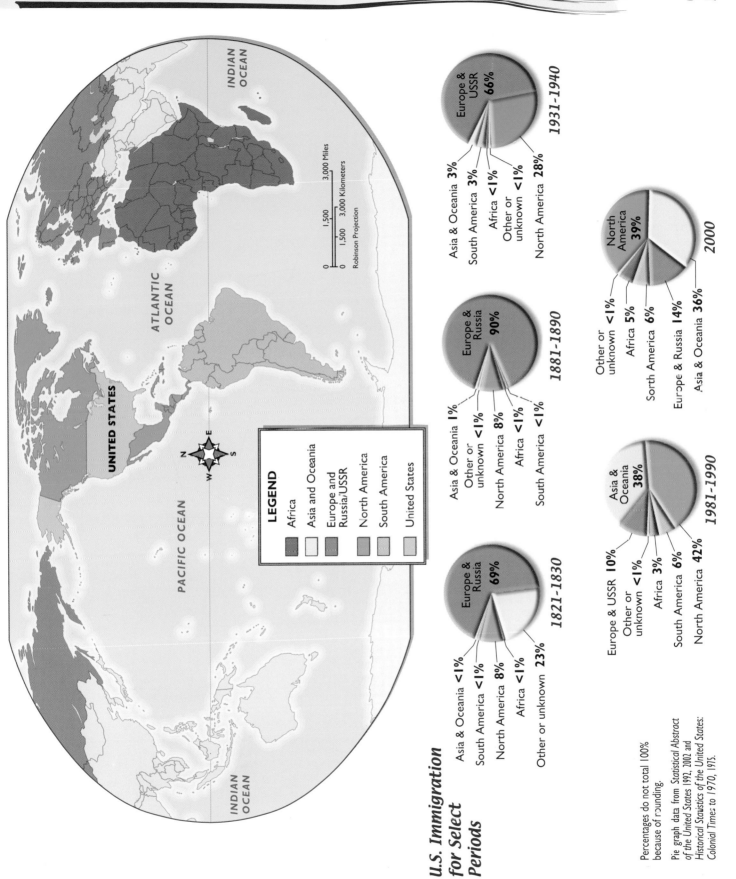

U.S. Immigration for Select Periods

1931-1940

- Europe & USSR **66%**
- Asia & Oceania **3%**
- South America **3%**
- Africa **<1%**
- Other or unknown **<1%**
- North America **28%**

1881-1890

- Europe & Russia **90%**
- Asia & Oceania **1%**
- Other or unknown **<1%**
- North America **8%**
- Africa **<1%**
- South America **<1%**

1821-1830

- Europe & Russia **69%**
- Asia & Oceania **<1%**
- South America **<1%**
- North America **8%**
- Africa **<1%**
- Other or unknown **23%**

2000

- North America **39%**
- Other or unknown **<1%**
- Africa **5%**
- South America **6%**
- Europe & Russia **14%**
- Asia & Oceania **36%**

1981-1990

- Asia & Oceania **38%**
- Europe & USSR **10%**
- Other or unknown **<1%**
- Africa **3%**
- South America **6%**
- North America **42%**

LEGEND
- Africa
- Asia and Oceania
- Europe and Russia/USSR
- North America
- South America
- United States

UNITED STATES

INDIAN OCEAN

ATLANTIC OCEAN

PACIFIC OCEAN

INDIAN OCEAN

3,000 Miles
1,500   3,000 Kilometers
0
0   1,500
Robinson Projection

Percentages do not total 100% because of rounding.

Pie graph data from *Statistical Abstract of the United States* 1992, 2002 and *Historical Statistics of the United States: Colonial Times to 1970*, 1975.

U.S. International Trade in Goods and Services

Billions of dollars

Imports

Trade Balance

Exports

January 2003
TRADE BALANCE
−$41.1 Billion

January 2001	January 2002	January 2003

Foreign Trade Statistics, U.S. Census Bureau

This graph indicates that the U.S. spends more money purchasing foreign products than it receives from selling domestic products abroad.

World Trade Organizations

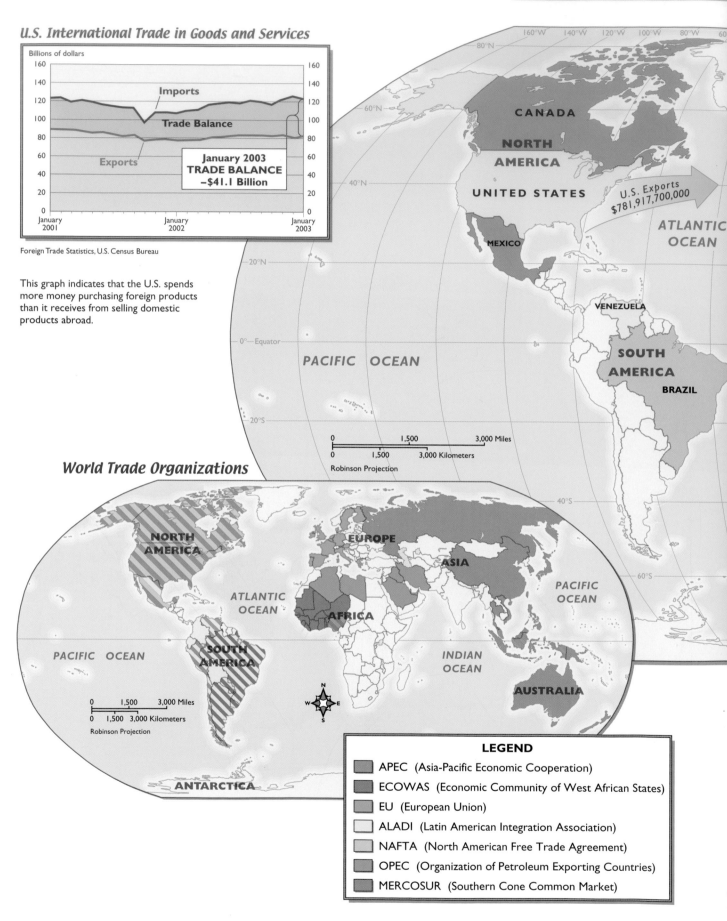

U.S. Exports
$781,917,700,000

LEGEND

- APEC (Asia-Pacific Economic Cooperation)
- ECOWAS (Economic Community of West African States)
- EU (European Union)
- ALADI (Latin American Integration Association)
- NAFTA (North American Free Trade Agreement)
- OPEC (Organization of Petroleum Exporting Countries)
- MERCOSUR (Southern Cone Common Market)

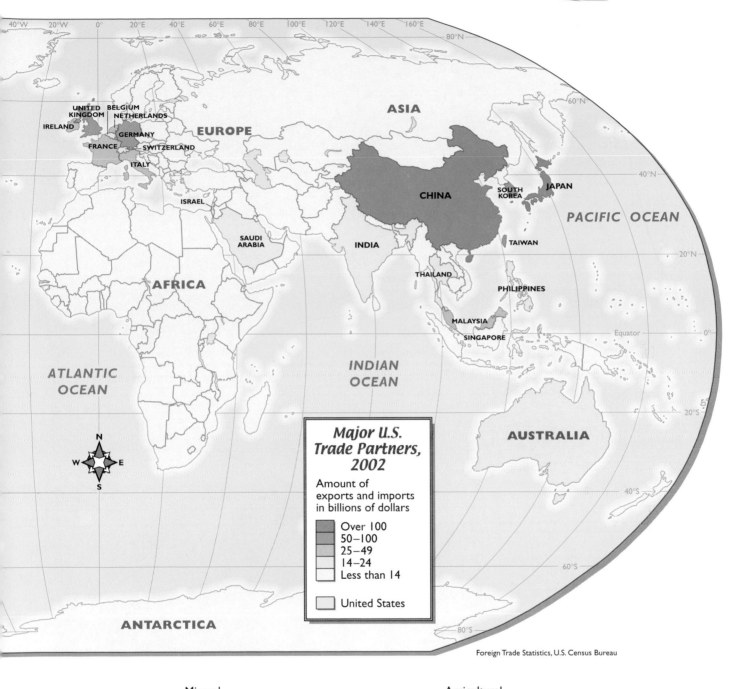

Major U.S.
Trade Partners,
2002

Amount of
exports and imports
in billions of dollars

Over 100
50–100
25–49
14–24
Less than 14

United States

Foreign Trade Statistics, U.S. Census Bureau

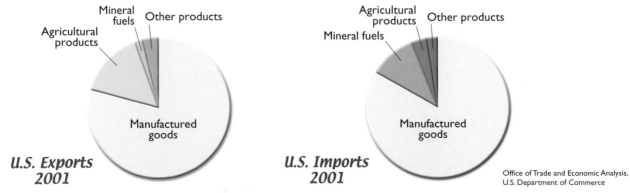

Mineral fuels
Other products
Agricultural products

Manufactured goods

U.S. Exports
2001

Agricultural products
Other products
Mineral fuels

Manufactured goods

U.S. Imports
2001

Office of Trade and Economic Analysis,
U.S. Department of Commerce

CANADA

Seattle
Olympia • WASHINGTON
Spokane •

Great Falls •
MONTANA
Helena •
Billings •

Grand Forks •
NORTH DAKOTA
Bismarck •
Fargo •
Duluth

MINNESOTA
St. Paul

Portland •
Salem •
Eugene •
OREGON

IDAHO
Boise •

Pocatello •

WYOMING
Casper •

SOUTH DAKOTA
Pierre •
Sioux Falls •

Minneapolis •

IOWA

Reno •
NEVADA
Carson City •

Ogden •
Salt Lake City • Provo •

Cheyenne •

NEBRASKA
Omaha •
Lincoln •

Des Moines •

Sacramento •
San Francisco • Oakland •
San Jose •
CALIFORNIA

UTAH

Denver •
COLORADO
Colorado Springs •
Pueblo •

Kansas City • Kansas City
Topeka •
KANSAS
MISSOURI

Las Vegas •

Wichita •

PACIFIC OCEAN

Los Angeles •
Long Beach •

San Diego •

ARIZONA

Phoenix •

Santa Fe •
Albuquerque •
NEW MEXICO

Tulsa •
OKLAHOMA
Oklahoma City •

Fort Smith •
ARKANSAS

Tucson •

El Paso •

Fort Worth • Dallas •
Shreveport •

TEXAS

Austin •

Houston •

130°W

40°N

30°N

120°W

San Antonio •

Laredo •
Corpus Christi •

MEXICO

RUSSIA
70°N
Arctic Circle
Nome •
Fairbanks •
ALASKA
CANADA
Anchorage •
60°N
Bering Sea
170°W
Juneau •
Gulf of Alaska

0   200   400 Miles
0   200   400 Kilometers
160°W   150°W   140°W

HAWAII
Honolulu •
PACIFIC OCEAN
20°N
Hilo •
0   100   200 Miles
0   100   200 Kilometers
160°W   155°W

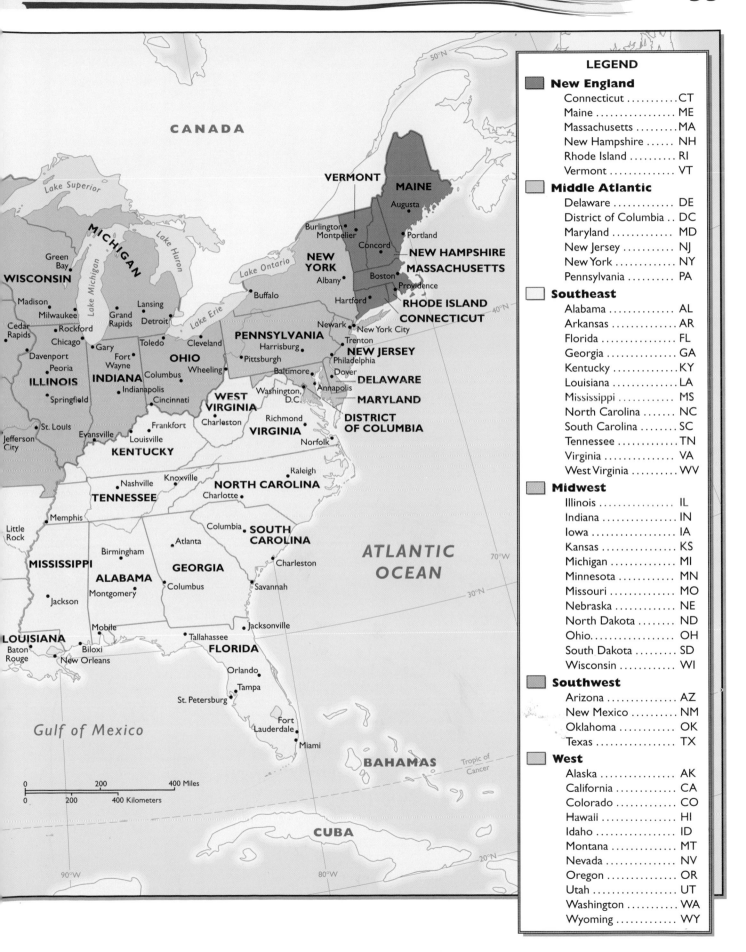

CANADA

Lake Superior

MICHIGAN

Green Bay

WISCONSIN

Lake Michigan

Lake Huron

Madison
Milwaukee
Cedar Rapids
Rockford
Chicago
Davenport
Peoria
ILLINOIS
Springfield

Lansing
Grand Rapids
Detroit

Lake Erie

St. Louis
Jefferson City
Evansville
Louisville
KENTUCKY

Gary
Fort Wayne
INDIANA
Indianapolis

Toledo
Cleveland
OHIO
Columbus
Cincinnati

Wheeling
Pittsburgh

Frankfort

WEST VIRGINIA
Charleston

Lake Ontario

Buffalo

PENNSYLVANIA
Harrisburg

VERMONT

MAINE
Augusta

Burlington
Montpelier
Concord
Portland

NEW YORK
Albany

NEW HAMPSHIRE
MASSACHUSETTS
Boston
Providence
Hartford
RHODE ISLAND
CONNECTICUT

Newark
New York City
Trenton
NEW JERSEY
Philadelphia
Dover
DELAWARE

Baltimore
Washington, D.C.
Annapolis
MARYLAND
DISTRICT OF COLUMBIA

Nashville
Knoxville
TENNESSEE
Charlotte

Memphis
Little Rock

MISSISSIPPI
Birmingham
ALABAMA
Montgomery
Jackson
Mobile

LOUISIANA
Baton Rouge
New Orleans
Biloxi

Richmond
VIRGINIA
Norfolk

Raleigh
NORTH CAROLINA

Columbia
SOUTH CAROLINA
Charleston

GEORGIA
Columbus
Atlanta
Savannah

Jacksonville
Tallahassee
FLORIDA

Orlando
Tampa
St. Petersburg
Fort Lauderdale
Miami

ATLANTIC OCEAN

70°W

30°N

50°N

40°N

Gulf of Mexico

0   200   400 Miles
0   200   400 Kilometers

BAHAMAS
Tropic of Cancer

CUBA

90°W   80°W   20°N

LEGEND

New England
Connecticut .... CT
Maine .... ME
Massachusetts .... MA
New Hampshire ...... NH
Rhode Island .... RI
Vermont .... VT

Middle Atlantic
Delaware .... DE
District of Columbia .. DC
Maryland .... MD
New Jersey .... NJ
New York .... NY
Pennsylvania .... PA

Southeast
Alabama .... AL
Arkansas .... AR
Florida .... FL
Georgia .... GA
Kentucky .... KY
Louisiana .... LA
Mississippi .... MS
North Carolina .... NC
South Carolina .... SC
Tennessee .... TN
Virginia .... VA
West Virginia .... WV

Midwest
Illinois IL
Indiana .... IN
Iowa .... IA
Kansas .... KS
Michigan .... MI
Minnesota .... MN
Missouri .... MO
Nebraska .... NE
North Dakota .... ND
Ohio................. OH
South Dakota .... SD
Wisconsin .... WI

Southwest
Arizona .... AZ
New Mexico .... NM
Oklahoma .... OK
Texas .... TX

West
Alaska .... AK
California .... CA
Colorado .... CO
Hawaii .... HI
Idaho .... ID
Montana .... MT
Nevada .... NV
Oregon .... OR
Utah .... UT
Washington .... WA
Wyoming .... WY

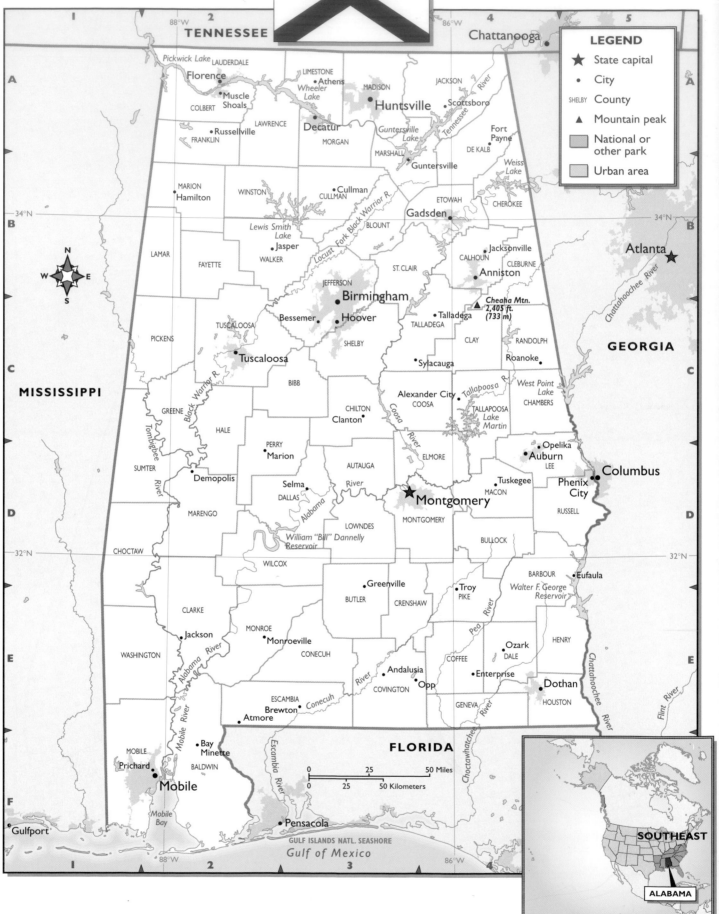

LEGEND
★ State capital
• City
SHELBY County
▲ Mountain peak
National or other park
Urban area

TENNESSEE

Pickwick Lake LAUDERDALE
Florence LIMESTONE
Muscle Shoals Athens MADISON JACKSON
COLBERT Wheeler Lake Huntsville Scottsboro
Russellville LAWRENCE Decatur Fort Payne
FRANKLIN MORGAN Guntersville Lake DE KALB
MARION WINSTON MARSHALL Guntersville Weiss Lake
Hamilton CULLMAN Cullman ETOWAH CHEROKEE
LAMAR Lewis Smith Lake BLOUNT Gadsden
FAYETTE Jasper Jacksonville CALHOUN CLEBURNE
WALKER ST. CLAIR Anniston
JEFFERSON Birmingham Cheaha Mtn. 2,405 ft. (733 m)
TUSCALOOSA Bessemer Hoover Talladega CLAY RANDOLPH
PICKENS SHELBY TALLADEGA Roanoke
Tuscaloosa Sylacauga West Point Lake
BIBB CHAMBERS
GREENE CHILTON Alexander City Tallapoosa
HALE Clanton COOSA Lake Martin
PERRY ELMORE Opelika Auburn
Marion AUTAUGA LEE
SUMTER Demopolis Selma Tuskegee Columbus
MARENGO DALLAS Montgomery MACON Phenix City
CHOCTAW LOWNDES MONTGOMERY RUSSELL
WILCOX BULLOCK
Greenville BARBOUR Eufaula
CLARKE BUTLER CRENSHAW Troy Walter F. George Reservoir
MONROE PIKE
Jackson Monroeville Ozark HENRY
WASHINGTON CONECUH COFFEE DALE
Andalusia Enterprise Dothan
ESCAMBIA Opp HOUSTON
Brewton COVINGTON GENEVA
Atmore Bay Minette
MOBILE BALDWIN FLORIDA
Prichard
Mobile Pensacola
Gulfport Mobile Bay GULF ISLANDS NATL. SEASHORE
Gulf of Mexico

MISSISSIPPI

GEORGIA

Atlanta

Chattanooga

Chattahoochee River

0 25 50 Miles
0 25 50 Kilometers

SOUTHEAST
ALABAMA

The shapes of Alabama and its neighbor Mississippi could almost be called mirror images of each other. However, that description must be used cautiously because Alabama is unique. The northern portion of the state includes hills and the southernmost ranges of the Appalachian Mountains. The Tennessee River, dammed for flood control and electric power, crosses this part of the state. Central and southern Alabama is primarily flat and is home to the best agricultural land. The state has a small segment of coastline along the Gulf of Mexico. Birmingham makes steel as well as a variety of other manufactured goods. All the elements used to make steel can be found within the state. Because of its industries, Alabama attracted immigrants 100 years ago, unlike the other southern states. High-tech, aerospace-related businesses can be found in Huntsville, while Mobile is an important seaport.

Alabama Almanac

Nicknames	Heart of Dixie, Camellia State
State capital	Montgomery
Date of statehood	Dec. 14, 1819; 22nd state
State bird	Yellowhammer
State flower	Camellia
State tree	Southern longleaf pine
State motto	We Dare Defend Our Rights
Total population & rank	4,464,356 (in 2001); 23rd
Population density	88 per sq. mile (34 per sq. km)
Population distribution	55% urban, 45% rural
Largest cities	Birmingham, Montgomery, Mobile, Huntsville
Highest elevation	Cheaha Mountain, 2,405 ft. (733 m)
Lowest elevation	sea level
Land area & rank	50,744 sq. miles (131,427 sq. km); 28th
Average January temperature	45°F (7°C)
Average July temperature	80°F (27°C)
Average yearly precipitation	56 inches (142 cm)
Major industries	pulp and paper, chemicals, electronics, apparel, textiles
Places to visit	Alabama Space and Rocket Center (Huntsville), Carver Museum (Tuskegee), Civil Rights Memorial (Montgomery)
Web site	www.alabama.gov

Did You Know?

Alabama honored an insect pest with a statue because it forced farmers to switch from cotton to more profitable crops: Boll Weevil Monument in Enterprise

Economy – Chief Products

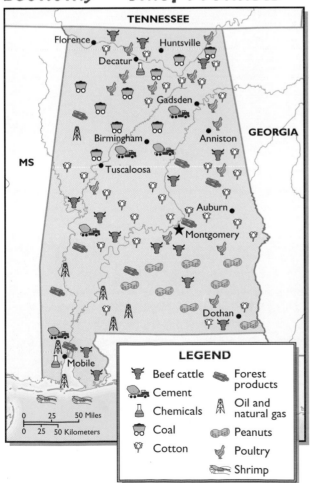

LEGEND

- 🐂 Beef cattle
- Cement
- Chemicals
- Coal
- Cotton
- Forest products
- Oil and natural gas
- Peanuts
- Poultry
- Shrimp

Physical

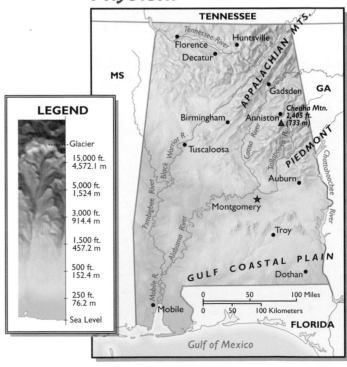

LEGEND

- Glacier
- 15,000 ft. / 4,572.1 m
- 5,000 ft. / 1,524 m
- 3,000 ft. / 914.4 m
- 1,500 ft. / 457.2 m
- 500 ft. / 152.4 m
- 250 ft. / 76.2 m
- Sea Level

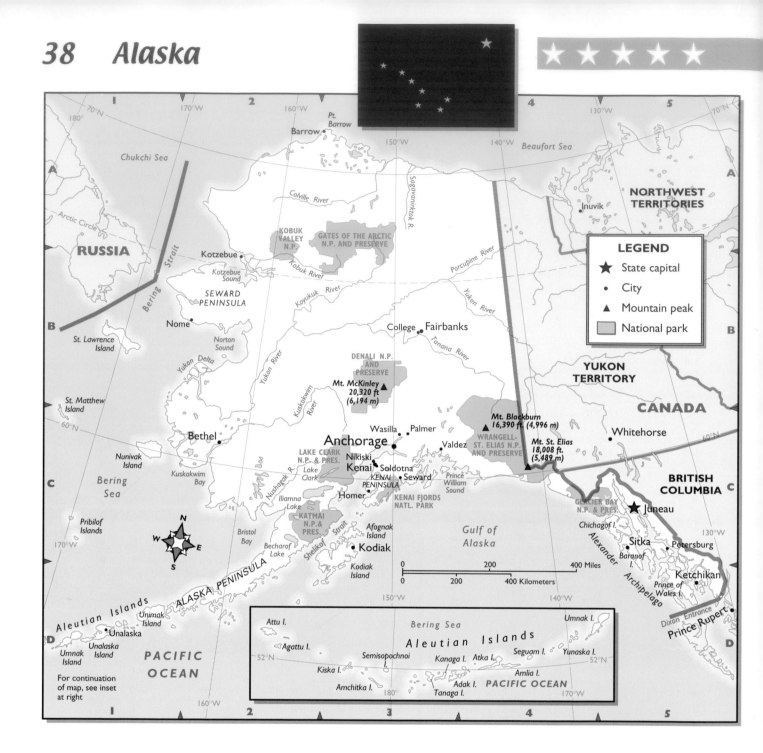

ALASKA

WEST

Twice the size of Texas, Alaska is the largest U.S. state. Sitting in the extreme northwest portion of North America, it is also the coldest. Above the Arctic Circle, winter means six months without sun, though in the summer the sun never sets. Many mountains here are very high: Mt. McKinley is the highest in North America. Many feel that the first people to settle North America may have come through Alaska from Asia many thousands of years ago. Alaska was settled on a large scale during and after the Gold Rush of the late 1890s, after it had become part of the United States. Today, most people earn a living by fishing, mining, oil extraction, transportation, and the service industry. Though almost 70% are of European descent, Native Alaskans still form about 16% of the population and actively maintain their heritage. Regardless of their origin, most people choose to live in Alaska rather than end up here by chance.

Alaska Almanac

Nickname	The Last Frontier	**Lowest elevation**	sea level
State capital	Juneau	**Land area & rank**	571,951 sq. miles (1,481,353 sq. km); 1st
Date of statehood	Jan. 3, 1959; 49th state	**Average January temperature**	10°F (−12°C)
State bird	Willow ptarmigan		
State flower	Forget-me-not	**Average July temperature**	54°F (12°C)
State tree	Sitka spruce		
State motto	North to the Future	**Average yearly precipitation**	22 inches (56 cm)
Total population & rank	634,892 (in 2001); 47th	**Major industries**	petroleum, tourism, fishing, mining, forestry
Population density	1.1 per sq. mile (0.4 per sq. km)		
Population distribution	66% urban, 34% rural	**Places to visit**	Glacier Bay National Park, Denali National Park, Inside Passage, Mendenhall Glacier, Skagway
Largest cities	Anchorage, Juneau, Fairbanks		
Highest elevation	Mt. McKinley, 20,320 ft. (6,194 m)	**Web site**	www.state.ak.us

Economy – Chief Products

Physical

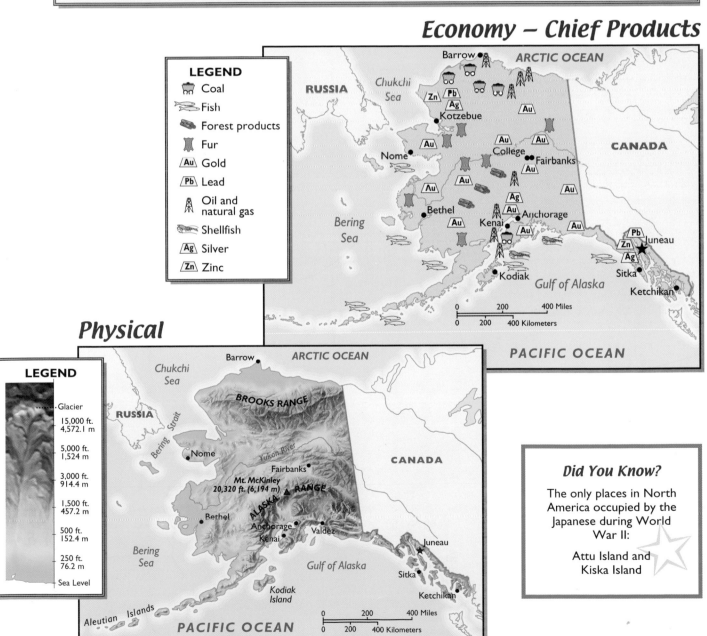

Did You Know?

The only places in North America occupied by the Japanese during World War II:

Attu Island and Kiska Island

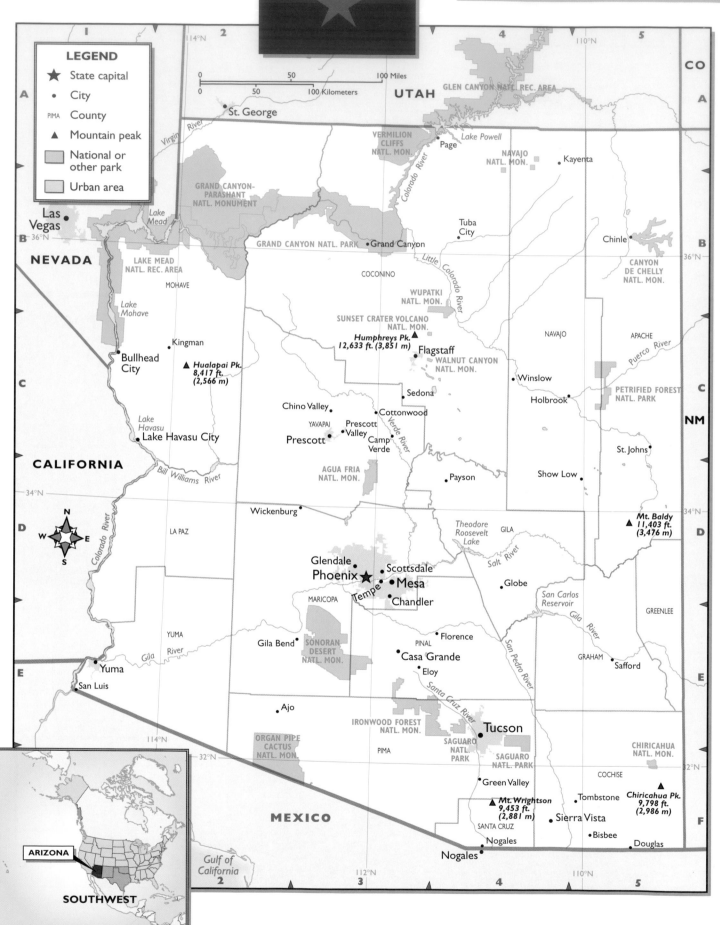

LEGEND
- ★ State capital
- • City
- PIMA County
- ▲ Mountain peak
- National or other park
- Urban area

50 Miles
50 100 Kilometers

UTAH

GLEN CANYON NATL. REC. AREA

St. George

VERMILION CLIFFS NATL. MON.
Page
Lake Powell
NAVAJO NATL. MON.
Kayenta

Las Vegas

NEVADA

36°N

LAKE MEAD NATL. REC. AREA

Lake Mead

GRAND CANYON-PARASHANT NATL. MONUMENT

GRAND CANYON NATL. PARK
Grand Canyon
Little Colorado River

CANYON DE CHELLY NATL. MON.

Chinle

36°N

MOHAVE

COCONINO

Lake Mohave

Tuba City

CO

NM

Kingman
Bullhead City

▲ Hualapai Pk. 8,417 ft. (2,566 m)

Humphreys Pk. 12,633 ft. (3,851 m) ▲
Flagstaff

WUPATKI NATL. MON.

SUNSET CRATER VOLCANO NATL. MON.

WALNUT CANYON NATL. MON.

NAVAJO

APACHE

Puerco River

Winslow

Holbrook

PETRIFIED FOREST NATL. PARK

Lake Havasu

Chino Valley

Sedona
Cottonwood

YAVAPAI
Prescott Valley
Prescott
Camp Verde

Verde River

St. Johns

Lake Havasu City

CALIFORNIA

Bill Williams River

34°N

AGUA FRIA NATL. MON.

Payson

Show Low

▲ Mt. Baldy 11,403 ft. (3,476 m)

34°N

Colorado River

N
W E
S

LA PAZ

Wickenburg

Theodore Roosevelt Lake

GILA

Glendale
Phoenix ★ Scottsdale
Tempe Mesa
Chandler

MARICOPA

Globe

San Carlos Reservoir

Salt River

GREENLEE

YUMA

Gila River

Gila Bend

SONORAN DESERT NATL. MON.

PINAL
Florence

Casa Grande
Eloy

San Pedro River

Gila River

GRAHAM
Safford

Yuma
San Luis

Ajo

IRONWOOD FOREST NATL. MON.

Santa Cruz River

PIMA

Tucson

SAGUARO NATL. PARK

CHIRICAHUA NATL. MON.

ORGAN PIPE CACTUS NATL. MON.

32°N

SAGUARO NATL. PARK

COCHISE

32°N

Green Valley

▲ *Mt. Wrightson* 9,453 ft. (2,881 m)

Tombstone

▲ Chiricahua Pk. 9,798 ft. (2,986 m)

Sierra Vista

MEXICO

SANTA CRUZ
Nogales

Bisbee

Douglas

F

Nogales

Gulf of California

112°N

110°N

ARIZONA

SOUTHWEST

While many think of Arizona as a dry, desert state, it also has many rivers and high, forested mountains. In the north, the raging Colorado River winds its way at the bottom of the spectacular Grand Canyon—which is as much as 1 mile (1.6 km) deep—before entering Lake Mead. Farther south, the land turns into a hot, dry desert with tall saguaro cacti dotting the landscape, and summertime high temperatures often top 110°F (43°C). Even though Arizona became a state only in 1912, Spanish explorers searching for gold were already here by 1539. Today, the people of Arizona are as mixed as the landscape. Mexican, Native American, European, and other cultures are all represented. Mining and ranching are common in the countryside, but services, tourism, and retail trade form the backbone of Arizona's economy. The sprawling capital city of Phoenix also has a vibrant high-technology industry, while the warm climate invites many to retire here.

Did You Know?

Pluto, the most distant planet from the sun, was discovered at this observatory:

Lowell Observatory in Flagstaff

Arizona Almanac

Nickname	Grand Canyon State
State capital	Phoenix
Date of statehood	Feb. 14, 1912; 48th state
State bird	Cactus wren
State flower	Blossom of the Saguaro cactus
State tree	Paloverde
State motto	*Ditat Deus* (God Enriches)
Total population & rank	5,307,331 (in 2001); 20th
Population density	47 per sq. mile (18 per sq. km)
Population distribution	88% urban, 12% rural
Largest cities	Phoenix, Tucson, Mesa, Glendale, Scottsdale, Chandler
Highest elevation	Humphreys Peak, 12,633 ft. (3,851 m)
Lowest elevation	Colorado River in Yuma Co., 70 ft. (21 m)
Land area & rank	113,635 sq. miles (294,315 sq. km); 6th
Average January temperature	44°F (7°C)
Average July temperature	83°F (28°C)
Average yearly precipitation	13 inches (33 cm)
Major industries	manufacturing, construction, tourism, mining, agriculture
Places to visit	Grand Canyon, Painted Desert, Petrified Forest, Navajo National Monument, Meteor Crater
Web site	www.state.az.gov

Economy – Chief Products

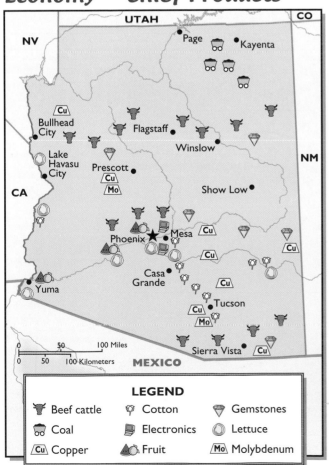

LEGEND

- 🐂 Beef cattle
- 🌱 Cotton
- 💎 Gemstones
- Coal
- 💻 Electronics
- Lettuce
- Cu Copper
- 🍇 Fruit
- Mo Molybdenum

Physical

LEGEND

- Glacier
- 15,000 ft. 4,572.1 m
- 5,000 ft. 1,524 m
- 3,000 ft. 914.4 m
- 1,500 ft. 457.2 m
- 500 ft. 152.4 m
- 250 ft. 76.2 m
- Sea Level

ARKANSAS

LEGEND

★ State capital
● City
GRANT County
▲ Mountain peak

National or other park
Urban area

MISSOURI

Joplin
Springfield

Grand Lake O'The Cherokees
Table Rock Lake
Bull Shoals Lake
Beaver Lake
Norfolk Lake

BENTON
Bentonville
Rogers
Springdale
Fayetteville

CARROLL
BOONE
Harrison

MARION
BAXTER
Mountain Home

FULTON
Pocahontas

RANDOLPH
CLAY

Black River

GREENE
Paragould

Blytheville

WASHINGTON
MADISON
NEWTON
BUFFALO NATL. RIVER
Buffalo River
SEARCY
STONE
Mountain View

SHARP
LAWRENCE

CRAIGHEAD
Jonesboro

Little River

MISSISSIPPI
Osceola

OKLAHOMA

CRAWFORD
FRANKLIN
JOHNSON

Clarksville

POPE
Lake Dardanelle
Russellville

VAN BUREN
Greers Ferry Lake
Heber Springs

CLEBURNE
Little

IZARD
Batesville
INDEPENDENCE

JACKSON
Newport
POINSETT
Trumann

St. Francis River

TENNESSEE

Van Buren
Fort Smith
SEBASTIAN
LOGAN
Magazine Mtn. ▲ 2,753 ft. (839 m)

Arkansas River

CONWAY
Morrilton
FAULKNER

White River
WHITE
Searcy

Red River

CROSS
WOODRUFF
Wynne

ST. FRANCIS
Forrest City

CRITTENDEN

West Memphis
Memphis

YELL
SCOTT

Fourche La Fave River

PERRY

Conway

PULASKI
North Little Rock
Little Rock
SALINE

LONOKE
PRAIRIE

De View

LEE
Marianna

MONROE
West Helena
Helena
PHILLIPS

Mena
POLK
MONTGOMERY
Lake Ouachita
GARLAND
HOT SPRINGS NATL. PARK
Hot Springs

Malvern
HOT SPRING
GRANT
JEFFERSON
Pine Bluff

Stuttgart
ARKANSAS

White River

MISSISSIPPI

De Queen
HOWARD
PIKE
Murfreesboro
Arkadelphia
CLARK

DALLAS

Saline River

CLEVELAND
LINCOLN

Arkansas River

SEVIER
Millwood Lake
Red River
Ashdown
LITTLE RIVER
HEMPSTEAD
Hope

NEVADA
OUACHITA
CALHOUN

Ouachita River

Warren
BRADLEY
DREW
Monticello

Dumas
DESHA

Mississippi River

Texarkana
Texarkana
MILLER

Camden
LAFAYETTE
COLUMBIA
Magnolia
UNION
El Dorado

Crossett
ASHLEY

CHICOT

TEXAS

LOUISIANA

Longview
Shreveport
Monroe

Vicksburg
Jackson

0   25   50 Miles
0   25   50 Kilometers

ARKANSAS

SOUTHEAST

Imagine a box with its right side beginning to tip out at the top, and you'll have the outline of Arkansas. The slanted eastern side is formed by the Mississippi River, a stream that looks as twisted and coiled as a phone cord. Crossing the state from west to southeast is the Arkansas River. Its valley divides the state's mountains. Year-round comfortable weather plus scenic beauty provided by forests, rivers, and lakes attract many visitors and residents to the mountains, especially to the northern portion known as the Ozarks. The southern portion features Hot Springs National Park, the country's oldest national park. Rivers flowing from the mountains cross a wide and flat plain on their way to the Mississippi. This is the state's prime farmland, used to raise a great variety of crops. Elsewhere in Arkansas, chickens, timber, and minerals are valuable, joined by important manufacturing and service businesses. The world headquarters of Wal-Mart is located near Bentonville.

Economy – Chief Products

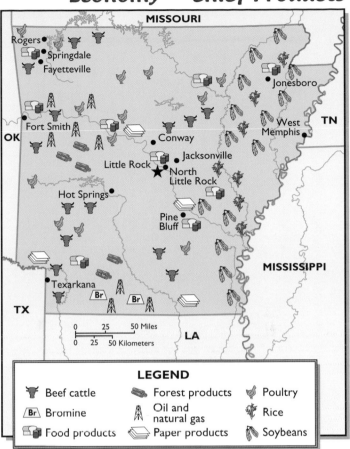

LEGEND

Beef cattle	Forest products	Poultry
Br Bromine	Oil and natural gas	Rice
Food products	Paper products	Soybeans

Physical

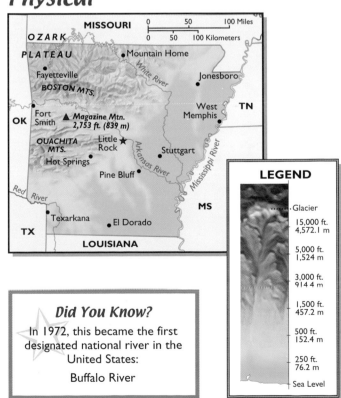

LEGEND

Glacier
15,000 ft. 4,572.1 m
5,000 ft. 1,524 m
3,000 ft. 914.4 m
1,500 ft. 457.2 m
500 ft. 152.4 m
250 ft. 76.2 m
Sea Level

Arkansas Almanac

Nicknames	Natural State, Razorback State
State capital	Little Rock
Date of statehood	June 15, 1836; 25th state
State bird	Mockingbird
State flower	Apple blossom
State tree	Pine
State motto	*Regnat Populus* (The People Rule)
Total population & rank	2,692,090 (in 2001); 33rd
Population density	52 per sq. mile (20 per sq. km)
Population distribution	52% urban, 48% rural
Largest cities	Little Rock, Fort Smith, North Little Rock, Fayetteville
Highest elevation	Magazine Mountain, 2,753 ft. (839 m)
Lowest elevation	Ouachita River, in Ashley & Union Counties, 55 ft. (17 m)
Land area & rank	52,068 sq. miles (134,856 sq. km); 27th
Average January temperature	40°F (4°C)
Average July temperature	80°F (27°C)
Average yearly precipitation	50 inches (127 cm)
Major industries	manufacturing, agriculture, tourism, forestry
Places to visit	Hot Springs National Park, Ozark Folk Center and Blanchard Springs Cavern (Mountain View), Crater of Diamonds (Murfreesboro)
Web site	www.state.ar.us

Did You Know?

In 1972, this became the first designated national river in the United States:

Buffalo River

CALIFORNIA REPUBLIC

OREGON

IDAHO

LEGEND

★ State capital
• City
SHASTA County
▲ Mountain peak
▽ Lowest point in United States
National or other park
Urban area

WEST

CALIFORNIA

Crescent City
REDWOOD NATL. PARK
DEL NORTE
•Yreka
SISKIYOU
MODOC
▲ Mt. Shasta 14,162 ft. (4,317 m)
•Alturas

Eureka •Arcata
HUMBOLDT
•Fortuna
TRINITY
Shasta Lake
SHASTA
LASSEN VOLCANIC NATL. PARK
LASSEN

Klamath River
Trinity River
Pit River

Redding
Anderson•
•Lassen Peak 10,457 ft. (3,187 m)
Red Bluff•
TEHAMA
•Susanville

Eel River
Fort Bragg•
MENDOCINO
Corning•
PLUMAS
40°N

Orland•
GLENN
Chico
BUTTE
SIERRA
Willits•
Oroville•
NEVADA

Ukiah•
COLUSA
LAKE
Grass Valley•
Reno
River

Clearlake•
Yuba City•
SUTTER
Marysville•
PLACER
Carson City

Healdsburg•
YOLO
Woodland•
Roseville•
Auburn•
South Lake Tahoe•

Santa Rosa•
Davis•
Placerville•
EL DORADO
Lake Tahoe
NEVADA

Sebastopol•
NAPA
Napa•
Sacramento★
AMADOR
ALPINE

Petaluma•
SOLANO
Vacaville•
SACRAMENTO
CALAVERAS

POINT REYES NATL. SEASHORE
Novato•
Vallejo•
MARIN
Lodi•
TUOLUMNE
YOSEMITE NATL. PARK
MONO

Berkeley•
Concord•
Stockton•
Mono Lake

San Francisco
CONTRA COSTA
SAN JOAQUIN
Manteca•
Boundary Pk. 13,140 ft (4,005 m)▲

SAN FRANCISCO
Oakland
Tracy•
Modesto•
Merced R.

San Mateo•
ALAMEDA
Milpitas•
STANISLAUS
MARIPOSA

SAN MATEO
Palo Alto
San Jose
Turlock•
MERCED
MADERA
Bishop•

SANTA CLARA
Morgan Hill•
Merced•
Chowchilla•

SANTA CRUZ
Gilroy•
Los Banos•
Madera•
FRESNO
KINGS CANYON NATL. PARK

Santa Cruz
Watsonville•
Clovis•

Monterey Bay
Hollister•
San Mendota•
Sanger•
Mt. Whitney 14,494 ft. (4,418 m)▲

Marina•
Salinas
BENITO
Fresno
INYO

Monterey•
PINNACLES NATL. MON.
SEQUOIA NATL. PARK
DEATH VALLEY NATL. PARK

POINT LOBOS STATE RESERVE
Soledad•
Kingsburg•
Las Vegas

Greenfield•
King City•
Hanford•
Visalia•
▽ Death Valley 282 ft. (86 m) below sea level

Salinas R.
Lemoore•
•Tulare
TULARE

MONTEREY
KINGS
•Porterville

•Avenal

Wasco•
•Delano
Ridgecrest•

Cambria•
Atascadero•
Oildale•
KERN

Morro Bay•
SAN LUIS OBISPO
•San Luis Obispo
Bakersfield
35°N

Pismo Beach•
•Tehachapi
Barstow•

Guadalupe•
Santa Maria
SAN BERNARDINO

SANTA BARBARA
Lancaster•
Lompoc•
VENTURA
LOS ANGELES
•Palmdale
Victorville•

Santa Barbara
Santa Paula•
Burbank•
Glendale
Pomona•
San Bernardino•

PACIFIC OCEAN

Ventura•
Camarillo•
Pasadena
Riverside
Palm Springs
JOSHUA TREE NATL. PARK

Oxnard•
Thousand Oaks
Santa Monica•
Los Angeles
Moreno Valley•
Cathedral City•
AZ

CHANNEL ISLANDS NATL. PARK
Torrance•
Anaheim•
Indio•
RIVERSIDE
Blythe•

Long Beach
Irvine•
ORANGE

Santa Catalina Island
San Clemente•
Temecula•

Vista•
San Marcos•
Salton Sea
IMPERIAL

Oceanside•
Escondido•
•Brawley

Carlsbad•
SAN DIEGO
Encinitas•
El Cajon•
•El Centro

San Diego
Chula Vista•
Mexicali
Yuma

Tijuana
MEXICO

NEVADA

Did You Know?
The highest and the lowest points in the contiguous United States are both in California:

Mount Whitney and Death Valley

0   50   100   150   200 Miles
0   50   100   150   200 Kilometers

With its 840-mile (1,352-km) coastline, California is probably the easiest western state to find on a map. California also has the largest population of any state in the United States. With its large size and population, California has many geographical features and many different kinds of people. It has hot, dry deserts and rich, green farmland; rolling foothills and rocky coastal regions; the nation's deepest valley and the highest mountain in the lower 48 states; and a variety of national parks and monuments. People have come to California from nearly every place on Earth, especially Asia and Latin America. Many come to live permanently, but many also come as tourists. For years, California has been famous as the home of movies and television. Many people work in these and other industries, including agriculture, tourism, and high-tech businesses.

California Almanac

Nickname	Golden State
State capital	Sacramento
Date of statehood	Sept. 9, 1850; 31st state
State bird	California valley quail
State flower	Golden poppy
State tree	California redwood
State motto	Eureka (I Have Found It)
Total population & rank	34,501,130 (in 2001); 1st
Population density	221 per sq. mile (85 per sq. km)
Population distribution	94% urban, 6% rural
Largest cities	Los Angeles, San Diego, San Jose, San Francisco, Long Beach
Highest elevation	Mt. Whitney, 14,494 ft. (4,418 m)
Lowest elevation	Death Valley, 282 ft. (86 m) below sea level
Land area & rank	155,959 sq. miles (403,934 sq. km); 3rd
Average January temperature	43°F (6°C)
Average July temperature	72°F (22°C)
Average yearly precipitation	22 inches (56 cm)
Major industries	agriculture, tourism, apparel, electronics, telecommunications, entertainment
Places to visit	Yosemite National Park, Lake Tahoe, Disneyland (Anaheim), San Diego Zoo, Hollywood, Sequoia Natl. Park, Pt. Lobos State Reserve
Web site	www.state.ca.us

Economy– Chief Products

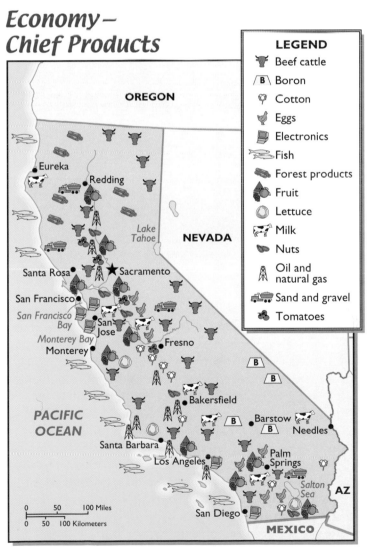

LEGEND
- 🐂 Beef cattle
- B Boron
- 🌸 Cotton
- 🐔 Eggs
- 💻 Electronics
- 🐟 Fish
- 🪵 Forest products
- 🍇 Fruit
- Lettuce
- 🐄 Milk
- Nuts
- Oil and natural gas
- 🚚 Sand and gravel
- Tomatoes

Physical

LEGEND
- ···· Glacier
- 15,000 ft. 4,572.1 m
- 5,000 ft. 1,524 m
- 3,000 ft. 914.4 m
- 1,500 ft. 457.2 m
- 500 ft. 152.4 m
- 250 ft. 76.2 m
- Sea Level

Map

WYOMING

NEBRASKA

★ Cheyenne

A

108°W
104°W
102°W

DINOSAUR NATL. MON.

MOFFAT — Craig — Steamboat Springs — JACKSON

LARIMER

Cache la Poudre R.

Fort Collins — WELD

Little Snake River

Loveland — Greeley

SEDGWICK — Julesburg

LOGAN — Sterling

PHILLIPS

Yampa River — ROUTT

ROCKY MOUNTAIN NATL. PARK

Estes Park

Longs Pk. 14,255 ft. (4,345 m) ▲

MORGAN — Brush — Fort Morgan

Yuma

40°N

White River

RIO BLANCO

GRAND

BOULDER

Boulder — Longmont

WASHINGTON

YUMA

40°N

ARAPAHO NATL. REC. AREA

BROOMFIELD

GILPIN

Arvada — Denver ★ — Aurora

ADAMS

GARFIELD — Rifle

Colorado River — Glenwood Springs

EAGLE — Vail

CLEAR CREEK — Lakewood — DENVER — Englewood

JEFFERSON — ARAPAHOE

Castle Rock

Arikaree River

B

SUMMIT

Mt. Evans 14,264 ft. (4,348 m) ▲

South Platte River

DOUGLAS

ELBERT

Limon

Burlington — KIT CARSON

PITKIN — Aspen

Leadville

LAKE

Mt. Elbert 14,433 ft. (4,399 m) ▲

PARK

TELLER

Colorado Springs

EL PASO — Fountain

LINCOLN

CHEYENNE

KS

Grand Junction

COLORADO NATL. MON.

Gunnison River — DELTA — Delta

MESA

Castle Pk. 14,265 ft. (4,348 m) ▲

Mt. Harvard 14,420 ft. (4,395 m) ▲

Buena Vista — CHAFFEE

GUNNISON

BLACK CANYON OF THE GUNNISON NATL. PARK

Gunnison

Pikes Pk. 14,110 ft. (4,301 m) ▲

FLORISSANT FOSSIL BEDS NATL. MON.

Horse Creek

South Fork Republican River

C

38°N

Dolores River

Montrose — MONTROSE

CURECANTI NATL. REC. AREA — Blue Mesa Reservoir

OURAY

SAN MIGUEL

Uncompahgre Pk. 14,309 ft. (4,361 m) ▲

Salida

SAGUACHE

FREMONT — Canon City

Arkansas River

CUSTER

Crestone Pk. 14,294 ft. (4,357 m) ▲

Pueblo — PUEBLO

CROWLEY

Rocky Ford

KIOWA

Las Animas — Lamar — PROWERS

OTERO — La Junta — BENT

Blue Sandy Creek

38°N

Telluride — SAN JUAN — HINSDALE

Mt. Wilson 14,246 ft. (4,342 m) ▲

ANASAZI B.L.M. REC. AREA

DOLORES

MINERAL

Rio Grande

MONTE VISTA — RIO GRANDE

Monte Vista

ALAMOSA — Alamosa

GREAT SAND DUNES NATL. PARK

Blanca Pk. 14,345 ft. (4,372 m) ▲

HUERFANO — Walsenburg

LAS ANIMAS

D

Cortez

MONTEZUMA — Durango — LA PLATA

MESA VERDE NATL. PARK

ARCHULETA

CONEJOS

COSTILLA

Purgatoire River — Trinidad

Springfield — BACA

Animas River

San Juan River

Farmington

NEW MEXICO

N W E S

108°W
106°W

0 25 50 75 100 Miles
0 25 50 75 100 Kilometers

104°W

OKLAHOMA

102°W

1 2 3 4 5

Legend

LEGEND

★ State capital
• City
ADAMS County
▲ Mountain peak
▭ National or other park
▭ Urban area

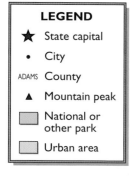

COLORADO

WEST

For many people, Colorado means the tall, snow-capped peaks of the Rocky Mountains and ski resorts. The state has more peaks over 14,000 feet (4,267 m)—known as "fourteeners"—than any of the lower 48 states. Having this scenery so close to the Front Range cities of Denver, Boulder, and Fort Collins causes even many city-dwellers to maintain an active outdoor lifestyle. The spectacular beauty of the mountains in the center of the state is balanced by dry, rugged ranchland in the west and prairie farmland in the east. Arid canyons in the southwest were once inhabited by Anasazi cliff dwellers, whose ancient structures can still be seen. Soon after settlers arrived in the 19th century, gold, silver, and lead were discovered and the population exploded. Today, a more diverse economy supplies a livelihood as ranching, farming, mining, tourism, and high technology all play major roles.

Colorado Almanac

Nickname	Centennial State	**Land area & rank**	103,718 sq. miles (268,630 sq. km); 8th
State capital	Denver		
Date of statehood	Aug. 1, 1876; 38th state	**Average January temperature**	23°F (−5°C)
State bird	Lark bunting		
State flower	Rocky Mountain columbine	**Average July temperature**	68°F (20°C)
State tree	Colorado blue spruce		
State motto	*Nil Sine Numine* (Nothing Without Providence)	**Average yearly precipitation**	15 inches (38 cm)
Total population & rank	4,417,714 (in 2001); 24th	**Major industries**	manufacturing, construction, government, tourism, agriculture, aerospace, electronics equipment
Population density	43 per sq. mile (17 per sq. km)		
Population distribution	84% urban, 16% rural		
Largest cities	Denver, Colorado Springs, Aurora, Lakewood	**Places to visit**	Rocky Mountain National Park, Mesa Verde National Park, Dinosaur National Monument, Pikes Peak, Central City
Highest elevation	Mt. Elbert, 14,433 ft. (4,399 m)		
Lowest elevation	Arikaree River in Yuma Co., 3,315 ft. (1,010 m)	**Web site**	www.colorado.gov

Physical

Did You Know?

The famous song "America the Beautiful" was inspired by the view from here:

Pikes Peak

Economy— Chief Products

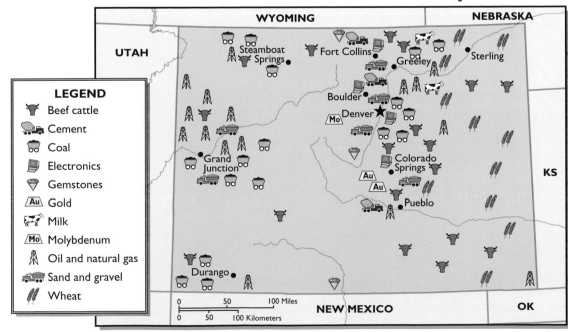

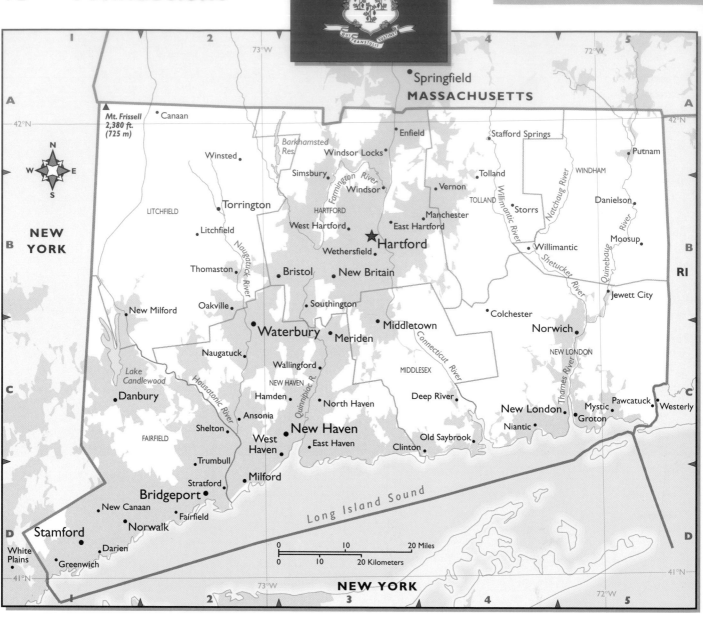

LEGEND

⭐ State capital   FAIRFIELD County   ▨ Urban area

● City   ▲ Mountain peak

New England's southernmost state is also the nation's third smallest state. The northwest and northeast portions are full of mountains and hills while the southern lowlands of the Atlantic coastal plain and the Connecticut River Valley, which bisects the state, are home to most of the state's population. The people of this state are mainly descendants of Western European immigrants who came to Connecticut in the 1800s. African Americans, Asians, and Latinos complete the make-up of this slow-growing state. Connecticut is rich in history, contributing the first state constitution based on the free consent of the people—the beginning of U.S. democracy. Most of the people in the state have jobs in the service industry (such as hotels), and finance industry (insurance, banking, and real estate). Because Connecticut has the highest percentage of workers with college degrees, high-tech manufacturing companies that make submarines, helicopters, and airplanes can find the qualified workers they need. Connecticut's beautiful coastline and charming New England towns attract many tourists.

Connecticut Almanac

Nicknames	Constitution State, Nutmeg State	**Lowest elevation**	sea level
State capital	Hartford	**Land area & rank**	4,845 sq. miles (12,549 sq. km); 48th
Date of statehood	Jan. 9, 1788; 5th state	**Average January temperature**	26°F (–3°C)
State bird	American robin		
State flower	Mountain laurel	**Average July temperature**	71°F (22°C)
State tree	White oak		
State motto	*Qui Transtulit Sustinet* (He Who Transplanted Still Sustains)	**Average yearly precipitation**	47 inches (119 cm)
Total population & rank	3,425,074 (in 2001); 29th	**Major industries**	manufacturing, retail trade, government, services, finance, insurance
Population density	707 per sq. mile (273 per sq. km)		
Population distribution	88% urban, 12% rural	**Places to visit**	Mystic Seaport, Marine Life Aquarium (Mystic), P.T. Barnum Museum (Bridgeport), Peabody Museum (New Haven)
Largest cities	Bridgeport, New Haven, Hartford, Stamford, Waterbury		
Highest elevation	south slope of Mt. Frissell, 2,380 ft. (725 m)	**Web site**	www.state.ct.us

Physical

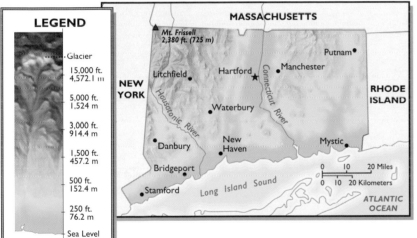

Did You Know?

The inspiration for that popular toy, the flying disk, was a baking company in Bridgeport:

Frisbee Baking Company

Economy– Chief Products

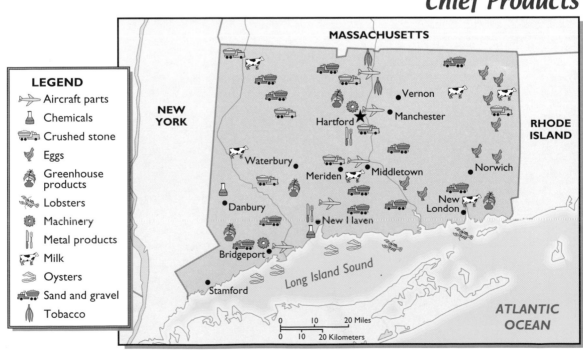

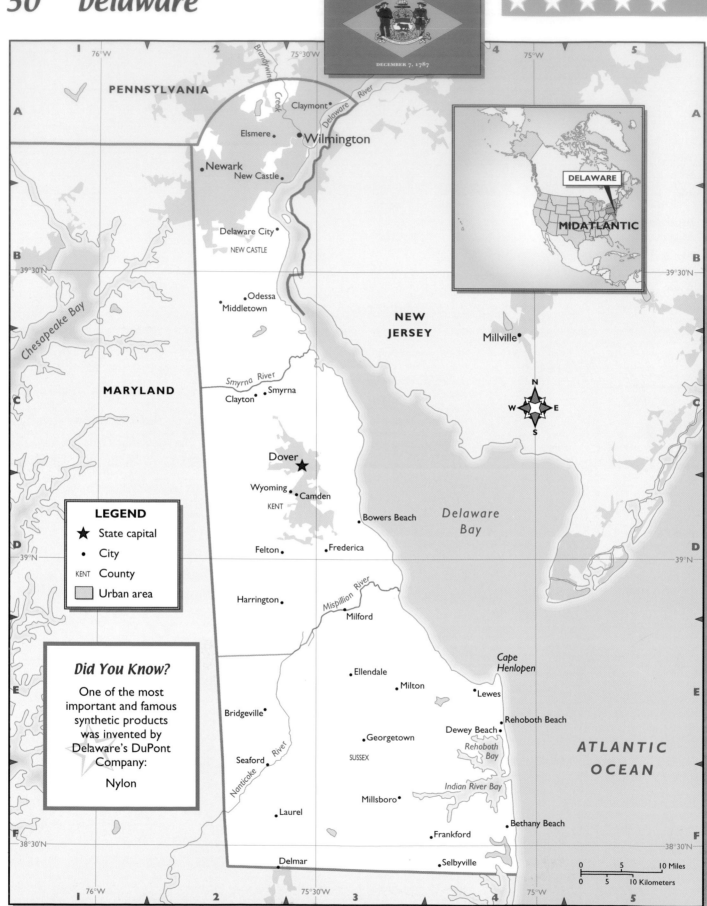

DECEMBER 7, 1787

PENNSYLVANIA

Claymont

Elsmere

Wilmington

Newark

New Castle

Delaware City

NEW CASTLE

Odessa

Middletown

MARYLAND

Smyrna River

Smyrna

Clayton

Dover

Wyoming

Camden

KENT

Bowers Beach

Felton

Frederica

Harrington

Mispillion River

Milford

Ellendale

Milton

Lewes

Bridgeville

Georgetown

SUSSEX

Rehoboth Bay

Seaford

Nanticoke River

Millsboro

Indian River Bay

Laurel

Frankford

Delmar

Selbyville

Chesapeake Bay

NEW JERSEY

Millville

Delaware Bay

Cape Henlopen

Rehoboth Beach

Dewey Beach

ATLANTIC OCEAN

Bethany Beach

DELAWARE

MIDATLANTIC

LEGEND

★ State capital

• City

KENT County

Urban area

Did You Know?

One of the most important and famous synthetic products was invented by Delaware's DuPont Company:

Nylon

0   5   10 Miles

0   5   10 Kilometers

Delaware is the second smallest state. Most of the wedge-shaped state is on the Delmarva Peninsula with the Atlantic Ocean and its beautiful white sand beaches on the east. Delaware is the flattest state and also the state with the overall lowest elevation. Most of the population of Delaware is in the north where E.I. du Pont established a gunpowder plant in 1802 that became one of the world's largest chemical companies. Since then, Delaware's taxes have favored corporations, encouraging many large banking, insurance, and real estate companies to open offices in the state's northern cities. These companies have made Delaware one of the wealthiest states. Southern Delaware has many farms. Poultry is the most important agricultural product in the state. In the last 20 years, tourism has grown because of the fine beach resorts, excellent museums, and the historic sites in colonial towns like New Castle and Lewes.

Economy – Chief Products

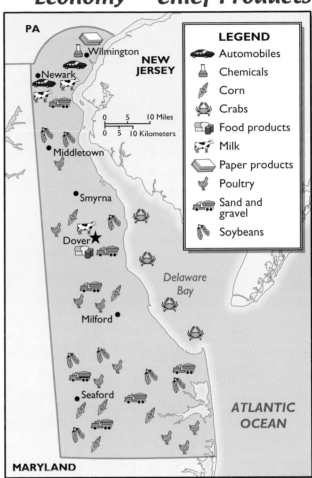

Physical

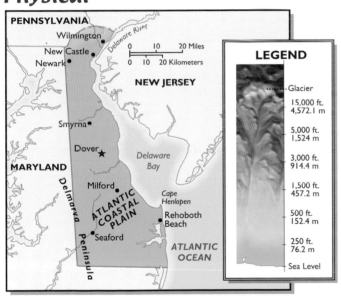

Delaware Almanac

Nicknames	First State, Diamond State	**Lowest elevation**	sea level
State capital	Dover	**Land area & rank**	1,954 sq. miles (5,061 sq. km); 49th
Date of statehood	Dec. 7, 1787; 1st state	**Average January temperature**	34°F (1°C)
State bird	Blue hen chicken		
State flower	Peach blossom	**Average July temperature**	76°F (24°C)
State tree	American holly		
State motto	Liberty and Independence	**Average yearly precipitation**	45 inches (114 cm)
Total population & rank	796,165 (in 2001); 45th		
Population density	408 per sq. mile (158 per sq. km)	**Major industries**	chemicals, agriculture, finance, poultry, shellfish, tourism
Population distribution	80% urban, 20% rural		
Largest cities	Wilmington, Dover, Newark	**Places to visit**	Wilmington: Winterthur Museum and Hagley Museum, Rehoboth Beach, New Castle
Highest elevation	Ebright Road in New Castle Co., 448 ft. (137 m)		
		Web site	www.delaware.gov

GEORGIA

LEGEND
★ State capital
• City
HENDRY County
National or other park
Swamp
Urban area

ATLANTIC OCEAN

Lake Seminole
Mariana
JACKSON
GADSDEN
★ Tallahassee
LEON
JEFFERSON
MADISON
HAMILTON
CALHOUN
LIBERTY
WAKULLA
Apalachicola River
Aucilla River
Perry
TAYLOR
SUWANNEE
Suwannee River
COLUMBIA
BAKER
Lake City
UNION
DUVAL
Jacksonville
NASSAU
Fernandina Beach
Amelia Island
St. Marys River
Ochlockonee River

GULF
FRANKLIN
Apalachee Bay
St. George Island

For continuation of map, see inset below

LAFAYETTE
GILCHRIST
DIXIE
ALACHUA
Gainesville
BRADFORD
CLAY
PUTNAM
St. Johns River
St. Augustine
FLAGLER
Palm Coast
ST. JOHNS

Waccasassa Bay
LEVY
MARION
Ocala
Lake George
VOLUSIA
Daytona Beach
Port Orange
CANAVERAL NATL. SEASHORE

N
W E
S

Gulf of Mexico

Withlacoochee River
CITRUS
Inverness
SUMTER
LAKE
Lake Apopka
SEMINOLE
Sanford
Deltona
HERNANDO
Spring Hill
ORANGE
Orlando
Titusville
BREVARD
Merritt Island
Cape Canaveral

New Port Richey
PASCO
Kissimmee
Tarpon Springs
Clearwater
PINELLAS
Tampa
HILLSBOROUGH
Lakeland
POLK
OSCEOLA
Lake Kissimmee
Melbourne
Palm Bay

SOUTHEAST
FLORIDA

St. Petersburg
Tampa Bay
MANATEE
Bradenton
Sarasota
SARASOTA
HARDEE
Peace River
DE SOTO
HIGHLANDS
Sebring
Lake Istokpoga
OKEECHOBEE
Kissimmee River
INDIAN RIVER
Vero Beach
Fort Pierce
ST. LUCIE
Port St. Lucie

Venice
Port Charlotte
CHARLOTTE
GLADES
Lake Okeechobee
MARTIN
Jupiter

Charlotte Harbor
Fort Myers
LEE
Cape Coral
HENDRY
Caloosahatchee River
PALM BEACH
Belle Glade
West Palm Beach
Delray Beach
Boca Raton

Sanibel Island
Immokalee
Coral Springs
Pompano Beach
BROWARD
Fort Lauderdale
Hollywood
Naples
COLLIER
Tamiami Canal
Hialeah
Miami Beach

Marco Island
Coral Gables
Miami
MIAMI-DADE
Biscayne Bay

EVERGLADES NATIONAL PARK
Homestead
BISCAYNE NATL. PARK

Whitewater Bay
MONROE
Cape Sable
Key Largo

Florida Bay

0   25   50 Miles
0   25   50 Kilometers

MONROE
Keys
Key West
Marathon
Florida

DRY TORTUGAS NATL. PARK

ALABAMA
Conecuh R.
Dothan
ESCAMBIA
SANTA ROSA
Escambia R.
OKALOOSA
Crestview
WALTON
HOLMES
Choctawhatchee R.
WASHINGTON
JACKSON
Marianna
Niceville
Pensacola
Fort Walton Beach
GULF ISLANDS NATL. SEASHORE
BAY
CALHOUN
Panama City
GULF
Gulf of Mexico

84°W   82°W   30°N   28°N   26°N   80°W   86°W

Florida is located in the southeastern corner of the United States. It has a narrow extension called the Panhandle that curves south to become a wide, flat peninsula separating the Gulf of Mexico and the Atlantic Ocean. Tropical summertime heat discouraged year-around residents before air conditioning was common. Now the state has the fourth-largest population in the United States, boosted by senior citizens and immigrants from nearby Caribbean and Central American nations. Florida is well known for its oranges and orange juice, but other leading farm products include vegetables and sugar cane. The space exploration facilities at Cape Canaveral gave birth to ever-growing electronic and high-tech businesses. Yet Florida is best known as a vacation destination, from the world famous attractions in Orlando to the mile after mile of beaches surrounding the state like a sandy skin.

Economy – Chief Products

LEGEND
- Aircraft parts
- Beef cattle
- Citrus fruit
- Electronics
- Fish and shellfish
- Forest products
- Oil
- Phosphate rock
- Potted plants
- Sugar cane
- Tomatoes
- Vegetables

Did You Know?

In 1564, the French established a colony on the St. Johns River. The following year, Spaniards killed the French and founded their own settlement, now the oldest permanent settlement in the United States:

St. Augustine

Physical

Florida Almanac

Nickname	Sunshine State
State capital	Tallahassee
Date of statehood	March 3, 1845; 27th state
State bird	Mockingbird
State flower	Orange blossom
State tree	Sabal palmetto palm
State motto	In God We Trust
Total population & rank	16,396,515 (in 2001); 4th
Population density	304 per sq. mile (117 per sq. km)
Population distribution	89% urban, 11% rural
Largest cities	Jacksonville, Miami, Tampa, St. Petersburg, Hialeah
Highest elevation	Sec. 30, T.6N, R.20W in Walton Co., 345 ft. (105 m)
Lowest elevation	sea level
Land area & rank	53,927 sq. miles (139,671 sq. km); 26th
Average January temperature	61°F (16°C)
Average July temperature	82°F (28°C)
Average yearly precipitation	54 inches (137 cm)
Major industries	tourism, agriculture, manufacturing, construction
Places to visit	Busch Gardens (Tampa), Spaceport USA at Kennedy Space Center, Everglades Natl. Park, St. Augustine, Orlando: Walt Disney World, Universal Studios
Web site	www.myflorida.com

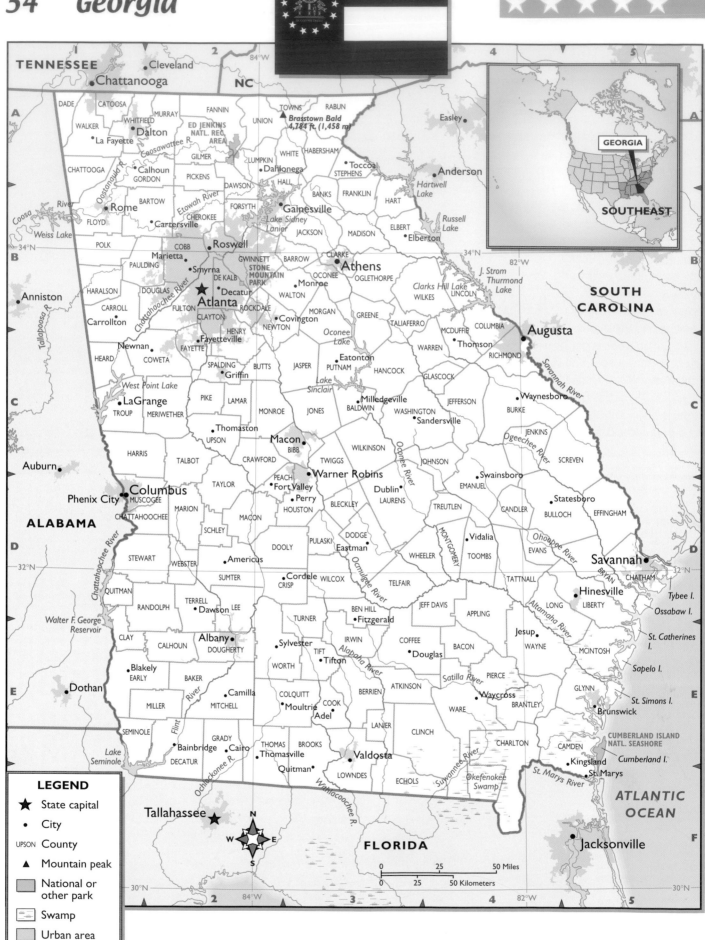

TENNESSEE
Cleveland
Chattanooga
NC

DADE
CATOOSA
WALKER
WHITFIELD
MURRAY
FANNIN
TOWNS
RABUN
Brasstown Bald
4,784 ft. (1,458 m)
Easley
Dalton
La Fayette
ED JENKINS NATL. REC. AREA
GILMER
UNION
Anderson
CHATTOOGA
Calhoun
GORDON
PICKENS
LUMPKIN
Dahlonega
WHITE
HABERSHAM
Toccoa
STEPHENS
Hartwell Lake
Rome
BARTOW
DAWSON
FORSYTH
HALL
BANKS
FRANKLIN
HART
Cartersville
CHEROKEE
Gainesville
Lake Sidney Lanier
JACKSON
MADISON
ELBERT
Russell Lake
Elberton
POLK
COBB
Roswell
GWINNETT
BARROW
CLARKE
Athens
OCONEE
OGLETHORPE
WILKES
LINCOLN
Clarks Hill Lake
J. Strom Thurmond Lake
SOUTH CAROLINA
Anniston
Marietta
PAULDING
Smyrna
DE KALB
STONE MOUNTAIN PARK
Monroe
WALTON
Decatur
Atlanta
FULTON
ROCKDALE
MORGAN
Covington
GREENE
TALIAFERRO
MCDUFFIE
Thomson
COLUMBIA
RICHMOND
Augusta
HARALSON
DOUGLAS
CARROLL
CLAYTON
Carrollton
HENRY
Fayetteville
FAYETTE
NEWTON
Oconee Lake
WARREN
GLASCOCK
Waynesboro
BURKE
Newnan
COWETA
HEARD
SPALDING
Griffin
BUTTS
JASPER
PUTNAM
Eatonton
HANCOCK
WASHINGTON
Sandersville
JEFFERSON
LaGrange
TROUP
PIKE
LAMAR
MONROE
JONES
Lake Sinclair
BALDWIN
Milledgeville
JENKINS
SCREVEN
West Point Lake
MERIWETHER
Thomaston
UPSON
CRAWFORD
Macon
BIBB
TWIGGS
WILKINSON
JOHNSON
Swainsboro
EMANUEL
Statesboro
BULLOCH
EFFINGHAM
HARRIS
TALBOT
Warner Robins
PEACH
Fort Valley
Perry
HOUSTON
BLECKLEY
Dublin
LAURENS
TREUTLEN
CANDLER
Auburn
TAYLOR
MARION
MACON
SCHLEY
DODGE
Eastman
Vidalia
TOOMBS
Ohoopee River
Phenix City
Columbus
MUSCOGEE
CHATTAHOOCHEE
PULASKI
WHEELER
MONTGOMERY
EVANS
ALABAMA
STEWART
WEBSTER
DOOLY
Americus
SUMTER
WILCOX
Cordele
CRISP
TELFAIR
TATTNALL
Savannah
CHATHAM
QUITMAN
RANDOLPH
TERRELL
LEE
Dawson
TURNER
BEN HILL
Fitzgerald
JEFF DAVIS
APPLING
Hinesville
LIBERTY
LONG
Walter F. George Reservoir
CLAY
CALHOUN
Albany
DOUGHERTY
WORTH
Sylvester
TIFT
Tifton
IRWIN
COFFEE
Douglas
BACON
Jesup
WAYNE
MCINTOSH
Blakely
EARLY
BAKER
Camilla
MITCHELL
COLQUITT
Moultrie
COOK
Adel
BERRIEN
ATKINSON
Satilla River
Waycross
WARE
PIERCE
GLYNN
Brunswick
Dothan
MILLER
SEMINOLE
Flint River
GRADY
Cairo
DECATUR
Bainbridge
THOMAS
Thomasville
Quitman
BROOKS
LANIER
CLINCH
Valdosta
LOWNDES
ECHOLS
Okefenokee Swamp
CHARLTON
Kingsland
CAMDEN
St. Marys
Lake Seminole
Ochlockonee R.
Tallahassee
FLORIDA
Withlacoochee R.
Suwannee River
St. Marys River
Cumberland I.
CUMBERLAND ISLAND NATL. SEASHORE
Tybee I.
Ossabaw I.
St. Catherines I.
Sapelo I.
St. Simons I.
ATLANTIC OCEAN
Jacksonville

LEGEND

★ State capital

• City

UPSON County

▲ Mountain peak

National or other park

Swamp

Urban area

0 25 50 Miles
0 25 50 Kilometers

The largest state east of the Mississippi River, Georgia sits at the turning point where the column of Atlantic Coast states bends to become the row of Gulf Coast states. Since 1990, Georgia has been among the fastest growing states. This growth rate has been elevated by new residents moving into the state, particularly people looking for a comfortable place to retire. The southern half of the state is a coastal plain: flat and primarily farmland. The southeastern corner contains the wet-and-wild Okefenokee Swamp. The northern half of the state rises from rolling hills to the peaks of the Appalachian Mountains. Many of the rivers within the mountains are popular for whitewater rafting. Georgia is well known for its farm products, especially peanuts, peaches, and chickens, but manufacturing and services are even more important. Many of these businesses are located in metropolitan Atlanta.

Did You Know?

Most people have heard about California's Gold Rush, but the first U.S. gold rush was near this town in the late 1820s:

Dahlonega

Georgia Almanac

Nicknames	Empire State of the South, Peach State
State capital	Atlanta
Date of statehood	Jan, 2, 1788; 4th state
State bird	Brown thrasher
State flower	Cherokee rose
State tree	Live oak
State motto	Wisdom, Justice and Moderation
Total population & rank	8,383,915 (in 2001); 10th
Population density	145 per sq. mile (56 per sq. km)
Population distribution	72% urban, 28% rural
Largest cities	Atlanta, Augusta, Columbus, Savannah, Athens
Highest elevation	Brasstown Bald, 4,784 ft. (1,458 m)
Lowest elevation	sea level
Land area & rank	57,906 sq. miles (149,977 sq. km); 21st
Average January temperature	46°F (8°C)
Average July temperature	80°F (27°C)
Average yearly precipitation	50 inches (127 cm)
Major industries	services, manufacturing, retail trade
Places to visit	Stone Mountain Park, Historic Savannah, Okefenokee Swamp, Atlanta: Six Flags Over Georgia, Martin Luther King, Jr. National Historic Site;
Web site	www.georgia.gov

Economy – Chief Products

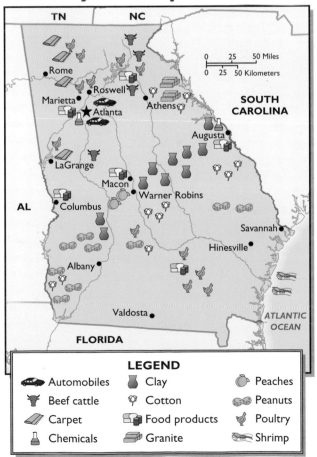

LEGEND

Automobiles		Clay		Peaches	
Beef cattle		Cotton		Peanuts	
Carpet		Food products		Poultry	
Chemicals		Granite		Shrimp	

Physical

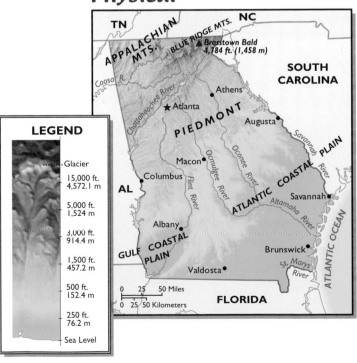

LEGEND

Glacier

15,000 ft. 4,572.1 m

5,000 ft. 1,524 m

3,000 ft. 914.4 m

1,500 ft. 457.2 m

500 ft. 152.4 m

250 ft. 76.2 m

Sea Level

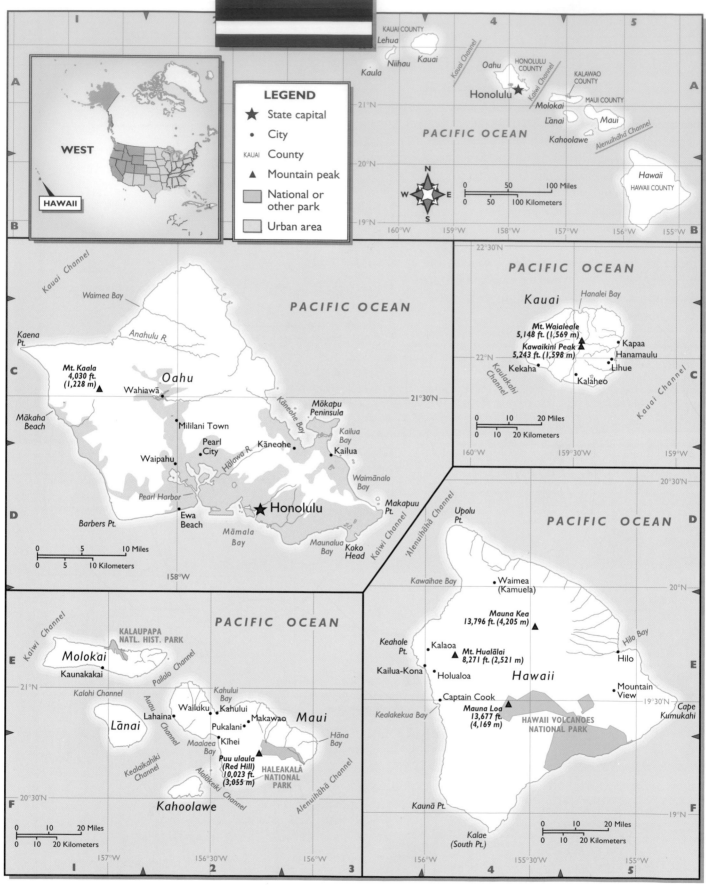

HAWAII

LEGEND

★ State capital

• City

KAUAI County

▲ Mountain peak

National or other park

Urban area

KAUAI COUNTY
Lehua
Kaula
Niihau
Kauai
Kauai Channel
Oahu
HONOLULU COUNTY
Honolulu ★
Kaiwi Channel
KALAWAO COUNTY
MAUI COUNTY
Molokai
Lānai
Maui
Kahoolawe
Alenuihāhā Channel

PACIFIC OCEAN

Hawaii
HAWAII COUNTY

0   50   100 Miles
0   50   100 Kilometers

Oahu
PACIFIC OCEAN
Kauai Channel
Waimea Bay
Anahulu R.
Kaena Pt.
Mt. Kaala 4,030 ft. (1,228 m) ▲
Wahiawā
Mākaha Beach
Mililani Town
Pearl City
Waipahu
Pearl Harbor
Hālawa R.
Kāneohe Bay
Kāneohe
Mōkapu Peninsula
Kailua Bay
Kailua
Waimānalo Bay
Barbers Pt.
Ewa Beach
Honolulu ★
Māmala Bay
Maunalua Bay
Koko Head
Makapuu Pt.
Kaiwi Channel

0   5   10 Miles
0   5   10 Kilometers

Kauai
PACIFIC OCEAN
Hanalei Bay
Mt. Waialeale 5,148 ft. (1,569 m) ▲
Kawaikini Peak 5,243 ft. (1,598 m) ▲
Kapaa
Hanamaulu
Kekaha
Lihue
Kalaheo
Kaulakahi Channel
Kauai Channel

0   10   20 Miles
0   10   20 Kilometers

Molokai / Lānai / Maui / Kahoolawe
Kaiwi Channel
KALAUPAPA NATL. HIST. PARK
PACIFIC OCEAN
Molokai
Kaunakakai
Pailolo Channel
Kalohi Channel
Lāhaina
Auau Channel
Lānai
Kealaikahiki Channel
Wailuku
Kahului Bay
Kahului
Pukalani
Kīhei
Maalaea Bay
Makawao
Maui
Hāna Bay
Puu ulaula (Red Hill) 10,023 ft. (3,055 m) ▲
HALEAKALĀ NATIONAL PARK
Alalākeiki Channel
Kahoolawe
Alenuihāhā Channel

0   10   20 Miles
0   10   20 Kilometers

Hawaii
Upolu Pt.
PACIFIC OCEAN
Alenuihāhā Channel
Kawaihae Bay
Waimea (Kamuela)
Mauna Kea 13,796 ft. (4,205 m) ▲
Keahole Pt.
Kalaoa
Mt. Hualālai 8,271 ft. (2,521 m) ▲
Kailua-Kona
Holualoa
Hilo Bay
Hilo
Mountain View
Captain Cook
Mauna Loa 13,677 ft. (4,169 m) ▲
Kealakekua Bay
Hawaii
HAWAII VOLCANOES NATIONAL PARK
Cape Kumukahi
Kaunā Pt.
Kalae (South Pt.)

0   10   20 Miles
0   10   20 Kilometers

Hawaii is often thought of as a tropical paradise, and it is that. Magnificent sun-drenched beaches stretch for miles on the state's many islands, and along the coast the temperature hovers around 85°F (29°C) every day. However, snow falls on Mauna Kea, which soars almost 14,000 feet (4,267 m) above the sea. Molokai has the highest sea cliffs in the world at 3,300 feet (1,006 m). On the island of Hawaii, Kilauea Volcano began erupting in 1983 with spectacular fountains of molten rock and is still active. Polynesians first settled on the islands around A.D. 300. In 1898, Hawaii was annexed by the United States, and it became the 50th state to enter the Union in 1959. The tourist industry has boomed, drawing visitors from around the globe and forming the mainstay of Hawaii's economy. Pineapple and sugar growing have declined in importance, while the military and service sectors are strong. Residents share a mix of cultures, with Hawaiian, European, and Japanese being most prominent.

Economy – Chief Products

LEGEND

- 🐂 Beef cattle
- ☕ Coffee
- 🚚 Crushed stone
- 🐟 Fish
- 🌿 Flowers
- 📦 Food products
- 🥜 Macadamia nuts
- 🍍 Pineapple
- 🌾 Sugar cane

Physical

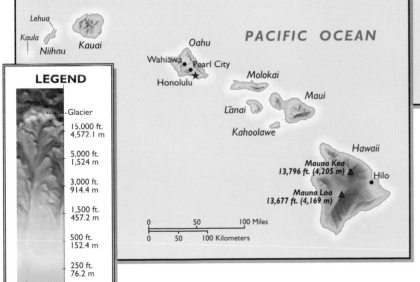

LEGEND

- Glacier
- 15,000 ft. / 4,572.1 m
- 5,000 ft. / 1,524 m
- 3,000 ft. / 914.4 m
- 1,500 ft. / 457.2 m
- 500 ft. / 152.4 m
- 250 ft. / 76.2 m
- Sea Level

Hawaii Almanac

Nickname	Aloha State	Lowest elevation	sea level
State capital	Honolulu	Land area & rank	6,423 sq. miles (16,636 sq. km); 47th
Date of statehood	Aug. 21, 1959; 50th state	Average January temperature	68°F (20°C)
State bird	Nēnē (Hawaiian goose)		
State flower	Yellow hibiscus	Average July temperature	74°F (23°C)
State tree	Kukui (candlenut)		
State motto	Ua mau ke ea o ka aina i ka pono (The Life of the Land Is Perpetuated in Righteousness)	Average yearly precipitation	67 inches (170 cm)
		Major industries	tourism, defense, agriculture
Total population & rank	1,224,398 (in 2001); 42nd	Places to visit	Hawaii Volcanoes National Park, Haleakalā National Park, Pearl Harbor and U.S.S. Arizona Memorial
Population density	191 per sq. mile (74 per sq. km)		
Population distribution	92% urban, 8% rural		
Largest cities	Honolulu, Hilo, Kailua, Kāneohe		
Highest elevation	Mauna Kea, 13,796 ft. (4,205 m)	Web site	www.hawaii.gov

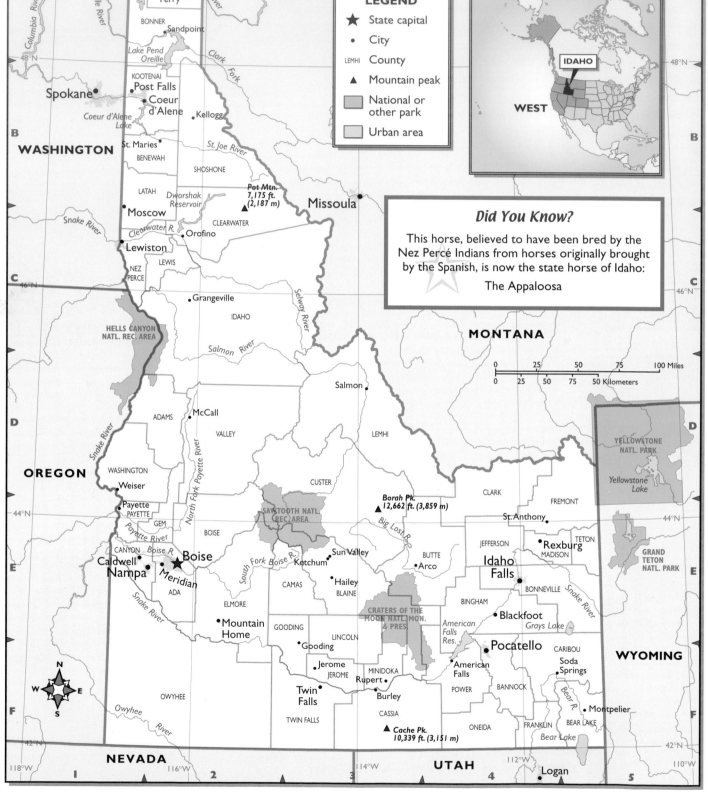

LEGEND

★ State capital
• City
LEMHI County
▲ Mountain peak
National or other park
Urban area

IDAHO

WEST

Did You Know?

This horse, believed to have been bred by the Nez Percé Indians from horses originally brought by the Spanish, is now the state horse of Idaho:

The Appaloosa

BRITISH COLUMBIA
ALBERTA CANADA

Priest Lake
BOUNDARY
Bonners Ferry
BONNER
Sandpoint
Lake Pend Oreille
Spokane
KOOTENAI
Post Falls
Coeur d'Alene
Coeur d'Alene Lake
Kellogg
WASHINGTON
St. Maries
BENEWAH
SHOSHONE
St. Joe River
Clark Fork
Pend Oreille River
Columbia River
Kootenai River

LATAH
Dworshak Reservoir
Pot Mtn.
7,175 ft.
(2,187 m)
Moscow
Missoula
CLEARWATER
Orofino
Clearwater R.
Snake River
LEWIS
Lewiston
NEZ PERCE

Grangeville
IDAHO
Selway River

HELLS CANYON NATL. REC. AREA

MONTANA

Salmon River
Salmon

0   25   50   75   100 Miles
0 25 50 75 50 Kilometers

McCall
ADAMS
VALLEY
LEMHI

YELLOWSTONE NATL. PARK
Yellowstone Lake

OREGON
WASHINGTON
Weiser
Snake River
Payette
PAYETTE
GEM
Payette River
North Fork Payette River

CUSTER

SAWTOOTH NATL. REC. AREA

Borah Pk.
12,662 ft. (3,859 m)
Big Lost R.
CLARK
FREMONT
St. Anthony

CANYON
Boise R.
Caldwell
Nampa
Meridian
ADA
BOISE
Boise
South Fork Boise R.
Ketchum
Sun Valley
Hailey
BLAINE
CAMAS
ELMORE

JEFFERSON
Rexburg
MADISON
TETON

BUTTE
Arco
Idaho Falls
BONNEVILLE
Snake River

GRAND TETON NATL. PARK

Snake River
Mountain Home
GOODING
CRATERS OF THE MOON NATL. MON. & PRES.
LINCOLN
American Falls Res.
BINGHAM
Blackfoot
Grays Lake

Gooding
Jerome
JEROME
MINIDOKA
Rupert
Pocatello
CARIBOU
Soda Springs
American Falls
POWER
BANNOCK
WYOMING

OWYHEE
Twin Falls
Burley
CASSIA
ONEIDA
FRANKLIN
BEAR LAKE
Bear R.
Montpelier

Owyhee River
TWIN FALLS
Cache Pk.
10,339 ft. (3,151 m)
Bear Lake

N
W   E
S

NEVADA
UTAH
Logan

The shape of Idaho is notable for its narrowing, northern extension called the Panhandle. This creates an outline that looks a little like a triangle but also could be described as a factory building with a tall chimney. Idaho is one of the Rocky Mountain States whose population growth has been greater than the U.S. average. Many of the cities in the state have grown to be twice the size they were in 1990. People are coming to Idaho to work in high-tech businesses and because they expect to be more comfortable in a state with a small population and an attractive environment. Making a large, U-shaped curve across the widest part of the state is the Snake River. The flat plain surrounding the river is where most of the people live and where most of the farming is done. Idaho is famous for growing potatoes. Potatoes are even mentioned on its automobile license plates. The rugged mountains north of the plain are the home of alpine lakes, dense forests, and roadless wilderness areas.

Idaho Almanac

Nickname	Gem State
State capital	Boise
Date of statehood	July 3, 1890; 43rd state
State bird	Mountain bluebird
State flower	Syringa
State tree	White pine
State motto	Esto Perpetua (It Is Perpetual)
Total population & rank	1,321,006 (in 2001); 39th
Population density	16 per sq. mile (6 per sq. km)
Population distribution	66% urban, 34% rural
Largest cities	Boise, Nampa, Pocatello
Highest elevation	Borah Peak, 12,662 ft. (3,859 m)
Lowest elevation	Snake River in Nez Perce Co., 710 ft. (216 m)
Land area & rank	82,747 sq. miles (214,315 sq. km); 11th
Average January temperature	24°F (–4°C)
Average July temperature	68°F (20°C)
Average yearly precipitation	19 inches (48 cm)
Major industries	manufacturing, agriculture, tourism, lumber, mining
Places to visit	Sun Valley, Hells Canyon, Craters of the Moon National Monument, World Center for Birds of Prey (Boise), Old Fort Hall (Pocatello)
Web site	www.state.id.us

Economy— Chief Products

LEGEND

- 🐂 Beef cattle
- 💻 Electronics
- 🪵 Forest products
- Au Gold
- ✖ Hay
- Pb Lead
- 🚛 Phosphate rock
- Potatoes
- 🐑 Sheep
- Ag Silver
- 🌱 Sugar beets
- 🌾 Wheat

Physical

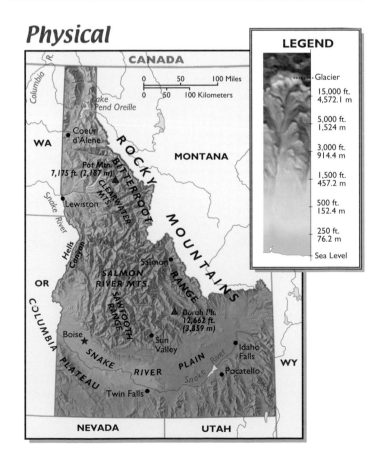

LEGEND

- ⋯⋯ Glacier
- 15,000 ft. 4,572.1 m
- 5,000 ft. 1,524 m
- 3,000 ft. 914.4 m
- 1,500 ft. 457.2 m
- 500 ft. 152.4 m
- 250 ft. 76.2 m
- Sea Level

ILLINOIS

LEGEND

★ State capital

• City

KNOX County

▲ Mountain peak

Urban area

WISCONSIN

IOWA

MISSOURI

INDIANA

KENTUCKY

Lake Michigan

MI

Racine
Kenosha
Waukegan
Evanston
Chicago
Hammond
Gary
South Bend

Dubuque
▲ Charles Mound
1,235 ft. (376 m)
Beloit
JO DAVIESS
STEPHENSON
WINNEBAGO
BOONE
MCHENRY
LAKE
Freeport
Rockford
CARROLL
OGLE
KANE
Elgin
De Kalb
DE KALB
DU PAGE
COOK
Aurora
Naperville
Joliet
Sterling
WHITESIDE
LEE

Davenport
Bettendorf
Rock Island
Moline
ROCK ISLAND
HENRY
BUREAU
Kewanee
MERCER
LA SALLE
Ottawa
Morris
Streator
GRUNDY
KANKAKEE
Kankakee
Kankakee River

PUTNAM
STARK
MARSHALL
LIVINGSTON
Pontiac
Watseka
IROQUOIS

Galesburg
WARREN
KNOX
Spoon River
PEORIA
WOODFORD
Peoria
Pekin
TAZEWELL
Normal
Bloomington
MCLEAN
FORD
VERMILION

HENDERSON
Macomb
HANCOCK
MCDONOUGH
FULTON
SCHUYLER
MASON
LOGAN
DE WITT
CHAMPAIGN
Champaign
Urbana
Danville
Lafayette

ADAMS
BROWN
Quincy
CASS
MENARD
Sangamon River
MACON
Decatur
PIATT
DOUGLAS
EDGAR
Paris

PIKE
SCOTT
MORGAN
Jacksonville
SANGAMON
Springfield
Taylorville
CHRISTIAN
Lake Shelbyville
MOULTRIE
COLES
Charleston
CLARK
Terre Haute
Bloomington

PETER
GREENE
Carlinville
MACOUPIN
MONTGOMERY
Litchfield
FAYETTE
EFFINGHAM
Effingham
JASPER
CRAWFORD

CALHOUN
JERSEY
Alton
St. Charles
MADISON
BOND
Vandalia
Olney
RICHLAND
LAWRENCE

Columbia
Collinsville
CLINTON
MARION
Centralia
CLAY
EDWARDS
WABASH

St. Louis
East St. Louis
Belleville
ST. CLAIR
WASHINGTON
Mount Vernon
JEFFERSON
WAYNE
WHITE
Carmi
Evansville

Jefferson City
MONROE
Kaskaskia River
Rend Lake
HAMILTON
Henderson
Owensboro

Chester
RANDOLPH
PERRY
FRANKLIN
Benton
SALINE
GALLATIN

Carbondale
JACKSON
Marion
WILLIAMSON
POPE
HARDIN

UNION
JOHNSON
ALEXANDER
PULASKI
MASSAC
Metropolis
KENTUCKY

Ohio River
Cairo

MIDWEST
ILLINOIS

Mississippi River
Rock River
Illinois River
Fox River
Des Plaines River
Vermilion River
Missouri River
Little Wabash River
Embarras River
Wabash River
Ohio River

92°W
90°W
88°W
42°N
40°N
38°N

0   25   50 Miles
0   25   50 Kilometers

Illinois is a tall and narrow state—tall like Abraham Lincoln, who lived there for many years, and tall like a skyscraper, which was a type of building invented in Chicago. The protruding western edge is formed by the Mississippi River. Illinois has more miles of Mississippi River boundary than any other state. Although the southern tip of the state has some modest, forest-covered hills, about 80% of the land is used for farming. Illinois farmers typically raise corn, soybeans, and livestock. The most valuable products of Illinois come from its cities, particularly Chicago. More than a transportation hub, food processing center, and corporate headquarters, Chicago has made many contributions to the state, the United States, and even the world. These contributions have involved art, music, literature, and architecture, as well as social welfare and the rights of workers.

Economy – Chief Products

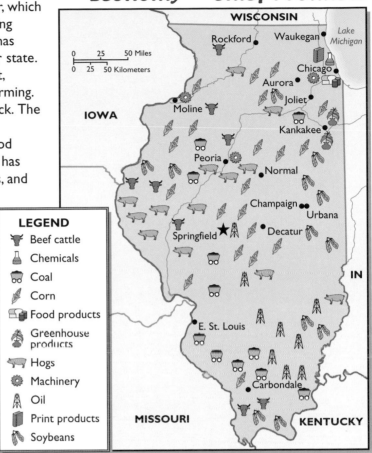

LEGEND

- 🐃 Beef cattle
- ⚗ Chemicals
- Coal
- 🌽 Corn
- 🍱 Food products
- 🌿 Greenhouse products
- 🐖 Hogs
- ⚙ Machinery
- Oil
- 📕 Print products
- 🌾 Soybeans

Physical

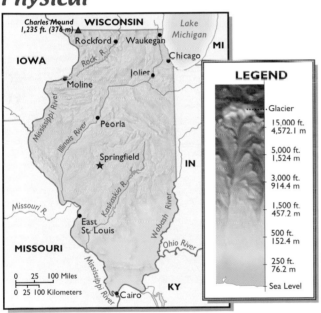

LEGEND

- .... Glacier
- 15,000 ft. 4,572.1 m
- 5,000 ft. 1,524 m
- 3,000 ft. 914.4 m
- 1,500 ft. 457.2 m
- 500 ft. 152.4 m
- 250 ft. 76.2 m
- Sea Level

Did You Know?

This southern Illinois region got its nickname because it supplied corn to other parts of the state during the severe winter of 1830–1831:

Little Egypt

Illinois Almanac

Nickname	Prairie State	**Lowest elevation**	Mississippi River in Alexander Co., 279 ft. (85 m)
State capital	Springfield	**Land area & rank**	55,584 sq. miles (143,963 sq. km); 24th
Date of statehood	Dec. 3, 1818; 21st state		
State bird	Cardinal	**Average January temperature**	26°F (−3°C)
State flower	Native violet		
State tree	White oak	**Average July temperature**	76°F (24°C)
State motto	State Sovereignty, National Union	**Average yearly precipitation**	38 inches (97 cm)
Total population & rank	12,482,301 (in 2001); 5th	**Major industries**	services, manufacturing, travel, wholesale and retail trade, finance, insurance, real estate
Population density	225 per sq. mile (87 per sq. km)		
Population distribution	88% urban, 12% rural		
Largest cities	Chicago, Rockford, Aurora, Naperville, Peoria	**Places to visit**	Chicago museums and parks, Lincoln shrines in Springfield, Cahokia Mounds (Collinsville)
Highest elevation	Charles Mound, 1,235 ft. (376 m)	**Web site**	www.state.il.us

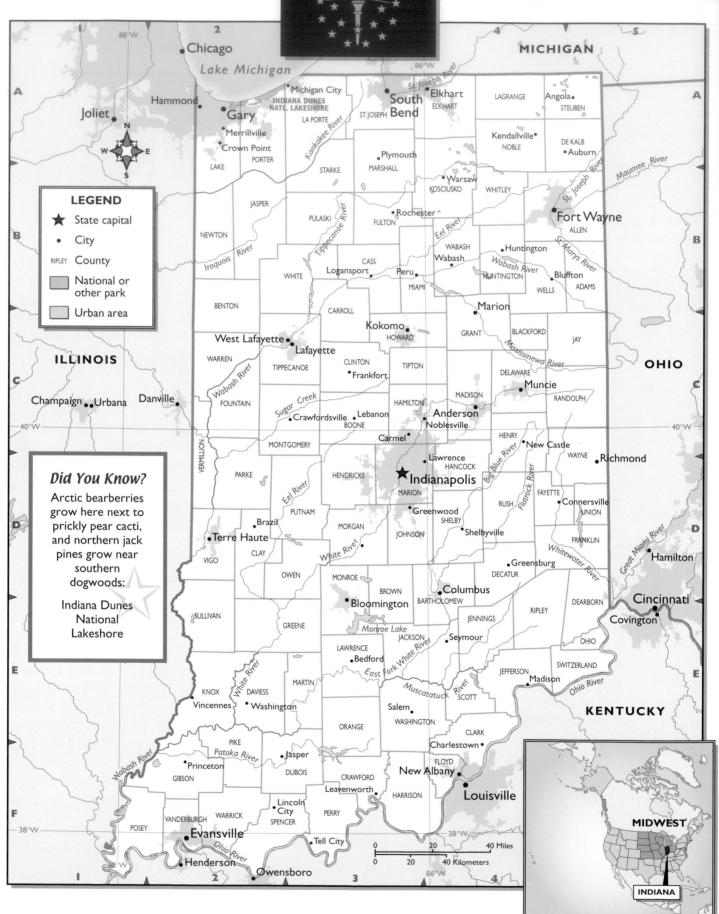

MICHIGAN

Chicago
Lake Michigan

Joliet
Hammond

Michigan City
INDIANA DUNES
NATL. LAKESHORE

South Bend
ST. JOSEPH

Elkhart
ELKHART

LAGRANGE

Angola
STEUBEN

Gary
Merrillville
Crown Point

LA PORTE

Plymouth
MARSHALL

Kendallville
NOBLE

DE KALB
Auburn

LEGEND

★ State capital
• City
RIPLEY County
National or other park
Urban area

PORTER
LAKE

STARKE

Warsaw
KOSCIUSKO

WHITLEY

St. Joseph River

Fort Wayne
ALLEN

NEWTON

JASPER

PULASKI

FULTON

Rochester

Eel River

WABASH

Wabash

Huntington

Maumee River

St. Marys River

Bluffton
ADAMS

ILLINOIS

BENTON

WHITE

CASS

Logansport

Peru
MIAMI

HUNTINGTON

WELLS

Wabash River

Mississinewa River

WARREN

West Lafayette

Lafayette

CARROLL

Kokomo
HOWARD

Marion

GRANT

BLACKFORD

JAY

Champaign Urbana

Danville

TIPPECANOE

CLINTON

Frankfort

TIPTON

MADISON

DELAWARE

Muncie

RANDOLPH

OHIO

40°W

FOUNTAIN

Sugar Creek

Crawfordsville
BOONE

Lebanon

HAMILTON

Noblesville

Anderson

Carmel

HENRY

New Castle

WAYNE

Richmond

40°W

Did You Know?

Arctic bearberries grow here next to prickly pear cacti, and northern jack pines grow near southern dogwoods:

Indiana Dunes National Lakeshore

VERMILION

PARKE

MONTGOMERY

Eel River

PUTNAM

HENDRICKS

Indianapolis

MARION

Lawrence
HANCOCK

RUSH

FAYETTE

Connersville
UNION

Big Blue River

Flatrock River

Whitewater River

Brazil

Terre Haute

CLAY

MORGAN

White River

Greenwood

JOHNSON

SHELBY

Shelbyville

FRANKLIN

Greensburg

DECATUR

Great Miami River

Hamilton

VIGO

OWEN

MONROE

BROWN

Bloomington

BARTHOLOMEW

Columbus

JENNINGS

RIPLEY

DEARBORN

Cincinnati

Covington

SULLIVAN

GREENE

Monroe Lake

JACKSON

Seymour

OHIO

KNOX

DAVIESS

MARTIN

LAWRENCE

Bedford

East Fork White River

Muscatatuck River

SCOTT

JEFFERSON

Madison

SWITZERLAND

Ohio River

KENTUCKY

Vincennes

Washington

ORANGE

Salem
WASHINGTON

CLARK

Charlestown

White River

PIKE

Patoka River

Jasper

DUBOIS

CRAWFORD

Leavenworth

FLOYD

New Albany

HARRISON

Louisville

Princeton
GIBSON

Lincoln City

SPENCER

PERRY

Wabash River

POSEY

VANDERBURGH

WARRICK

Evansville

Tell City

Henderson

Owensboro

Ohio River

38°W

38°W

86°W

0   20   40 Miles
0   20   40 Kilometers

MIDWEST

INDIANA

The shape of Indiana resembles the letter "J" drawn by a very thick crayon. The southernmost quarter, curving west to a point, is bordered by the Ohio River and the Wabash River. Nearly all of the state's rivers flow south, even those in areas very close to Lake Michigan. Indiana calls itself the Crossroads of America, a reference to the spider web of interstate highways interlinked within the state and to its central location among the major cities of the central and northeastern United States. The initial occupation by settlers from Kentucky continues to influence the personality of the state. Indiana's southern hills contain most of the forested land and can be quite steep. Other portions of the state are flat and are used for farming. Massive industrial plants on the shores of Lake Michigan allow Indiana to lead all states in the production of steel. Indianapolis is the most important city and attracts visitors to its museums, historic sites, and sports facilities.

Indiana Almanac

Nickname	Hoosier State
State capital	Indianapolis
Date of statehood	Dec. 11, 1816; 19th state
State bird	Cardinal
State flower	Peony
State tree	Tulip poplar
State motto	The Crossroads of America
Total population & rank	6,114,745 (in 2001); 14th
Population density	170 per sq. mile (66 per sq. km)
Population distribution	71% urban, 29% rural
Largest cities	Indianapolis, Fort Wayne, Evansville, South Bend, Gary
Highest elevation	Franklin Township in Wayne Co., 1,257 ft. (383 m)
Lowest elevation	Ohio River in Posey Co., 320 ft. (98 m)
Land area & rank	35,867 sq. miles (92,896 sq. km); 38th
Average January temperature	27°F (−3°C)
Average July temperature	75°F (24°C)
Average yearly precipitation	40 inches (102 cm)
Major industries	manufacturing, services, agriculture, government, wholesale and retail trade
Places to visit	Connor Prairie Pioneer Settlement (Noblesville), Children's Museum (Indianapolis), Indiana Dunes National Lakeshore, Lincoln Boyhood National Memorial (Lincoln City), Wyandotte Cave (Leavenworth)
Web site	www.ai.org

Economy – Chief Products

LEGEND

- Automobiles
- Cement
- Chemicals
- Coal
- Corn
- Crushed stone
- Hogs
- Milk
- Oil and natural gas
- Poultry
- Soybeans
- Steel

Physical

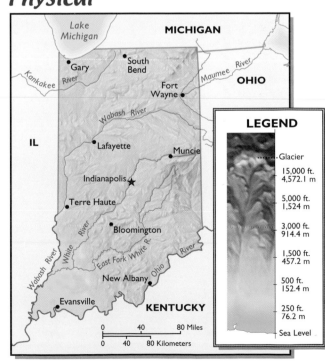

LEGEND

- Glacier
- 15,000 ft. 4,572.1 m
- 5,000 ft. 1,524 m
- 3,000 ft. 914.4 m
- 1,500 ft. 457.2 m
- 500 ft. 152.4 m
- 250 ft. 76.2 m
- Sea Level

IOWA

MINNESOTA

WISCONSIN

Some people point out a human profile on the eastern side of Iowa, with the sweeping curves of the Mississippi River forming the forehead, nose, and chin. Another famous river lies on its western edge. The Missouri River was a pathway of exploration and commerce, and for many years the gateway to the disputed Native American lands of the frontier. Though bridging east and west, Iowa has always been unified by its fundamental physical geography and its people. This is a land with dependable water, a long growing season, and dark prairie topsoil extending down for many feet. No other state grows as much corn as Iowa or raises as many hogs. Few other states produce as much beef or have as many people living and working on farms. Manufacturing has historically been connected to farming and food, but the well-educated population has been attracting an increasing variety of businesses, including publishing, banking, and insurance.

LEGEND

★ State capital

• City

PAGE County

Urban area

MIDWEST

IOWA

Iowa Almanac

Nickname	Hawkeye State	**Lowest elevation**	Mississippi River in Lee Co., 480 ft, (146 m)
State capital	Des Moines	**Land area & rank**	55,869 sq. miles (144,701 sq. km); 23rd
Date of statehood	Dec. 28, 1846; 29th state		
State bird	Eastern goldfinch	**Average January temperature**	18°F (–8°C)
State flower	Wild rose		
State tree	Oak	**Average July temperature**	74°F (23°C)
State motto	Our Liberties We Prize, and Our Rights We Will Maintain	**Average yearly precipitation**	33 inches (84 cm)
Total population & rank	2,923,179 (in 2001); 30th	**Major industries**	agriculture, communications, construction, finance, insurance, trade, services, manufacturing
Population density	52 per sq. mile (20 per sq. km)		
Population distribution	61% urban, 39% rural		
Largest cities	Des Moines, Cedar Rapids, Davenport, Sioux City	**Places to visit**	Effigy Mounds National Monument (Marquette), Living History Farms (Des Moines), Amana Colonies
Highest elevation	Sec. 29, T.100N, R.41W in Osceola Co., 1,670 ft. (509 m)	**Web site**	www.state.ia.us

Physical

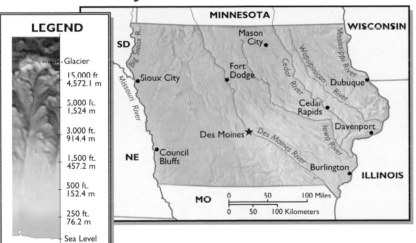

Did You Know?

The number of Iowans who fought in the Civil War—measured as a percent of total residents—was greater than any other Union state:

About 12% or 80,000

Economy— Chief Products

LEGEND
- Beef cattle
- Coal
- Corn
- Crushed stone
- Food products
- Hay
- Hogs
- Machinery
- Milk
- Oats
- Soybeans

KANSAS

NEBRASKA

IOWA

MISSOURI

OKLAHOMA

TEXAS

CHEYENNE | RAWLINS | DECATUR | NORTON | PHILLIPS | SMITH | JEWELL | REPUBLIC | WASHINGTON | MARSHALL | NEMAHA | BROWN | DONIPHAN

Frenchman Creek
Little Blue R.
Missouri River

40°N

S. Fork Republican River
Beaver Creek
Sappa Creek
North Fork Solomon R.
Waconda Lake
Republican R.
Big Blue R.

Norton
• Phillipsburg
Concordia
• Beloit

SHERMAN | THOMAS | SHERIDAN | GRAHAM | ROOKS | OSBORNE | MITCHELL | CLOUD

• Goodland
• Colby

South Fork Solomon River
Solomon R.
Tuttle Creek Lake
POTTAWATOMIE | JACKSON | ATCHISON
Leavenworth
LEAVENWORTH
Kansas City

Mt. Sunflower
4,039 ft.
(1,231 m)

Oakley •

WALLACE | LOGAN | GOVE | TREGO | ELLIS | RUSSELL | LINCOLN

Big Creek
Smoky Hill River
• Hays
• Russell
Saline River
Milford Lake
Clay Center
CLAY
RILEY
• Manhattan
Junction City
GEARY
Abilene •
Kansas R.
Topeka ★
Lawrence
SHAWNEE

Kansas City
WYANDOTTE
JEFFERSON
JOHNSON
Olathe •
Overland Park

CO

38°N

Ladder Creek
GREELEY | WICHITA | SCOTT | LANE | NESS | RUSH | BARTON | RICE
Scott City •
Walnut Creek
Great Bend •
PAWNEE
• Lyons
McPherson •
MCPHERSON
MARION
ELLSWORTH
SALINE
• Salina
DICKINSON
MORRIS
Cottonwood R.
Emporia •
LYON
OSAGE
Ottawa •
FRANKLIN
Marais des Cygnes R.
MIAMI
• Paola
DOUGLAS
Ottawa •
WABAUNSEE

HAMILTON | KEARNY | FINNEY | HODGEMAN | EDWARDS | STAFFORD | RENO | HARVEY | BUTLER | GREENWOOD | WOODSON | ALLEN | BOURBON

Garden City
Arkansas River
Dodge City
Larned •
Hutchinson •
• Newton
• El Dorado
Iola •
Fort Scott

• Ulysses
STANTON | GRANT | HASKELL | GRAY | FORD | KIOWA | PRATT | KINGMAN | SEDGWICK
Wichita
Haysville •
Augusta •
Chanute •
WILSON
NEOSHO
CRAWFORD
Pittsburg •

MORTON | STEVENS | SEWARD | MEADE | CLARK | COMANCHE | BARBER | HARPER | SUMNER | COWLEY | ELK | MONTGOMERY | LABETTE | CHEROKEE

North Fork Cimarron River
• Hugoton
• Liberal
CLARK
Wellington •
• Derby
Arkansas River
Winfield •
Arkansas City •
Independence •
CHAUTAUQUA
Coffeyville •
Parsons •
Joplin •
Verdigris River
Neosho R.

OKLAHOMA

Cimarron River

0 25 50 75 100 Miles
0 25 50 75 100 Kilometers

98°W 96°W

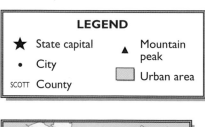

MIDWEST

KANSAS

Physical

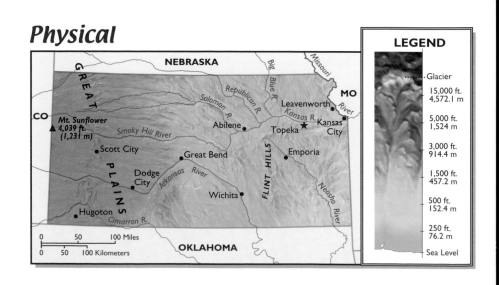

NEBRASKA

GREAT PLAINS

CO
Mt. Sunflower
4,039 ft.
(1,231 m)
Scott City •
Smoky Hill River
Dodge City •
Arkansas River
• Great Bend
Abilene •
Solomon R.
Republican R.
Big Blue R.
Missouri R.
Leavenworth •
Topeka ★
Kansas R.
Kansas City
MO
FLINT HILLS
Emporia •
Wichita •
Neosho River
• Hugoton
Cimarron R.

OKLAHOMA

0 50 100 Miles
0 50 100 Kilometers

If you guessed that Kansas is in the exact center of the United States, you'd be partly right. The geographical center of the lower 48 states is in Smith County, Kansas. The state just barely avoids having four straight sides. A short portion of its northeastern boundary lies along the Missouri River. A large amount of Kansas farmland is devoted to growing wheat. It produces more wheat than any other state. Corn and other grains are also important crops. The western part of Kansas is dry, but farmers obtain water from deep wells. Although much of the state is relatively flat, the Flint Hills are steep, and the land is still covered in grass and used for cattle ranching. Tourists in Kansas often visit famous Old West towns like Dodge City, where large herds of cattle driven north from Texas reached the railroad and cowboys confronted lawmen. Food processing is an important business, but Wichita is home to a unique industry. More than two out of every three private airplanes sold in the world are manufactured and tested there.

Did You Know?

Clashes between pro-slavery and anti-slavery groups before the Civil War earned Kansas a scary but temporary nickname:

Bleeding Kansas

Kansas Almanac

Nickname	Sunflower State
State capital	Topeka
Date of statehood	Jan. 29, 1861; 34th state
State bird	Western meadowlark
State flower	Native sunflower
State tree	Cottonwood
State motto	Ad Astra per Aspera (To the Stars Through Difficulties)
Total population & rank	2,694,641 (in 2001); 32nd
Population density	33 per sq. mile (13 per sq. km)
Population distribution	71% urban, 29% rural
Largest cities	Wichita, Overland Park, Kansas City, Topeka
Highest elevation	Mt. Sunflower, 4,039 ft. (1,231 m)
Lowest elevation	Verdigris River in Montgomery Co., 679 ft. (207 m)
Land area & rank	81,815 sq. miles (211,901 sq. km); 13th
Average January temperature	29°F (–2°C)
Average July temperature	79°F (26°C)
Average yearly precipitation	28 inches (71 cm)
Major industries	manufacturing, finance, insurance, real estate, services
Places to visit	Fort Larned Natl. Historic Site (Larned), Kansas Cosmosphere and Space Discovery Center (Hutchinson), Dodge City, Eisenhower Center (Abilene)
Web site	www.accesskansas.org

Economy – Chief Products

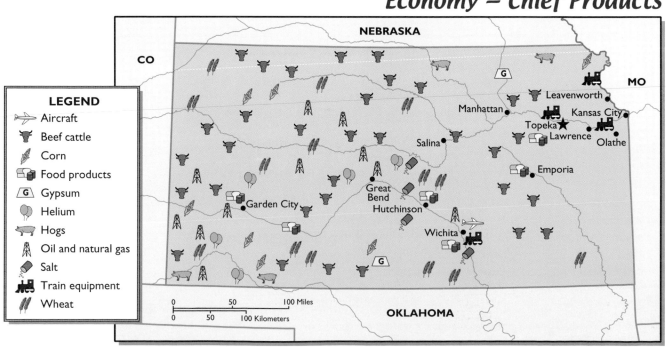

LEGEND

- ✈ Aircraft
- 🐂 Beef cattle
- 🌽 Corn
- 🥫 Food products
- Ⓖ Gypsum
- 🎈 Helium
- 🐖 Hogs
- Oil and natural gas
- Salt
- Train equipment
- 🌾 Wheat

Kentucky Almanac

Nickname	Bluegrass State	**Land area & rank**	39,728 sq. miles (102,896 sq. km); 36th
State capital	Frankfort	**Average January temperature**	34°F (1°C)
Date of statehood	June 1, 1792; 15th state		
State bird	Cardinal	**Average July temperature**	76°F (24°C)
State flower	Goldenrod		
State tree	Tulip poplar	**Average yearly precipitation**	47 inches (119 cm)
State motto	United We Stand, Divided We Fall		
Total population & rank	4,065,556 (in 2001); 25th	**Major industries**	manufacturing, services, finance, insurance and real estate
Population density	102 per sq. mile (39 per sq. km)		
Population distribution	56% urban, 44% rural	**Places to visit**	Mammoth Cave National Park, Lincoln's Birthplace (Hodgenville), Cumberland Gap National Historical Park
Largest cities	Lexington, Louisville, Owensboro		
Highest elevation	Black Mountain, 4,145 ft. (1,263 m)		
Lowest elevation	Mississippi River in Fulton Co., 257 ft. (78 m)	**Web site**	www.kydirect.net

With its nearly-flat bottom and its bulging, irregular top, the profile of Kentucky might be compared to a submarine cruising on calm surface waters: that bumpy top is the Ohio River, squirming its way downstream. Kentucky has more miles of Ohio River boundary than any other state. Kentucky was one of the first areas across the Appalachians to be settled, and it is one of the oldest noncolonial states. Isolated areas in the mountains retain the character of early American life. Coal has been widely mined in the mountains, although the environment has suffered. The most famous part of the state is the Bluegrass Region, where immaculate horse farms raise some of the best thoroughbred race horses in the world. The most valuable farm crop is tobacco, while car manufacturing is an important industry. Louisville attracts many visitors who enjoy its Southern manners and hospitality.

LEGEND

Glacier
15,000 ft. 4,572.1 m
5,000 ft. 1,524 m
3,000 ft. 914.4 m
1,500 ft. 457.2 m
500 ft. 152.4 m
250 ft. 76.2 m
Sea Level

Did You Know?

Kentucky is home to the longest—about 350 miles (563 km)—known cave system in the world: Mammoth Cave

Physical

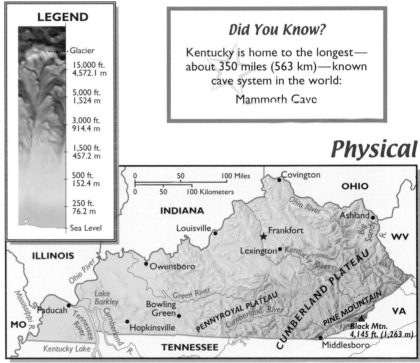

Economy–Chief Products

LEGEND

- Automobiles
- Beef cattle
- Chemicals
- Coal
- Corn
- Horses
- Limestone
- Natural gas
- Tobacco

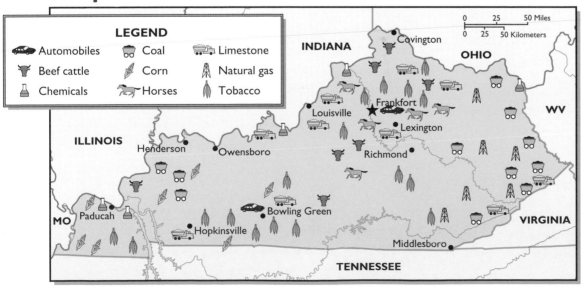

70   Louisiana

UNION JUSTICE & CONFIDENCE

ARKANSAS

Springhill
CADDO
WEBSTER
Minden
BOSSIER
Bossier City
Shreveport
CLAIBORNE
UNION
LINCOLN
Grambling • Ruston
▲ Driskill Mtn.
535 ft. (163 m)
BIENVILLE
JACKSON
OUACHITA
MOREHOUSE
Bastrop
WEST CARROLL
EAST CARROLL
Lake Providence
Monroe
RICHLAND
Tallulah
MADISON
Vicksburg
DE SOTO
RED RIVER
Mansfield
WINN
Winnfield
Winnsboro
CALDWELL
FRANKLIN
TENSAS
Natchitoches
NATCHITOCHES
LA SALLE
CATAHOULA
Catahoula Lake
GRANT
Vidalia
CONCORDIA
MISSISSIPPI
Toledo Bend Reservoir
SABINE
Alexandria
Pineville
RAPIDES
Marksville
AVOYELLES
Red River
Hattiesburg
TEXAS
Leesville
VERNON
Bunkie
WEST FELICIANA
EAST FELICIANA
ST. HELENA
WASHINGTON
Bogalusa
De Ridder
Oakdale
EVANGELINE
Ville Platte
ALLEN
ST. LANDRY
Opelousas
POINTE COUPEE
New Roads
EAST BATON ROUGE
TANGIPAHOA
Hammond
ST. TAMMANY
Gulfport
Biloxi
BEAUREGARD
Eunice
ACADIA
Crowley
Lafayette
WEST BATON ROUGE
Baton Rouge
LIVINGSTON
Lake Maurepas
Slidell
Sulphur
Lake Charles
CALCASIEU
JEFFERSON DAVIS
LAFAYETTE
Plaquemine
IBERVILLE
Gonzales
ASCENSION
Lake Pontchartrain
Kenner
Metairie
New Orleans
Beaumont
New Iberia
IBERIA
ST. MARTIN
ST. JOHN THE BAPTIST
Laplace
ORLEANS
Lake Borgne
Port Arthur
Sabine Lake
Calcasieu Lake
CAMERON
Grand Lake
Abbeville
VERMILION
Franklin
ST. MARTIN
ASSUMPTION
ST. JAMES
ST. CHARLES
Gretna
ST. BERNARD
White Lake
Vermilion Bay
ST. MARY
Morgan City
Thibodaux
JEFFERSON
Chandeleur Sound
Atchafalaya Bay
Houma
TERREBONNE
LAFOURCHE
PLAQUEMINES
Port Sulphur
Breton Sound
Terrebonne Bay
Barataria Bay
Mississippi Delta

Gulf of Mexico

0 25 50 75 100 Miles
0 25 50 75 100 Kilometers

SOUTHEAST
LOUISIANA

LEGEND
★ State capital
• City
ACADIA Parish
▲ Mountain peak
Swamp
Urban area

Did You Know?
British troops were crushed in the final battle of the War of 1812, but it actually occurred after a peace treaty had been signed in Europe:
The Battle of New Orleans

Boot-shaped Louisiana, the state standing prominently at the center of the Gulf Coast, is a shadow of its former self. In 1803, the territory of Louisiana stretched all the way to the present state of Montana. In a sense, the Mississippi River is its parent. Much of the land within the state is the result of the mud carried south and dumped at the edge of the Gulf of Mexico by the river. Southern Louisiana is the home of the Cajuns, the descendants of French Canadians who were transported to the area 250 years ago. The Creole culture, a mix of Spanish and French traditions, began to form at about the same time. African-American traditions influenced music and laid foundations for the development of jazz and the blues. Louisiana's Gulf Coast is a supermarket of resources, providing shrimp, oysters, and crawfish as well as salt, sulphur, and natural gas. New Orleans is an immensely popular tourist destination. Visitors come for jazz and Cajun music, its famous regional cooking, and the multi-day festival and street party called Mardi Gras, usually held in February.

Louisiana Almanac

Nickname	Pelican State
State capital	Baton Rouge
Date of statehood	April 30, 1812; 18th state
State bird	Eastern brown pelican
State flower	Magnolia
State tree	Cypress
State motto	Union, Justice and Confidence
Total population & rank	4,465,430 (in 2001); 22nd
Population density	103 per sq. mile (40 per sq. km)
Population distribution	73% urban, 27% rural
Largest cities	New Orleans, Baton Rouge, Shreveport, Metairie
Highest elevation	Driskill Mountain, 535 ft. (163 m)
Lowest elevation	New Orleans, 8 ft. (2.4 m) below sea level
Land area & rank	43,562 sq. miles (112,826 sq. km); 33rd
Average January temperature	49°F (9°C)
Average July temperature	82°F (28°C)
Average yearly precipitation	58 inches (147 cm)
Major industries	wholesale and retail trade, tourism, manufacturing, construction, transportation
Places to visit	Natchitoches, New Orleans: Aquarium of the Americas, Audubon Zoo and Gardens, French Quarter, Jackson Square, Confederate Museum
Web site	www.state.la.us

Economy— Chief Products

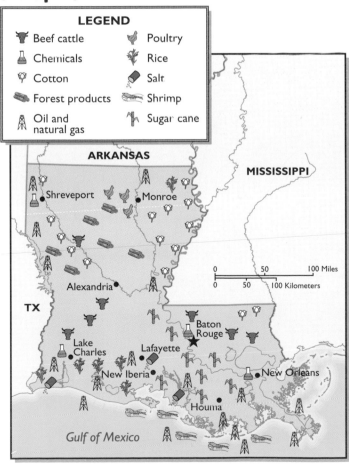

LEGEND

- 🐄 Beef cattle
- ⚗️ Chemicals
- 🌿 Cotton
- 🪵 Forest products
- 🛢️ Oil and natural gas
- 🐔 Poultry
- 🌾 Rice
- 🧂 Salt
- 🦐 Shrimp
- 🌱 Sugar cane

Physical

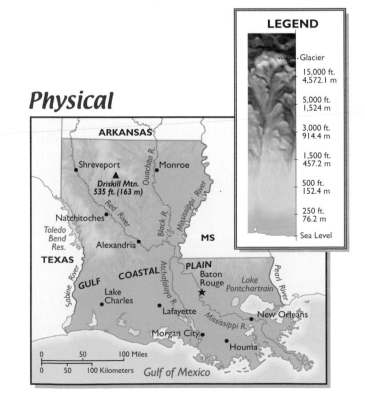

LEGEND

- Glacier
- 15,000 ft. 4,572.1 m
- 5,000 ft. 1,524 m
- 3,000 ft. 914.4 m
- 1,500 ft. 457.2 m
- 500 ft. 152.4 m
- 250 ft. 76.2 m
- Sea Level

★ ★ ★ ★ ★

LEGEND

★ State capital
• City
KNOX County
▲ Mountain peak
National or other park
Urban area

Did You Know?

The winters are cold in Maine, and this wintertime accessory was invented here:

Earmuffs

QUÉBEC

CANADA

CANADA

NEW BRUNSWICK

St. Lawrence River

70°W

St. John River

Madawaska

Fort Kent

Van Buren

Caribou

AROOSTOOK

Aroostook River

Presque Isle

Houlton

68°W

46°N

Eagle Lake

Chesuncook Lake

BAXTER STATE PARK

▲ Mt. Katahdin 5,267 ft. (1,605 m)

St. John River

46°N

Allagash River

St. John River

Moosehead Lake

PISCATAQUIS

SOMERSET

Pemadumcook Lake

Millinocket

PENOBSCOT

Lincoln

West Grand Lake

St. Croix River

Big Lake

Calais

WASHINGTON

Eastport

Dover-Foxcroft

Piscataquis River

Penobscot River

Flagstaff Lake

Kennebago R.

FRANKLIN

Mooselookmeguntic Lake

Skowhegan

Bangor

Orono

HANCOCK

Machias

Connecticut River

Farmington

Rumford

Androscoggin River

OXFORD

Waterville

KENNEBEC

Kennebec River

WALDO

Belfast

Ellsworth

Bar Harbor

ACADIA NATL. PARK

Augusta

Gardiner

KNOX

Penobscot Bay

Rockland

Auburn

Lewiston

ANDROSCOGGIN

LINCOLN

44°N

NEW HAMPSHIRE

SAGADAHOC

Sebago Lake

Brunswick

Bath

Boothbay

ACADIA NATL. PARK

44°N

CUMBERLAND

Westbrook

Portland

South Portland

ATLANTIC OCEAN

Lake Winnipesaukee

YORK

Saco

Biddeford

Sanford

Kennebunkport

Concord

Kittery

Manchester

Portsmouth

70°W

68°W

| 0 | 25 | 50 Miles |
| 0 | 25 | 50 Kilometers |

MAINE

NEW ENGLAND

Maine, the easternmost state and the largest of the New England states, is wedged between the Canadian provinces of New Brunswick and Quebec. Maine is most famous for the rugged beauty of its 228-mile (367 km) rocky coast. There are many port cities and fishing villages along the coast, where tourism, fishing, and ship-building prosper. Maine's lobster catch is the largest of any state. Lobster is its most well-known product and the Maine Lobster Festival one of its outstanding annual events. Forests cover about 90% of the state— more woodland area than any other state. These forests are a beautiful wilderness area for hiking and other outdoor sports as well as the natural resource for Maine's largest industry—lumber, wood, and paper products. The people here, descendants of English, French, French-Canadian, Irish, and German immigrants, are noted for their tough independent spirit. Because Maine's economy relies on its natural resources, the state's residents take conservation very seriously.

Maine Almanac

Nickname	Pine Tree State
State capital	Augusta
Date of statehood	March 15, 1820; 23rd state
State bird	Chickadee
State flower	White pine cone and tassel
State tree	Eastern white pine
State motto	Dirigo (I Direct)
Total population & rank	1,286,670 (in 2001); 40th
Population density	42 per sq. mile (16 per sq. km)
Population distribution	40% urban, 60% rural
Largest cities	Portland, Lewiston, Bangor
Highest elevation	Mt. Katahdin, 5,267 ft. (1,605 m)
Lowest elevation	sea level
Land area & rank	30,862 sq. miles (79,933 sq. km); 39th
Average January temperature	17°F (–8°C)
Average July temperature	67°F (19°C)
Average yearly precipitation	41 inches (104 cm)
Major industries	manufacturing, agriculture, fishing, services, trade
Places to visit	Acadia National Park, Portland Head Lighthouse, Boothbay Railway Museum
Web site	www.state.me.us

Economy – Chief Products

LEGEND

- 🫐 Blueberries
- 🌾 Oats
- 🐔 Eggs
- 📄 Paper products
- 🐟 Fish
- 🥔 Potatoes
- 💎 Gemstones
- 🚚 Sand and gravel
- 🐄 Milk
- 🦐 Shellfish

Physical

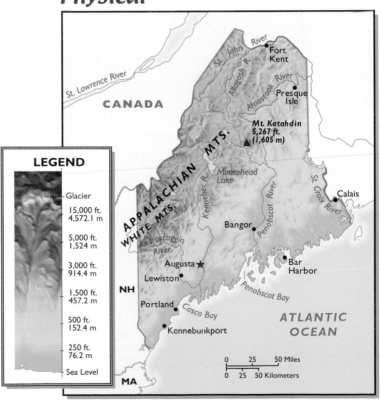

LEGEND

- Glacier
- 15,000 ft. 4,572.1 m
- 5,000 ft. 1,524 m
- 3,000 ft. 914.4 m
- 1,500 ft. 457.2 m
- 500 ft. 152.4 m
- 250 ft. 76.2 m
- Sea Level

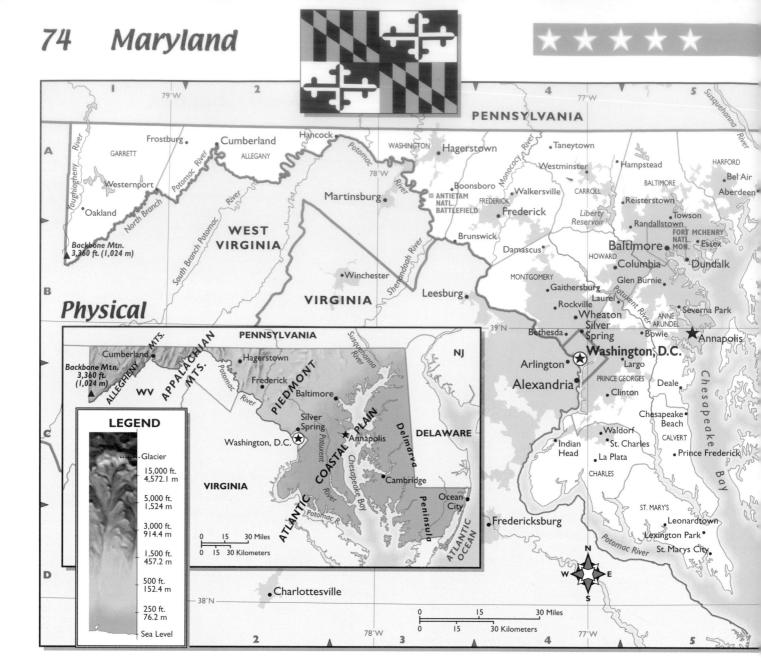

Physical

LEGEND

Glacier

15,000 ft.
4,572.1 m

5,000 ft.
1,524 m

3,000 ft.
914.4 m

1,500 ft.
457.2 m

500 ft.
152.4 m

250 ft.
76.2 m

Sea Level

Maryland Almanac

Nicknames	Old Line State, Free State
State capital	Annapolis
Date of statehood	April 28, 1788; 7th state
State bird	Baltimore oriole
State flower	Black-eyed Susan
State tree	White oak
State motto	*Fatti Maschii, Parole Femine* (Manly Deeds, Womanly Words)
Total population & rank	5,375,156 (in 2001); 19th
Population density	550 per sq. mile (212 per sq. km)
Population distribution	86% urban, 14% rural
Largest cities	Baltimore, Columbia, Silver Spring, Dundalk, Wheaton-Glenmont
Highest elevation	Backbone Mountain, 3,360 ft. (1,024 m)
Lowest elevation	sea level
Land area & rank	9,774 sq. miles (25,315 sq. km); 42nd
Average January temperature	33°F (1°C)
Average July temperature	75°F (24°C)
Average yearly precipitation	43 inches (109 cm)
Major industries	manufacturing, biotechnology, information technology, services, tourism
Places to visit	Antietam National Battlefield (Sharpsburg), Fort McHenry National Monument (Baltimore), Assateague Island National Seashore
Web site	www.state.md.us

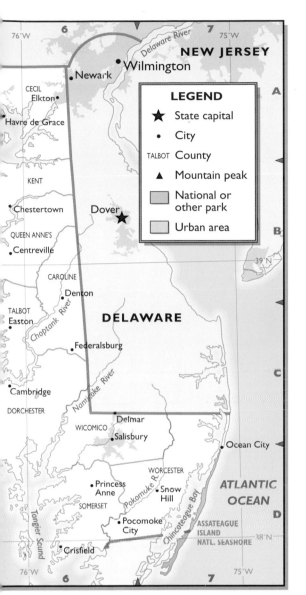

Maryland's unique shape is divided into two parts by the Chesapeake Bay. The coastal regions of the Chesapeake and Atlantic are flat and home to Maryland's commercial and recreational harbors. The western section is a mix of mountains, hills, plains, valleys, and forests. There is good farmland throughout the state, where nursery stock, fruit, grains, poultry, and tobacco are grown. In 1791, the state gave part of its land to create the new national capital, Washington, D.C. Many people who work in Washington, D.C. live in Maryland. In this densely populated state, 86% of the people live and work in urban areas such as Baltimore and Hagerstown. The border between Maryland and Pennsylvania is called the Mason-Dixon Line and is the unofficial line between the northern and southern states. Even though considered a southern state, Maryland fought with the north during the Civil War. "The Star Spangled Banner" was written by Francis Scott Key at Fort McHenry near Baltimore. There are many other historic sites as well as fabulous beaches and urban centers like the renowned Inner Harbor of Baltimore attracting visitors to Maryland.

MIDATLANTIC

MARYLAND

Did You Know?

Not many states have an official sport, and Maryland's is an ancient one:

Jousting

Economy – Chief Products

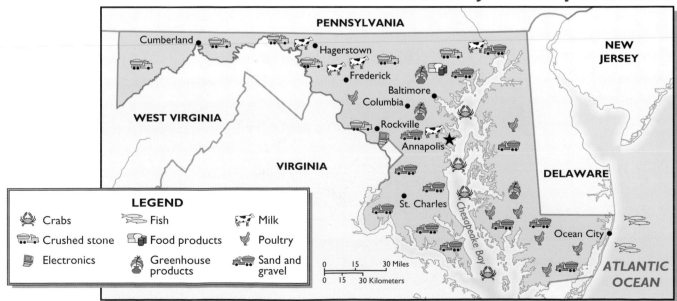

LEGEND

Crabs	Fish	Milk
Crushed stone	Food products	Poultry
Electronics	Greenhouse products	Sand and gravel

0   15   30 Miles
0   15   30 Kilometers

Map Labels

VERMONT
NEW HAMPSHIRE
NEW YORK
Nashua
Williamstown
North Adams
Mt. Greylock 3,487 ft. (1,063)
Adams
Deerfield R.
FRANKLIN
Greenfield
Millers River
Athol
Gardner
Fitchburg
Leominster
Amesbury
Newburyport
Haverhill
Methuen
Lawrence
Andover
ESSEX
Lowell
Billerica
Beverly
Peabody
Salem
Dalton
Pittsfield
Connecticut River
Quabbin Reservoir
Amherst
WORCESTER
Clinton
Concord
MINUTEMAN NATL. HISTORIC PARK
Woburn
Lexington
Medford
Lynn
MIDDLESEX
HAMPSHIRE
Northampton
Easthampton
Ware River
Marlborough
Cambridge
Newton
Boston
NORFOLK
SUFFOLK
Stockbridge
Housatonic River
Holyoke
Worcester
Spencer
Framingham
Quincy
NORFOLK
Great Barrington
BERKSHIRE
HAMPDEN
Westfield River
Chicopee R.
Chicopee
Auburn
Norwood
Milford
Randolph
Stoughton
NORFOLK
Westfield
Springfield
Sturbridge
Southbridge
Franklin
Foxboro
Brockton
Agawam
Windsor Locks
Bridgewater
PLYMOUTH
Attleboro
Taunton
Middleboro
CONNECTICUT
Providence
BRISTOL
Somerset
RHODE ISLAND
Fall River
New Bedford
Buzzards
Rhode Island Sound
Merrimack River
Nashua River
Concord R.
Westfield River

LEGEND

★ State capital
• City
ESSEX County
▲ Mountain peak
National or other park
Urban area

MASSACHUSETTS
NEW ENGLAND

N W E S

0 10 20 30 40 Miles
0 10 20 30 40 Kilometers

Massachusetts Almanac

Nicknames	Bay State, Old Colony
State capital	Boston
Date of statehood	Feb. 6, 1788; 6th state
State bird	Chickadee
State flower	Mayflower
State tree	American elm
State motto	*Ense Petit Placidam Sub Libertate Quietem* (By the Sword We Seek Peace, but Peace Only Under Liberty)
Total population & rank	6,379,304 (in 2001); 13th
Population density	814 per sq. mile (314 per sq. km)
Population distribution	91% urban, 9% rural
Largest cities	Boston, Worcester, Springfield, Lowell, Cambridge

Highest elevation	Mt. Greylock, 3,487 ft. (1,063 m)
Lowest elevation	sea level
Land area & rank	7,840 sq. miles (20,306 sq. km); 45th
Average January temperature	25°F (−4°C)
Average July temperature	70°F (21°C)
Average yearly precipitation	45 inches (114 cm)
Major industries	services, trade, manufacturing
Places to visit	Minute Man National Historical Park, Freedom Trail (Boston), Old Sturbridge Village, Plymouth: Plymouth Rock, Plimouth Plantation,
Web site	www.mass.gov

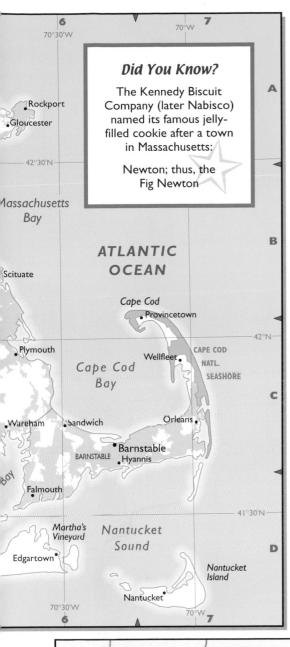

The shape of Massachusetts is defined by the curl of Cape Cod on the Atlantic coast. Massachusetts is a key state in U.S. history. It is the home of Plymouth Rock, the landing point of the Pilgrims in 1620, as well as many U.S. firsts: Harvard (the first college in the United States), the first newspaper, printing press, library, and post office. There are also many famous Revolutionary War sites. Its ports and fine harbors contributed to the success of the fishing and shipping industries. Technology came early to Massachusetts with the first power loom and continues to this day with many people working for high-tech businesses. Although Massachusetts is a very industrialized state, both its coastal lowlands and its western river valleys support agriculture. Nursery stock and cranberries are the state's leading products. The world-class museums, cultural events, historic sites, lovely New England coastal resorts, and ski areas and the natural beauty of the western forests have fostered a strong tourist business.

Physical

Economy– Chief Products

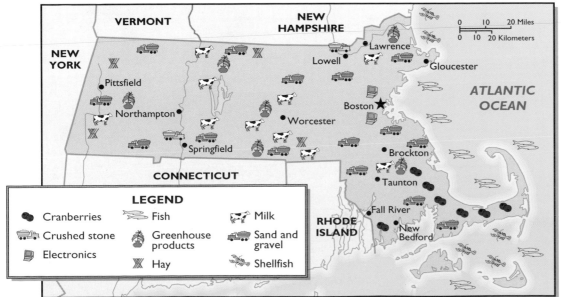

LEGEND

- Cranberries
- Crushed stone
- Electronics
- Fish
- Greenhouse products
- Hay
- Milk
- Sand and gravel
- Shellfish

LEGEND

- Glacier
- 15,000 ft. 4,572.1 m
- 5,000 ft. 1,524 m
- 3,000 ft. 914.4 m
- 1,500 ft. 457.2 m
- 500 ft. 152.4 m
- 250 ft. 76.2 m
- Sea Level

For continuation of map, see insets at right

CANADA

WISCONSIN

CANADA

Lake Superior

Copper Harbor
KEWEENAW
Houghton
HOUGHTON
ONTONAGON
BARAGA
Mt. Arvon 1,979 ft. (603 m)
MARQUETTE
Marquette
Ishpeming
IRON
DICKINSON
Iron Mountain
Escanaba
DELTA
MENOMINEE
Menominee
Marinette

Ontonagon
ONTONAGON
HOUGHTON
Ironwood
GOGEBIC
IRON

WISCONSIN

Lake Superior

Isle Royale
Lake Superior
ISLE ROYALE NATL. PARK

PICTURED ROCKS NATIONAL LAKESHORE
GRAND ISLAND NATL. REC. AREA
Munising
ALGER
SCHOOLCRAFT
LUCE
Whitefish Bay
Sault Ste. Marie
CHIPPEWA
MACKINAC
Manistique
St. Ignace
Mackinaw City
Mackinac Island
Bois Blanc Island
Cheboygan
Drummond Island

Escanaba River
Menominee River
Big Bay de Noc
Green Bay

WISCONSIN

Beaver Island
North Manitou Island
South Manitou Island
SLEEPING BEAR DUNES NATL. LAKESHORE
LEELANAU
Traverse City
BENZIE
GRAND TRAVERSE
MANISTEE
Manistee
Cadillac
WEXFORD
MISSAUKEE
EMMET
Petoskey
CHARLEVOIX
ANTRIM
OTSEGO
MONTMORENCY
ALPENA
Alpena
CRAWFORD
OSCODA
ALCONA
KALKASKA
Au Sable River
ROSCOMMON
OGEMAW
IOSCO
Tawas City
Houghton Lake
PRESQUE ISLE
CHEBOYGAN
Grand Traverse Bay
Manistee River

Lake Michigan

Ludington
MASON
LAKE
OSCEOLA
CLARE
GLADWIN
ARENAC
HURON
Bad Axe
OCEANA
NEWAYGO
MECOSTA
Big Rapids
ISABELLA
Mount Pleasant
MIDLAND
Midland
BAY
Bay City
Saginaw Bay
SANILAC
Sandusky
Muskegon River
MONTCALM
Alma
GRATIOT
Saginaw
TUSCOLA
Cass River
MUSKEGON
Muskegon
KENT
Grand Rapids
Wyoming
OTTAWA
Holland
IONIA
Ionia
Grand River
CLINTON
Owosso
SHIAWASSEE
GENESEE
Flint
LAPEER
Lapeer
Port Huron
ST. CLAIR
St. Clair River
Saginaw R.

Lansing
East Lansing
EATON
INGHAM
LIVINGSTON
OAKLAND
Pontiac
MACOMB
Sterling Heights
Warren
BARRY
Kalamazoo River
ALLEGAN
South Haven
KALAMAZOO
Kalamazoo
Portage
VAN BUREN
Benton Harbor
St. Joseph
BERRIEN
CALHOUN
Battle Creek
JACKSON
Jackson
WASHTENAW
Ann Arbor
Livonia
Dearborn
Detroit
WAYNE
Windsor
MONROE
Monroe
Lake St. Clair
St. Clair River
Detroit R.
ONTARIO CANADA

CASS
ST. JOSEPH
Niles
St. Joseph River
Sturgis
BRANCH
HILLSDALE
LENAWEE
Adrian

ILLINOIS
Chicago
Gary
South Bend
INDIANA
OHIO
Toledo
Lake Erie

Lake Huron

LEGEND
★ State capital
• City
GRATIOT County
National or other park
Urban area

MICHIGAN
MIDWEST

0   25   50 Miles
0   25   50 Kilometers

Michigan is unique among the lower 48 states by being divided into two large pieces. Lower Michigan resembles a mitten with its thumb protruding to the right, while the Upper Peninsula sits above it, spreading from west to east like a crooked tree branch. Both parts of the state are nearly surrounded by waters of the Great Lakes. Michigan has the longest freshwater coastline in the United States. With just a small fraction of the state's population, the Upper Peninsula is largely involved with forestry, dairy farming, and outdoor recreation. Agriculture is important in Lower Michigan, particularly in the southern half. Cherries and other fruits are common along the Lake Michigan shore where the trees are protected from frost damage. Michigan has long been known for manufacturing, and the automobile industry and food processing lead the way. Industrial demand for workers has attracted many immigrants, including a large number from the southern United States.

Economy – Chief Products

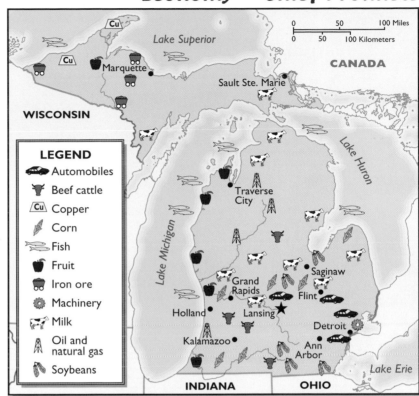

LEGEND
- 🚗 Automobiles
- 🐂 Beef cattle
- Cu Copper
- Corn
- Fish
- Fruit
- Iron ore
- Machinery
- Milk
- Oil and natural gas
- Soybeans

Did You Know?

Native Americans were mining copper here long before the arrival of Europeans: Upper Peninsula

Physical

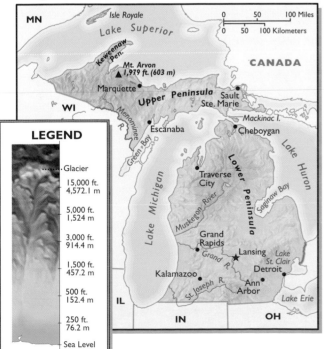

LEGEND
- Glacier
- 15,000 ft. 4,572.1 m
- 5,000 ft. 1,524 m
- 3,000 ft. 914.4 m
- 1,500 ft. 457.2 m
- 500 ft. 152.4 m
- 250 ft. 76.2 m
- Sea Level

Michigan Almanac

Nicknames	Great Lakes State, Wolverine State
State capital	Lansing
Date of statehood	Jan. 26, 1837; 26th state
State bird	Robin
State flower	Apple blossom
State tree	White pine
State motto	*Si Quaeris Peninsulam Amoenam, Circumspice* (If You Seek a Pleasant Peninsula, Look About You)
Total population & rank	9,990,871 (in 2001); 8th
Population density	176 per sq. mile (70 per sq. km)
Population distribution	75% urban, 25% rural
Largest cities	Detroit, Grand Rapids, Warren, Flint, Sterling Heights
Highest elevation	Mt. Arvon, 1,979 ft. (603 m)
Lowest elevation	Lake Erie, 571 ft. (174 m)
Land area & rank	56,804 sq. miles (147,122 sq. km); 22nd
Average January temperature	20°F (–7°C)
Average July temperature	69°F (21°C)
Average yearly precipitation	32 inches (81 cm)
Major industries	manufacturing, services, tourism, agriculture, forestry/lumber
Places to visit	Greenfield Village (Dearborn), Motown Historical Museum (Detroit), Mackinac Island
Web site	www.michigan.gov

MINNESOTA

★ ★ ★ ★

MANITOBA

CANADA

ONTARIO

Red River

Lake of the Woods

Rainy River

Rainy Lake

International Falls

Kabetogama Lake

VOYAGEURS NATL. PARK

Basswood R.

Pigeon River

Grand Portage

KITTSON

Roseau

ROSEAU

LAKE OF THE WOODS

KOOCHICHING

Vermilion Lake

Ely

Eagle Mtn. 2,301 ft. (701 m) ▲ COOK

Grand Portage

MARSHALL

Mud Lake

Upper Red Lake

Thief River Falls

PENNINGTON

Red Lake River

East Grand Forks

Grand Forks

Crookston

RED LAKE

Lower Red Lake

POLK

CLEARWATER

BELTRAMI

Lake Winnibigoshish

Big Fork River

SAINT LOUIS

LAKE

Lake Superior

NORTH DAKOTA

NORMAN

MAHNOMEN

Bemidji

Cass Lake

ITASCA

Chisholm

Virginia

Hibbing

HUBBARD

Leech Lake

Grand Rapids

St. Louis River

West Fargo

Fargo

Moorhead

CLAY

BECKER

CASS

Two Harbors

Detroit Lakes

WADENA

CROW

Hermantown

Duluth

Cloquet

Superior

MICHIGAN

WILKIN

Otter Tail Cr.

OTTER TAIL

Fergus Falls

Brainerd

Mille Lacs Lake

AITKIN

CARLTON

TODD

MILLE LACS

PINE

GRANT

DOUGLAS

Little Falls

MORRISON

KANABEC

Bois de Sioux River

TRAVERSE

Alexandria

BENTON

Sartell

Sauk Rapids

STEARNS

St. Cloud

SHERBURNE

Elk River

ISANTI

CHISAGO

St. Croix River

BIG STONE

STEVENS

Morris

POPE

Chippewa River

SWIFT

KANDIYOHI

Willmar

MEEKER

WRIGHT

Buffalo

HENNEPIN

Coon Rapids

RAMSEY

ANOKA

WASHINGTON

LAC QUI PARLE

CHIPPEWA

Montevideo

Minnesota River

Minneapolis

St. Paul

Bloomington

Eau Claire

SOUTH DAKOTA

YELLOW MEDICINE

RENVILLE

MCLEOD

CARVER

Shakopee

SCOTT

DAKOTA

WISCONSIN

Marshall

LINCOLN

LYON

Redwood River

REDWOOD

SIBLEY

NICOLLET

Northfield

LE SUEUR

RICE

Red Wing

GOODHUE

WABASHA

Mississippi River

New Ulm

Faribault

BROWN

Mankato

BLUE EARTH

WASECA

Owatonna

DODGE

Rochester

Winona

La Crosse

PIPESTONE

MURRAY

COTTONWOOD

WATONWAN

STEELE

OLMSTED

WINONA

Des Moines River

Sioux Falls

ROCK

NOBLES

JACKSON

Worthington

MARTIN

Fairmont

FARIBAULT

Albert Lea

FREEBORN

Austin

MOWER

FILLMORE

HOUSTON

IOWA

LEGEND

★ State capital

• City

PINE County

▲ Mountain peak

National or other park

Swamp

Urban area

N W E S

0 25 50 75 100 Miles

0 25 50 75 100 Kilometers

Taller than it is wide and capped with a small wedge of land thrusting up into Canada, Minnesota is associated with fresh water. Lake Superior washes against the remote northeastern shoreline, thousands of small lakes speckle the woodlands, and a modest lake is the source of the mighty Mississippi River. Scandinavian immigrants saw a landscape that looked familiar, and many stayed to make their home. The north, like Canada, has miles and miles of forests and a celebrated history of lumberjacks and trappers. Iron ore from its mountain ranges was crucial to the U.S. steel industry. The south, like Iowa, is fertile farmland, producing corn and soybeans. Although many U.S. cities lie close to each other, the expression "Twin Cities" means just one thing—Minneapolis and St. Paul. Each has its distinctive character, but together they blend into an attractive and comfortable metropolitan area.

Did You Know?

A commonly expressed statement says that Minnesota is the land of 10,000 lakes, but it has many more:

15,000

Minnesota Almanac

Nicknames	North Star State, Gopher State
State capital	St. Paul
Date of statehood	May 11, 1858; 32nd state
State bird	Common loon
State flower	Pink and white lady's-slipper
State tree	Norway (red) pine
State motto	L'Etoile du Nord (The Star of the North)
Total population & rank	4,972,294 (in 2001); 21st
Population density	62 per sq. mile (24 per sq. km)
Population distribution	71% urban, 29% rural
Largest cities	Minneapolis, St. Paul, Duluth, Rochester, Bloomington
Highest elevation	Eagle Mountain, 2,301 ft. (701 m)
Lowest elevation	Lake Superior, 602 ft. (183 m)
Land area & rank	79,610 sq. miles (206,190 sq. km); 14th
Average January temperature	9°F (–13°C)
Average July temperature	70°F (21°C)
Average yearly precipitation	26 inches (66 cm)
Major industries	agribusiness, forest products, mining, manufacturing, tourism
Places to visit	Voyageurs National Park, Walker Art Center (Minneapolis), Ironworld (Chisholm), St. Paul: Minnesota State Fair, Fort Snelling
Web site	www.state.mn.us

Economy – Chief Products

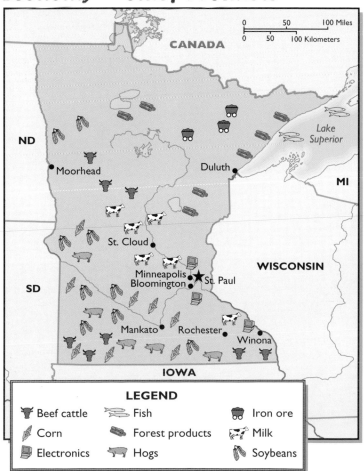

LEGEND

- 🐄 Beef cattle
- 🌽 Corn
- 💻 Electronics
- 🐟 Fish
- 🪵 Forest products
- 🐖 Hogs
- ⛏ Iron ore
- 🥛 Milk
- 🫘 Soybeans

Physical

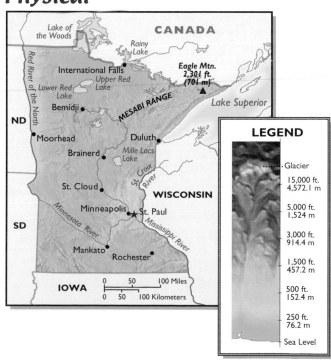

LEGEND

- ...... Glacier
- 15,000 ft. / 4,572.1 m
- 5,000 ft. / 1,524 m
- 3,000 ft. / 914.4 m
- 1,500 ft. / 457.2 m
- 500 ft. / 152.4 m
- 250 ft. / 76.2 m
- Sea Level

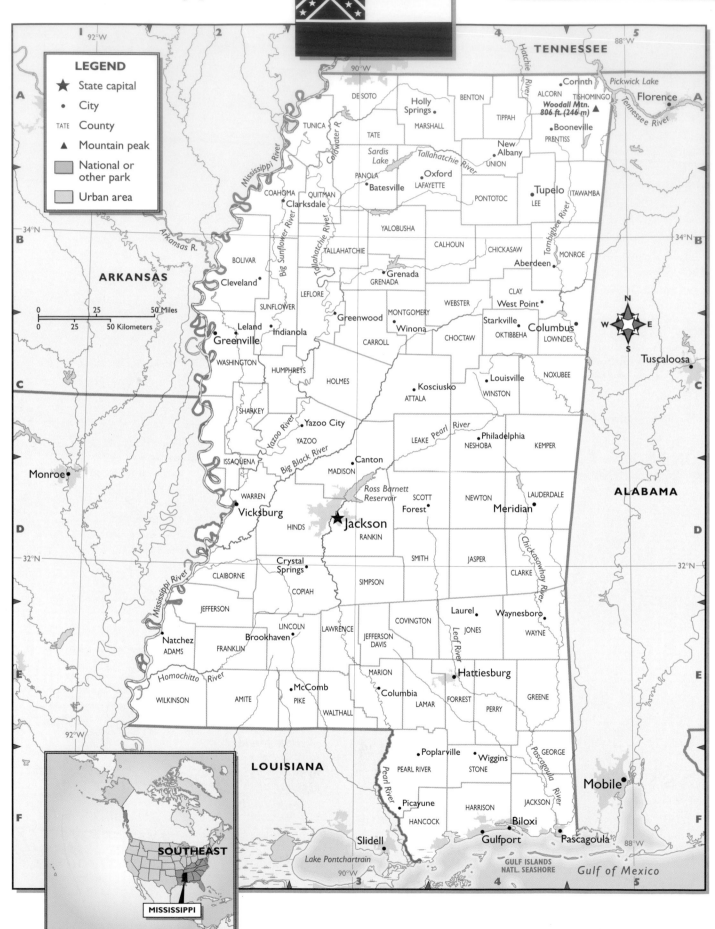

LEGEND
★ State capital
• City
TATE County
▲ Mountain peak
National or other park
Urban area

TENNESSEE

0 25 50 Miles
0 25 50 Kilometers

ARKANSAS

92°W

34°N

32°N

Pickwick Lake
Corinth
ALCORN TISHOMINGO
Florence
Woodall Mtn. 806 ft. (246 m) ▲
Booneville
PRENTISS
New Albany
Tennessee River
DE SOTO
Holly Springs
BENTON
TIPPAH
MARSHALL
TUNICA
TATE
Sardis Lake
Tallahatchie River
PANOLA
Oxford
LAFAYETTE
UNION
Tupelo
ITAWAMBA
LEE
Batesville
PONTOTOC
Coldwater R.
COAHOMA
QUITMAN
Clarksdale
YALOBUSHA
CALHOUN
CHICKASAW
MONROE
Aberdeen
Mississippi River
Big Sunflower River
Tallahatchie River
TALLAHATCHIE
BOLIVAR
Grenada
GRENADA
CLAY
West Point
Starkville
Columbus
LOWNDES
Cleveland
LEFLORE
MONTGOMERY
WEBSTER
OKTIBBEHA
Tombigbee River
SUNFLOWER
Greenwood
Winona
CHOCTAW
Leland
Indianola
CARROLL
Tuscaloosa
Greenville
WASHINGTON
HUMPHREYS
Kosciusko
Louisville
NOXUBEE
HOLMES
ATTALA
WINSTON
SHARKEY
Yazoo River
Yazoo City
YAZOO
Pearl River
Philadelphia
KEMPER
ISSAQUENA
Big Black River
LEAKE
NESHOBA
Monroe
Canton
MADISON
Ross Barnett Reservoir
SCOTT
NEWTON
LAUDERDALE
ALABAMA
WARREN
Vicksburg
HINDS
Jackson
RANKIN
Forest
Meridian
Crystal Springs
CLAIBORNE
SMITH
JASPER
Chickasawhay River
COPIAH
SIMPSON
CLARKE
JEFFERSON
Laurel
Waynesboro
Natchez
ADAMS
LINCOLN
LAWRENCE
COVINGTON
JONES
WAYNE
Brookhaven
JEFFERSON DAVIS
Leaf River
FRANKLIN
Hattiesburg
Homochitto River
MARION
Columbia
LAMAR
FORREST
PERRY
GREENE
McComb
PIKE
WALTHALL
WILKINSON
AMITE
GEORGE
Poplarville
Wiggins
PEARL RIVER
STONE
Pascagoula River
Mobile
LOUISIANA
Pearl River
Picayune
HARRISON
JACKSON
HANCOCK
Biloxi
Slidell
Gulfport
Pascagoula
Lake Pontchartrain
GULF ISLANDS NATL. SEASHORE
Gulf of Mexico

SOUTHEAST
MISSISSIPPI

90°W

The state of Mississippi takes its name from the celebrated waterway that forms its irregular, western-facing border—the Mississippi River. By its geography, culture, and history, Mississippi is one of the states belonging to the Deep South. Within the state, the Delta region, an oval-shaped cluster of counties next to the Mississippi River, best matches the popular image of the Deep South. The Delta has tropical heat, unbroken flat fields growing cotton and soybeans, and the highest concentration of African Americans (60% of the Delta's population) in the United States. The rest of the state rolls from the northeastern hills to the Gulf Coast and produces a mix of crops, livestock, and forest products. As in all the South today, there is much in Mississippi that is new—manufacturing, catfish farming, plus visitors who flock to the Delta to hear the blues, enjoy themselves at the beaches and bays, or spend time at casino facilities.

Economy – Chief Products

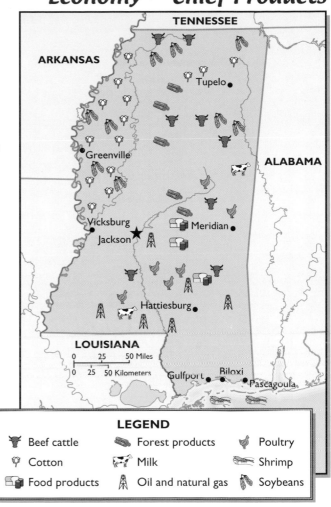

LEGEND

Beef cattle	Forest products		Poultry
Cotton	Milk		Shrimp
Food products	Oil and natural gas		Soybeans

Did You Know?

Because a river's course shifts over time, some land belonging to Mississippi lies in an unexpected location: West of the Mississippi River

Physical

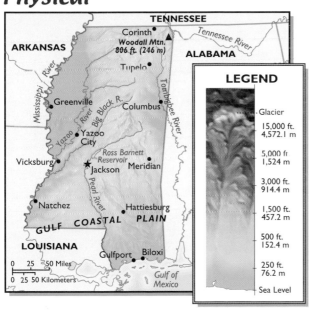

LEGEND

- Glacier
- 15,000 ft. 4,572.1 m
- 5,000 ft 1,524 m
- 3,000 ft. 914.4 m
- 1,500 ft. 457.2 m
- 500 ft. 152.4 m
- 250 ft. 76.2 m
- Sea Level

Mississippi Almanac

Nickname	Magnolia State	**Land area & rank**	46,907 sq. miles (121,489 sq. km); 31st
State capital	Jackson		
Date of statehood	Dec. 10, 1817; 20th state	**Average January temperature**	45°F (7°C)
State bird	Mockingbird		
State flower	Magnolia	**Average July temperature**	81°F (27°C)
State tree	Magnolia		
State motto	*Virtute et Armis* (By Valor and Arms)	**Average yearly precipitation**	56 inches (142 cm)
Total population & rank	2,858,029 (in 2001); 31st	**Major industries**	warehousing and distribution, services, manufacturing, government, wholesale and retail trade
Population density	61 per sq. mile (24 per sq. km)		
Population distribution	49% urban, 51% rural		
Largest cities	Jackson, Gulfport, Biloxi	**Places to visit**	Vicksburg National Military Park, Natchez Trace Parkway (from Natchez to Nashville, TN), Old Spanish Fort and Museum (Pascagoula)
Highest elevation	Woodall Mountain, 806 ft. (246 m)		
Lowest elevation	sea level	**Web site**	www.ms.gov

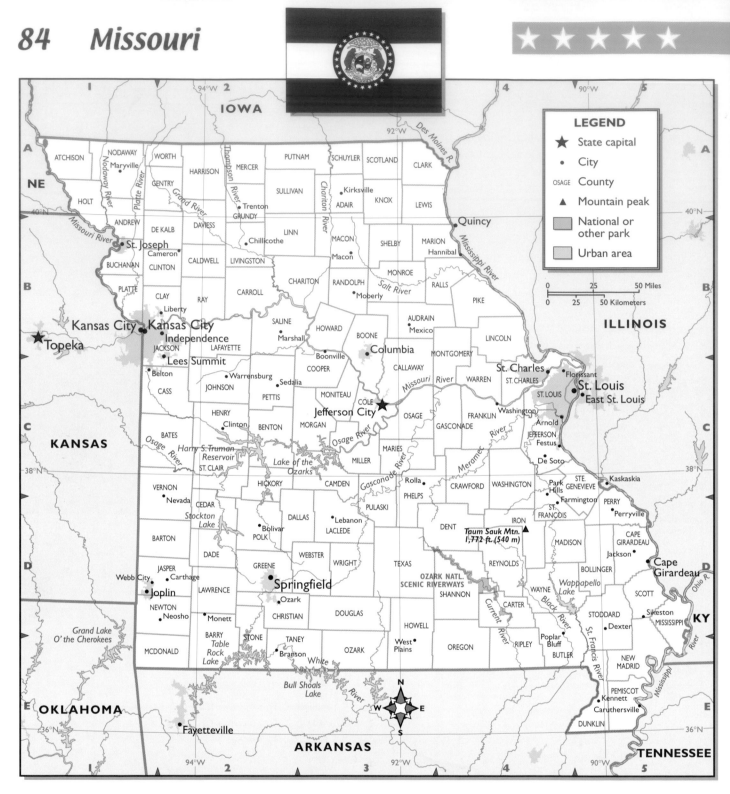

Positioned near the center of the lower 48 states, Missouri can be recognized by the small projection dangling from the southeast corner like a toe being dipped into a swimming pool. Missouri is a state with neighbors—eight states surround it—and with two celebrated rivers. The Mississippi River forms the entire eastern boundary, and the Missouri River crosses the center of the state. The southern half, particularly the portion known as the Ozarks, is a hilly region of lakes and forests. Fertile soil provided by the rivers supports extensive farming. Like its neighbors to the north and east, the state produces plenty of corn, soybeans, and livestock. Branson, a small town in the Ozarks, attracts millions of people to its music theaters and nearby lakes. An imaginary point in Missouri is called the U.S. center of population. That means an equal number of people live north, south, east, and west of the point.

Physical

LEGEND

Glacier

15,000 ft.
4,572.1 m

5,000 ft.
1,524 m

3,000 ft.
914.4 m

1,500 ft.
457.2 m

500 ft.
152.4 m

250 ft.
76.2 m

Sea Level

Missouri Almanac

Nickname	Show Me State
State capital	Jefferson City
Date of statehood	Aug. 10, 1821; 24th state
State bird	Bluebird
State flower	Hawthorn
State tree	Dogwood
State motto	Salus Populi Suprema Lex Esto (The Welfare of the People Shall Be the Supreme Law)
Total population & rank	5,629,707 (in 2001); 17th
Population density	82 per sq. mile (32 per sq. km)
Population distribution	69% urban, 31% rural
Largest cities	Kansas City, St. Louis, Springfield, Independence
Highest elevation	Taum Sauk Mountain, 1,772 ft. (540 m)
Lowest elevation	St Francis River in Dunklin Co., 230 ft. (70 m)
Land area & rank	68,886 sq. miles (178,415 sq. km); 18th
Average January temperature	31°F (−1°C)
Average July temperature	78°F (26°C)
Average yearly precipitation	41 inches (104 cm)
Major industries	agriculture, manufacturing, aerospace, tourism
Places to visit	Gateway Arch (St. Louis), Mark Twain Area (Hannibal), Pony Express Museum (St. Joseph)
Web site	www.state.mo.us

Economy – Chief Products

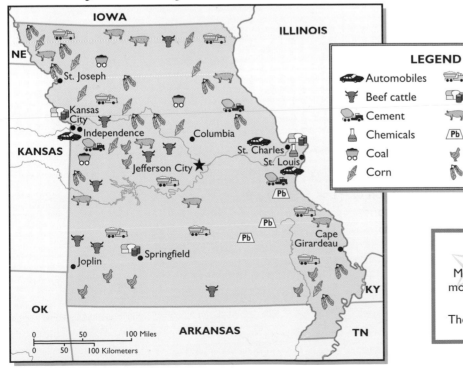

LEGEND

Automobiles
Beef cattle
Cement
Chemicals
Coal
Corn
Crushed stone
Food products
Hogs
Pb Lead
Poultry
Soybeans

Did You Know?

Missouri was the epicenter of some of the most powerful earthquakes ever to occur in the United States:

The New Madrid earthquakes of 1811–1812

MONTANA

Map labels

116°W · I · 2 · 112°W · 3 · 108°W · 4 · 5 · 104°W

BRITISH COLUMBIA · ALBERTA · CANADA · SASKATCHEWAN

Milk River · Frenchman Creek

A

Kootenai R. · Lake Koocanusa · Flathead River · GLACIER NATL. PARK · GLACIER · Cut Bank · TOOLE · LIBERTY · HILL · Fresno Res. · Chinook · VALLEY · DANIELS · Poplar River · SHERIDAN · Plentywood

LINCOLN · Libby · Whitefish · FLATHEAD · Browning · Shelby · Havre · BLAINE · Malta · PHILLIPS · Glasgow · Wolf Point · ROOSEVELT

48°N · Kalispell · Flathead Lake · PONDERA · Conrad · Marias River · UPPER MISSOURI RIVER BREAKS NATL. MON. · Missouri River · RICHLAND · Sidney · ND

Clark · Thompson Falls · Polson · SANDERS · LAKE · TETON · Choteau · Teton River · CHOUTEAU · River · Fort Benton · Judith R. · GARFIELD · Big Dry Cr. · MCCONE · DAWSON

MINERAL · RATTLESNAKE NATL. REC. AREA · LEWIS AND CLARK · CASCADE · Great Falls · Missouri · FERGUS · PETROLEUM · Glendive · WIBAUX · B

Bitterroot River · Lolo · MISSOULA · Missoula · Helena · POWELL · BROADWATER · Canyon Ferry Lake · MEAGHER · JUDITH BASIN · Lewistown · MUSSELSHELL · Roundup · Musselshell River · PRAIRIE · Baker · FALLON

GRANITE · Deer Lodge · JEFFERSON · Boulder · Townsend · WHEATLAND · GOLDEN VALLEY · Forsyth · Miles City · CUSTER

Hamilton · Anaconda · Butte · DEER LODGE · SILVER BOW · Jefferson R. · GALLATIN · Belgrade · SWEET GRASS · Big Timber · Billings · Hardin · TREASURE · ROSEBUD · Colstrip · POWDER RIVER · CARTER · C

RAVALLI · Big Hole R. · Bozeman · Yellowstone · River · Livingston · STILLWATER · YELLOWSTONE · Laurel · BIG HORN · LITTLE BIGHORN BATTLEFIELD NATL. MON. · Bighorn R. · Tongue River · Powder R.

Dillon · MADISON · Gallatin R. · PARK · Granite Pk. 12,799 ft. (3,901 m) ▲ · CARBON · Red Lodge · BIGHORN CANYON NATL. REC. AREA · SD

BEAVERHEAD · Madison River · YELLOWSTONE NATL. PARK · Yellowstone Lake

IDAHO · WYOMING · 44°N · D

GRAND TETON NATL. PARK

Idaho Falls · 112°W · 108°W · 104°W

1 · 2 · 3 · 4 · 5

0 · 50 · 100 Miles
0 · 50 · 100 Kilometers

N · W · E · S

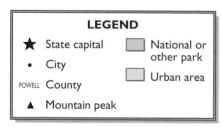

MONTANA
WEST

Physical

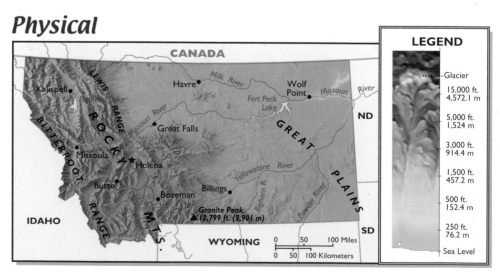

CANADA

Kalispell · LEWIS RANGE · Havre · Milk River · Wolf Point · Missouri · River · ND

BITTERROOT RANGE · ROCKY · Missouri River · Great Falls · Fort Peck Lake · GREAT · PLAINS

Missoula · Helena · Yellowstone · River

Butte · Bozeman · Billings · Bighorn R. · Powder River · SD

IDAHO · MTS. · Granite Peak ▲ 12,799 ft. (3,901 m) · WYOMING

0 · 50 · 100 Miles
0 · 50 · 100 Kilometers

LEGEND

·········· Glacier
15,000 ft. 4,572.1 m
5,000 ft. 1,524 m
3,000 ft. 914.4 m
1,500 ft. 457.2 m
500 ft. 152.4 m
250 ft. 76.2 m
Sea Level

Montana earns its "Big Sky Country" reputation from the seemingly endless horizon above the vast prairies covering the eastern two-thirds of the state. Rugged, glaciated mountains occupy the western third. Lewis and Clark explored along the Missouri River here in 1805–1806, bringing back the first descriptions of grizzly bears and other amazing plants and animals. Native Americans fought to keep their share of the land as well. General George Armstrong Custer made an ill-advised attack against a large Sioux encampment at the Battle of Little Bighorn in 1876, losing the lives of his entire company. Things have settled down since then, but Montana is still cowboy country. Rodeos, recreated cattle drives, and other ranching-related celebrations recall the heritage of this state. While many people still earn a living as real cowboys, many more work in industries such as mining, agriculture, oil, or the service sector.

Did You Know?

Montana is the only state whose rivers drain into three oceans:

Pacific, Atlantic, and Arctic Oceans

Montana Almanac

Nickname	Treasure State
State capital	Helena
Date of statehood	Nov. 8, 1889; 41st state
State bird	Western meadowlark
State flower	Bitterroot
State tree	Ponderosa pine
State motto	Oro y Plata (Gold and Silver)
Total population & rank	904,433 (in 2001); 44th
Population density	6 per sq. mile (2.3 per sq. km)
Population distribution	54% urban, 46% rural
Largest cities	Billings, Missoula, Great Falls, Butte
Highest elevation	Granite Peak, 12,799 ft. (3,901 m)
Lowest elevation	Kootenai River in Lincoln Co., 1,800 ft. (549 m)
Land area & rank	145,552 sq. miles (376,980 sq. km); 4th
Average January temperature	17°F (−8°C)
Average July temperature	70°F (21°C)
Average yearly precipitation	15 inches (38 cm)
Major industries	agriculture, timber, mining, tourism, oil and gas
Places to visit	Glacier National Park, Little Bighorn Battlefield National Monument, Museum of the Rockies (Bozeman), Museum of the Plains Indian (Browning)
Web site	www.state.mt.us

Economy – Chief Products

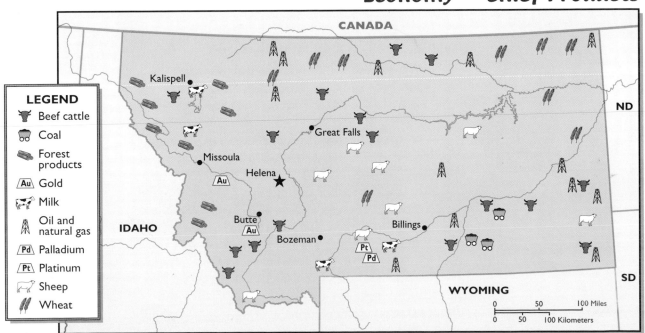

LEGEND

- 🐂 Beef cattle
- Coal
- Forest products
- Au Gold
- Milk
- Oil and natural gas
- Pd Palladium
- Pt Platinum
- Sheep
- Wheat

LEGEND

⭐ State capital

• City

SIOUX County

National or other park

Urban area

MIDWEST

NEBRASKA

Nebraska lies in the middle of the five states that are stacked on top of Texas and has a wide western extension called the Panhandle. The Missouri River is its eastern boundary, but another important river is the Platte. The gentle valley of the Platte River provided an easy way to travel west and was used by the Oregon Trail, Mormon pioneers, and the first transcontinental railroad. Originally covered by mile after mile of tall prairie grasses, the eastern half of Nebraska is now devoted to farming and contains most of the state's residents. The primary crops are corn and other grains. The dry and hilly western half is ranching country, particularly in the Sand Hills. The Sand Hills are permanent, grass-covered sand dunes that are ideal for raising cattle. Not surprisingly, one of the most important industries is meat packing, and many other businesses in the state are involved with food processing.

Did You Know?

Unlike those in other states, the national forests of Nebraska were created by an unusual method:

Hand-planted tree seedlings

Nebraska Almanac

Nickname	Cornhusker State	**Land area & rank**	76,872 sq. miles (199,098 sq. km); 15th
State capital	Lincoln	**Average January temperature**	23°F (−5°C)
Date of statehood	March 1, 1867; 37th state	**Average July temperature**	76°F (24°C)
State bird	Western meadowlark		
State flower	Goldenrod	**Average yearly precipitation**	22 inches (56 cm)
State tree	Cottonwood	**Major industries**	agriculture, manufacturing
State motto	Equality Before the Law	**Places to visit**	Scotts Bluff National Monument, Stuhr Museum of the Prairie Pioneer (Grand Island), Agate Fossil Beds National Monument
Total population & rank	1,713,235 (in 2001); 38th		
Population density	22 per sq. mile (8 per sq. km)		
Population distribution	70% urban, 30% rural		
Largest cities	Omaha, Lincoln		
Highest elevation	Johnson Township, 5,424 ft. (1,653 m)	**Web site**	www.state.ne.us
Lowest elevation	Missouri River in Richardson Co., 840 ft. (256 m)		

Physical

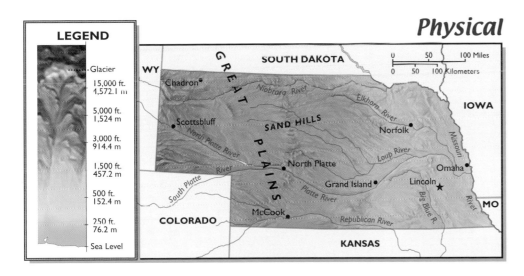

Economy – Chief Products

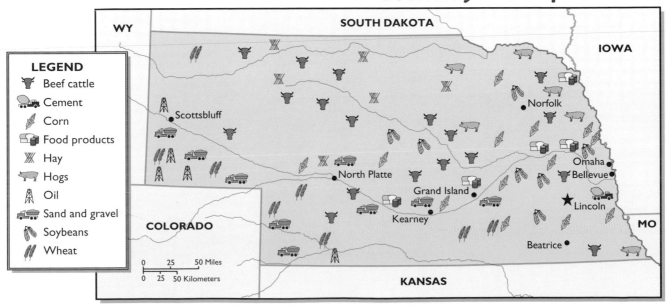

OREGON

IDAHO

A

McDermitt
Owyhee
Jackpot

Quinn River

HUMBOLDT

River

ELKO

Marys R.

Wells

B
WASHOE
Empire

Winnemucca

PERSHING

Humboldt River

Battle Mountain

Carlin

Elko

West Wendover

Humboldt R.

Pyramid Lake

Lovelock

LANDER

40°N

EUREKA

40°N

UTAH

Sparks
STOREY
Fernley
Carson R.
Reno
Fallon

Stillwater Marsh

CHURCHILL

Austin

Eureka

WHITE PINE

McGill

Virginia City
★ Carson City

Reese River

Ruth

Ely

Lake Tahoe
DOUGLAS

LYON

Gardnerville
Yerington

Walker R.

Gabbs

GREAT BASIN NATL. PARK

C

N
W E
S

Walker Lake

Hawthorne
MINERAL

LEGEND

★ State capital

• City

CLARK County

▲ Mountain peak

National or other park

Urban area

NYE

CALIFORNIA

Boundary Pk.
13,143 ft. (4,006 m)

Tonopah

Pioche

Meadow Valley Wash

Panaca

D

Goldfield

ESMERALDA

White River

Caliente

LINCOLN

St. George

120°W

Amargosa R.

Beatty

Mesquite

Virgin River

E

NEVADA

WEST

DEATH VALLEY NATL. PARK

SPRING MOUNTAINS NATL. REC. AREA

CLARK

Pahrump

North Las Vegas
Las Vegas
Paradise
Boulder City

Henderson

Colorado River

LAKE MEAD NATL. REC. AREA

ARIZONA

0   25   50   75   100 Miles

0 25 50 75 100 Kilometers

Cal Nev Ari

Laughlin

Bullhead City

35°N

115°W

35°N

The long and angled border that Nevada shares with California gives the state an outline that looks like a triangle attached to the bottom of a rectangle. Nevada lies within the U.S. geographical region called the Great Basin, the very driest part of the country. Despite this limitation, since 1990 Nevada has been the fastest growing state, climbing to the rank of 35th most populous. The distinctive terrain is called basin and range. Small mountain ranges are separated by wide, flat valleys, making a physical map of the state resemble corduroy fabric. Long known for its deposits of precious metals, Nevada leads the United States in the production of gold. Although irrigation makes farming possible and ranching occupies most of the rural land, the state's biggest business is tourism. Skiers swoosh in the mountains around Lake Tahoe, and millions of people arrive year-round to enjoy the hotels and casinos, the golf courses, and the shows and spectacles of Las Vegas.

Did You Know?

While working for a Virginia City newspaper, Samuel Clemens took the pen name for which he would be famous: Mark Twain

Nevada Almanac

Nicknames	Sagebrush State, Battle Born State, Silver State
State capital	Carson City
Date of statehood	Oct. 31, 1864; 36th state
State bird	Mountain bluebird
State flower	Sagebrush
State trees	Single-leaf piñon, bristlecone pine
State motto	All for Our Country
Total population & rank	2,106,074 (in 2001); 35th
Population density	19 per sq. mile (7.3 per sq. km)
Population distribution	92% urban, 8% rural
Largest cities	Las Vegas, Paradise, Reno, Henderson
Highest elevation	Boundary Peak, 13,143 ft. (4,006 m)
Lowest elevation	Colorado River in Clark Co., 479 ft. (146 m)
Land area & rank	109,826 sq. miles (284,449 sq. km); 7th
Average January temperature	32°F (0°C)
Average July temperature	75°F (24°C)
Average yearly precipitation	9 inches (23 cm)
Major industries	gaming, tourism, mining, manufacturing, government
Places to visit	Great Basin National Park, Hoover Dam (Boulder City), Lake Tahoe, Las Vegas
Web site	www.silver.state.nv.us

Economy – Chief Products

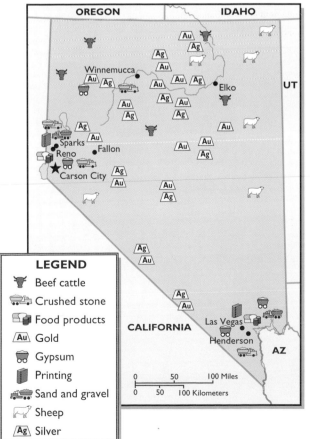

LEGEND
- 🐂 Beef cattle
- 🚚 Crushed stone
- 📦 Food products
- Au\ Gold
- Gypsum
- Printing
- Sand and gravel
- 🐑 Sheep
- Ag\ Silver

Physical

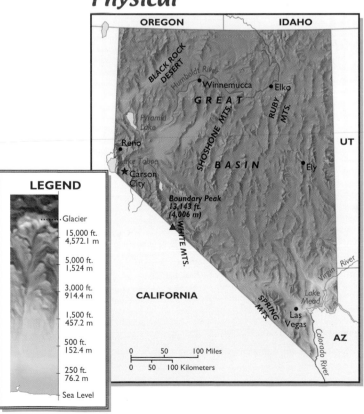

LEGEND
- Glacier
- 15,000 ft. 4,572.1 m
- 5,000 ft. 1,524 m
- 3,000 ft. 914.4 m
- 1,500 ft. 457.2 m
- 500 ft. 152.4 m
- 250 ft. 76.2 m
- Sea Level

LEGEND

- ★ State capital
- • City
- COOS County
- ▲ Mountain peak
- National or other park
- National forest
- Urban area

★ Montpelier

Did You Know?

The highest non-tornadic gust of wind was 231 mph (372 km/h), and it was recorded in this state:

Mount Washington

CANADA

QUÉBEC

VERMONT

MAINE

NEW HAMPSHIRE

NEW ENGLAND

Colebrook

COOS

Connecticut River

Androscoggin River

Groveton
WHITE MOUNTAIN NATL. FOREST

Lancaster

Berlin

Whitefield

Gorham

Littleton

Ammonoosuc River

Mt. Washington
6,288 ft. (1,917 m) ▲

Lisbon

FRANCONIA NOTCH STATE PARK

Woodsville

WHITE MOUNTAIN NATL. FOREST

North Conway

Lincoln

GRAFTON

Lewiston

Pemigewasset River

Conway

Baker River

CARROLL

Plymouth

Lake Winnipesaukee

Hanover

Newfound Lake

Portland

Lebanon

Bristol

Wolfeboro

Laconia

Winnisquam Lake

BELKNAP

Franklin

Farmington

Claremont

Lake Sunapee

Newport

SULLIVAN

MERRIMACK

Shaker Village (Canterbury)

Rochester

STRAFFORD

Somersworth

Dover

Contoocook R.

Merrimack River

Concord

Durham

Salmon Falls River

Piscataqua River

Hillsborough

Great Bay

Portsmouth

Keene

HILLSBOROUGH

Manchester

Exeter

Hampton

CHESHIRE

Peterborough

ROCKINGHAM

Derry

ATLANTIC OCEAN

Milford

Jaffrey

Salem

Haverhill

Nashua

Lawrence

MASSACHUSETTS

Lowell

Saco River

Scale:
0 — 15 — 30 Miles
0 — 15 — 30 Kilometers

New Hampshire, the New England state shaped like a wedge between Maine and Vermont, is a state of great natural beauty. Its mountains, forests, and lakes, home to countless species of fish and wildlife, attract outdoor enthusiasts year-round. People of New Hampshire have been known for their rugged individualism even before becoming the first of the original 13 colonies to separate from Great Britain. Since 1952, New Hampshire has had the first presidential primary, which gives it a big impact on presidential politics. It has more members in its house of representatives than any other state. Most of New Hampshire's residents live in cities in the southeastern part of the state. Cities like

Portsmouth, New Hampshire's port city, and Manchester are industrial centers that produce computers and electronic equipment and metal goods. Because of the abundance of tourists to the state, the biggest part of the workforce works in the service industry, staffing hotels, restaurants, museums, stores, ski resorts, and historic sites.

Economy – Chief Products

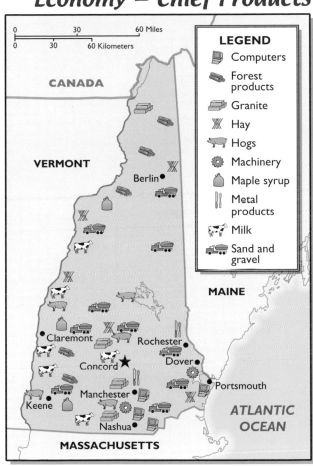

Physical

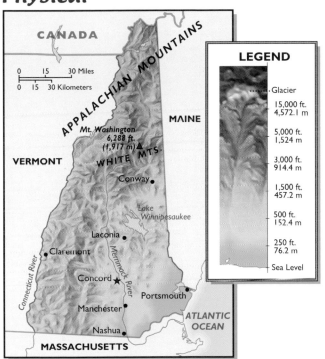

New Hampshire Almanac

Nickname	Granite State	**Land area & rank**	8,968 sq. miles (23,227 sq. km); 44th
State capital	Concord	**Average January temperature**	17°F (–8°C)
Date of statehood	June 21, 1788; 9th state		
State bird	Purple finch	**Average July temperature**	67°F (19°C)
State flower	Purple lilac		
State tree	White birch	**Average yearly precipitation**	42 inches (107 cm)
State motto	Live Free or Die		
Total population & rank	1,259,181 (in 2001); 41st	**Major industries**	tourism, manufacturing, agriculture, trade, mining
Population density	140 per sq. mile (54 per sq. km)		
Population distribution	59% urban, 41% rural	**Places to visit**	White Mountain National Forest, Mt. Washington, Canterbury Shaker Village, Franconia Notch State Park
Largest cities	Manchester, Nashua, Concord		
Highest elevation	Mt. Washington, 6,288 ft. (1,917 m)	**Web site**	www.state.nh.us
Lowest elevation	sea level		

★ ★ ★ ★ ★

LEGEND

★ State capital

• City

SALEM County

▲ Mountain peak

National or other park

Urban area

76°W
Scranton

1 2 75°W 3 4 74°W 5

High Point
1,803 ft. (550 m)

NEW YORK

DELAWARE WATER GAP
NATL. REC. AREA

Danbury

CT

Norwalk

Stamford

SUSSEX
Wallkill River

Newton • Sparta
Ringwood
Ramsey

PASSAIC
Paramus
Yonkers

41°N
Hopatcong

New Rochelle

Paterson
BERGEN
Hackensack
41°N

PENNSYLVANIA
Hackettstown
WARREN
Dover
MORRIS
Clifton
Passaic

Washington
Morristown
EDISON NATL.
HISTORIC SITE
ESSEX
HUDSON
Jersey City

Easton • Phillipsburg
Passaic R.
Newark
New York City

Bethlehem
Elizabeth
Bayonne

Allentown
UNION
Plainfield
Staten
Island

HUNTERDON
SOMERSET
Somerville
GATEWAY
NATL.
REC. AREA

Did You Know?
Raritan R.
Edison
Sandy Hook

New Jersey is one of the most densely populated states in the nation, but its truck farms, orchards, and flower gardens gave the state its nickname:

The Garden State

New Brunswick
Perth Amboy

Sayreville

MIDDLESEX
Red Bank
Long Branch

Princeton
Freehold
Asbury Park

MERCER
MONMOUTH

Trenton
Lakewood
Point Pleasant

40°N
Burlington
Mount Holly
Browns Mills
Toms River
N
40°N

Philadelphia
Camden
Rancocas River
W • E

Cherry Hill
BURLINGTON
OCEAN
S

Woodbury
**ATLANTIC
OCEAN**

Wilmington
Lindenwold
Barnegat Bay

Newark
GLOUCESTER
CAMDEN
Penns Grove
Barnegat Inlet

Glassboro
0   15   30 Miles

SALEM
Hammonton
0 15 30 Kilometers

Salem
ATLANTIC
Little Egg Inlet

Vineland
E

Bridgeton
Pleasantville
Brigantine
NEW JERSEY

Millville
CUMBERLAND
Atlantic City
MIDATLANTIC

DELAWARE
Great Egg Inlet
Ocean
City

MD
Dover
CAPE MAY
Sea Isle City
Avalon

39°N
Delaware
Bay
Hereford Inlet
39°N

Wildwood

1 2 75°W Cape May 3 4 74°W 5

New Jersey's shape is delineated by the Delaware and Hudson Rivers as well as the Atlantic coast. Its location between two of the largest U.S. cities, Philadelphia and New York, has given New Jersey access to immense markets for its products and encouraged economic growth. New Jersey is one of the largest producers of medicines, chemicals, electronics, and also food products like Campbell's Soup from its many truck farms and orchards. This economic success has also led to New Jersey's standing as one of the most densely populated state, with 94% of the people living in cities. Some of the world's most famous inventors like Thomas Edison, Samuel Morse, and Albert Einstein lived in New Jersey, adding to its reputation as an innovative state. New Jersey has many colonial and Revolutionary War historic sites including Monmouth Battlefield, Trenton, and Morristown. The Atlantic coastal region is famous for its resort towns with boardwalks, casinos, and white sand beaches. Tourism has increased the number of people with jobs in the service industry.

New Jersey Almanac

Nickname	Garden State
State capital	Trenton
Date of statehood	Dec. 18, 1787; 3rd state
State bird	Eastern goldfinch
State flower	Purple violet
State tree	Red oak
State motto	Liberty and Prosperity
Total population & rank	8,484,431 (in 2001); 9th
Population density	1,144 per sq. mile (442 per sq. km)
Population distribution	94% urban, 6% rural
Largest cities	Newark, Jersey City, Paterson, Elizabeth
Highest elevation	High Point, 1,803 ft. (550 m)
Lowest elevation	sea level
Land area & rank	7,417 sq. miles (19,210 sq. km); 46th
Average January temperature	31°F (−1°C)
Average July temperature	74°F (23°C)
Average yearly precipitation	45 inches (114 cm)
Major industries	pharmaceuticals/drugs, telecommunications, biotechnology, printing and publishing
Places to visit	Edison National Historic Site (West Orange), Liberty State Park (Jersey City), Pine Barrens wilderness area, Atlantic City
Web site	www.state.nj.us

Economy – Chief Products

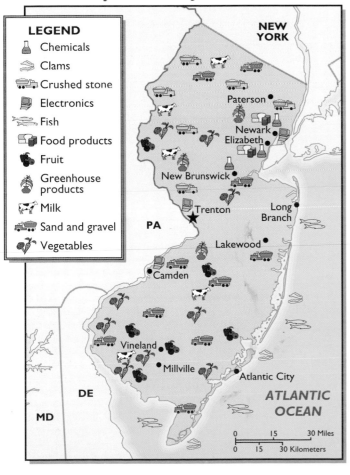

LEGEND
- Chemicals
- Clams
- Crushed stone
- Electronics
- Fish
- Food products
- Fruit
- Greenhouse products
- Milk
- Sand and gravel
- Vegetables

Physical

UT

COLORADO   106°W

108°W   2   4   104°W   5

OK

A

Shiprock

Aztec

Farmington

Bloomfield

Chama

SAN JUAN

RIO ARRIBA

Navajo Reservoir

Raton

Cimarron River

Questa

COLFAX

UNION

Clayton

▲ Wheeler Pk. 13,161 ft (4,011 m)

TAOS

Taos

San Juan River

Chaco River

CHACO CULTURE NATL. HISTORIC PARK

Abiquiu Res.

Rio Chama

MORA

HARDING

36°N   Espanola   Chimayo   36°N

Mora River

B

LOS ALAMOS

Los Alamos

BANDELIER NATL. MON.

Santa Fe

Las Vegas

Conchas Lake

SANTA FE

SAN MIGUEL

Canadian River

MCKINLEY

SANDOVAL

Gallup

Puerco River

Bernalillo

Rio Grande

Rio Puerco

Tucumcari

Zuni Pueblo

Grants

Rio Rancho

Albuquerque

BERNALILLO

QUAY

C

EL MALPAIS NATL. MON. AND CONS. AREA

CIBOLA

Los Lunas

VALENCIA

Belen

TORRANCE

Santa Rosa

GUADALUPE

CURRY

Clovis

Portales

DE BACA

AZ

34°N   Socorro   34°N

CATRON

SOCORRO

LINCOLN

ROOSEVELT

D

Elephant Butte Reservoir

Ruidoso

Roswell

CHAVES

Pecos River

Caballo Reservoir

Truth or Consequences

SIERRA

Tularosa

Alamogordo

Lovington

Silver City

Bayard

GRANT

Gila River

WHITE SANDS NATL. MON.

Artesia

Hobbs

LEA

Eunice

DONA ANA

OTERO

EDDY

E

Lordsburg

Deming

LUNA

Las Cruces

Rio Grande

Carlsbad

Jal

32°N   Anthony   CARLSBAD CAVERNS NATL. PARK   Red Bluff Reservoir   32°N

HIDALGO

Sunland Park

El Paso

TEXAS

106°W   104°W

F

Ciudad Juárez

MEXICO

N
W   E
S

SOUTHWEST

NEW MEXICO

LEGEND

★ State capital

• City

SIERRA County

▲ Mountain peak

National or other park

Urban area

0   25   50   75   100 Miles

0   25   50   75   100 Kilometers

108°W

1   2   3   4

New Mexico earns its nickname, "The Land of Enchantment," from its diverse landscape and people. From the stark beauty of the northern desert landscape to the large areas of forested mountains and streams, the state is an outdoor paradise. A state since only 1912, it became part of the United States after the 1846–1848 Mexican-American War. Founded in 1610, Santa Fe is both the oldest capital city in the United States, and the highest at 6,989 feet (2,130 m) above sea level. In 1945, New Mexico witnessed the first detonation of an atomic bomb near Alamogordo. Native American culture is strong. The Navajo Reservation, the nation's largest, is in the northwest corner of the state. The small city of Taos hosts a vibrant art scene. Farther south, Albuquerque, New Mexico's largest city, serves as the economic hub of the state. New Mexico mines many fuels and minerals, while high-tech businesses, tourism, and service industries employ many people.

Economy – Chief Products

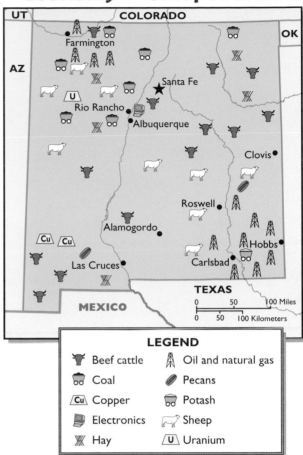

LEGEND

🐂	Beef cattle	🛢	Oil and natural gas
Coal		Pecans
Cu Copper		Potash
Electronics		Sheep
Hay		U Uranium

Physical

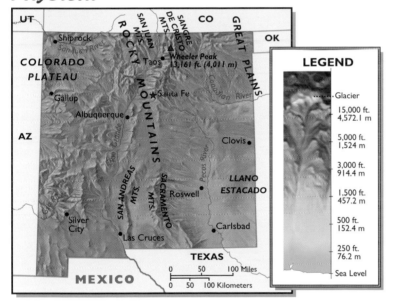

LEGEND

...... Glacier

15,000 ft.
4,572.1 m

5,000 ft.
1,524 m

3,000 ft.
914.4 m

1,500 ft.
457.2 m

500 ft.
152.4 m

250 ft.
76.2 m

Sea Level

Did You Know?

This bear cub was found clinging to a tree during a human-caused forest fire in New Mexico. He was rescued and soon became the symbol for forest fire prevention:

Smokey Bear

New Mexico Almanac

Nickname	Land of Enchantment	**Lowest elevation**	Red Bluff Reservoir in Eddy Co., 2,842 ft. (866 m)
State capital	Santa Fe	**Land area & rank**	121,356 sq. miles (314,312 sq. km); 5th
Date of statehood	Jan. 6, 1912; 47th state		
State bird	Roadrunner	**Average January temperature**	33°F (1°C)
State flower	Yucca		
State tree	Piñon	**Average July temperature**	73°F (23°C)
State motto	*Crescit Eundo* (It Grows as It Goes)		
Total population & rank	1,829,146 (in 2001); 36th	**Average yearly precipitation**	14 inches (36 cm)
Population density	15 per sq. mile (5.8 per sq. km)	**Major industries**	government, services, trade
Population distribution	75% urban, 25% rural	**Places to visit**	Carlsbad Caverns National Park, Chaco Culture National Historic Park, Mission San Miguel (Santa Fe)
Largest cities	Albuquerque, Las Cruces, Santa Fe		
Highest elevation	Wheeler Peak, 13,161 ft. (4,011 m)	**Web site**	www.state.nm.us

CATSKILL PARK · ULSTER · DUTCHESS · SULLIVAN · Monticello · Poughkeepsie · Waterbury · CONNECTICUT · Newburgh · Middletown · ORANGE · Danbury · New Haven · Port Jervis · PUTNAM · Bridgeport · Fishers I. · PA · ROCKLAND · WESTCHESTER · New City · White Plains · Stamford · Greenwich · Riverhead · Paterson · Yonkers · New Rochelle · Long Island · SUFFOLK · Jersey City · NEW YORK · BRONX · Long Island Sound · Newark · QUEENS · NASSAU · Hempstead · NEW JERSEY · Staten I. · KINGS · New York City · FIRE ISLAND NATL. SEASHORE · RICHMOND · GATEWAY NATL. REC. AREA · ATLANTIC OCEAN

CANADA · ONTARIO · St. Lawrence River · Cornwall · Massena · Malone · Ogdensburg · Canton · ST. LAWRENCE · FRANKLIN · Black Lake · Raquette River · Oswegatchie River · Tupper Lake · JEFFERSON · ADIRONDACK · Watertown · HAMILTON · LEWIS · Black River · HERKIMER · Lake Ontario · Oswego · OSWEGO · Oswego R. · Fulton · Oneida Lake · ONEIDA · Rome · Hamilton · CANADA · NIAGARA · Lockport · ORLEANS · MONROE · Irondequoit · WAYNE · Syracuse · Utica · Mohawk River · FULTON · Niagara Falls · Rochester · CAYUGA · ONONDAGA · MADISON · MONTGOMERY · Buffalo · Batavia · GENESEE · Canandaigua · Seneca R. · Auburn · Lackawanna · ERIE · Geneseo · ONTARIO · Geneva · SENECA · Cooperstown · Otsego Lake · OTSEGO · SCHOHARIE · Lake Erie · WYOMING · Genesee River · LIVINGSTON · Canandaigua Lake · YATES · Penn Yan · Cayuga Lake · Skaneateles Lake · CORTLAND · Norwich · Dunkirk · Keuka Lake · Seneca Lake · Cortland · CHENANGO · Oneonta · Fredonia · CHAUTAUQUA · CATTARAUGUS · Hornell · Bath · SCHUYLER · Ithaca · TOMPKINS · Chautauqua Lake · ALLEGANY · STEUBEN · Susquehanna River · DELAWARE · Jamestown · Salamanca · Corning · CHEMUNG · TIOGA · BROOME · Binghamton · Allegheny River · Olean · Elmira · Delaware R. · CATSKILL PARK · SULLIVAN · Allegheny Reservoir · PENNSYLVANIA · For continuation of map, see inset above

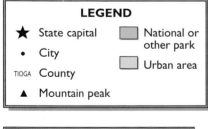

LEGEND

★ State capital
• City
TIOGA County
▲ Mountain peak

National or other park
Urban area

NEW YORK · MIDATLANTIC

Physical

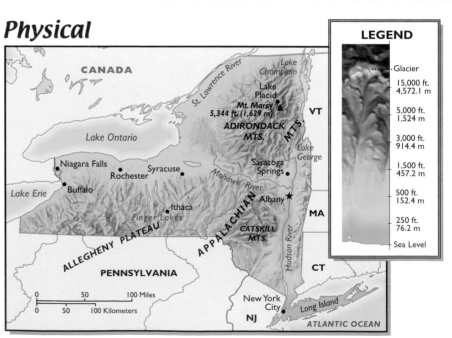

CANADA · St. Lawrence River · Lake Champlain · Lake Placid · Mt. Marcy 5,344 ft. (1,629 m) · ADIRONDACK MTS. · VT · Lake Ontario · Niagara Falls · Syracuse · Rochester · Saratoga Springs · Lake George · Buffalo · Mohawk River · Albany · MA · Lake Erie · Ithaca · Finger Lakes · ALLEGHENY PLATEAU · APPALACHIAN · CATSKILL MTS. · Hudson River · CT · PENNSYLVANIA · New York City · Long Island · NJ · ATLANTIC OCEAN

LEGEND

Glacier
15,000 ft. 4,572.1 m
5,000 ft. 1,524 m
3,000 ft. 914.4 m
1,500 ft. 457.2 m
500 ft. 152.4 m
250 ft. 76.2 m
Sea Level

New York's shape has been described as a "lopsided funnel," with all of the wealth of the state flowing through the southernmost funnel of New York City. It is a state with two separate cultures: the big city, world-class culture of New York City, and the rural, small-town, natural beauty of "Upstate" New York. New York City is a world leader in trade, manufacturing, and business. The dazzling array of cultural activities, museums, theaters, art, and music in the city make it an international tourist destination as well. Because of the United Nations Headquarters, the city is often viewed as a world capital. Upstate New York is home to many amazing natural wonders including Niagara Falls, the Finger Lakes region, and Adirondack Park (the nation's largest), as well as many historic sites. The Port of New York is among the busiest anywhere. In its harbor stands the Statue of Liberty—a symbol of freedom throughout the world.

New York Almanac

Nickname	Empire State
State capital	Albany
Date of statehood	July 26, 1788; 11th state
State bird	Bluebird
State flower	Rose
State tree	Sugar maple
State motto	*Excelsior* (Ever Upward)
Total population & rank	19,011,378 (in 2001); 3rd
Population density	403 per sq. mile (156 per sq. km)
Population distribution	88% urban, 12% rural
Largest cities	New York City, Buffalo, Rochester, Yonkers, Syracuse
Highest elevation	Mt. Marcy, 5,344 ft. (1,629 m)
Lowest elevation	sea level
Land area & rank	47,214 sq. miles (122,284 sq. km); 30th
Average January temperature	21°F (–6°C)
Average July temperature	69°F (21°C)
Average yearly precipitation	40 inches (102 cm)
Major industries	manufacturing, finance, communications, tourism, transportation, services
Places to visit	National Baseball Hall of Fame (Cooperstown), Niagara Falls, New York City: Central Park, Statue of Liberty and Ellis Island, Bronx Zoo, World Trade Center Site
Web site	www.state.ny.us

Did You Know?

In 1853, a resort in this town was home to the invention of this all-time favorite snack food—the potato chip:

Saratoga Springs

Economy – Chief Products

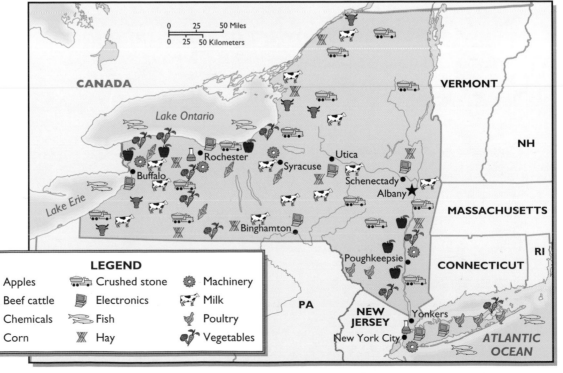

LEGEND

- Apples
- Beef cattle
- Chemicals
- Corn
- Crushed stone
- Electronics
- Fish
- Hay
- Machinery
- Milk
- Poultry
- Vegetables

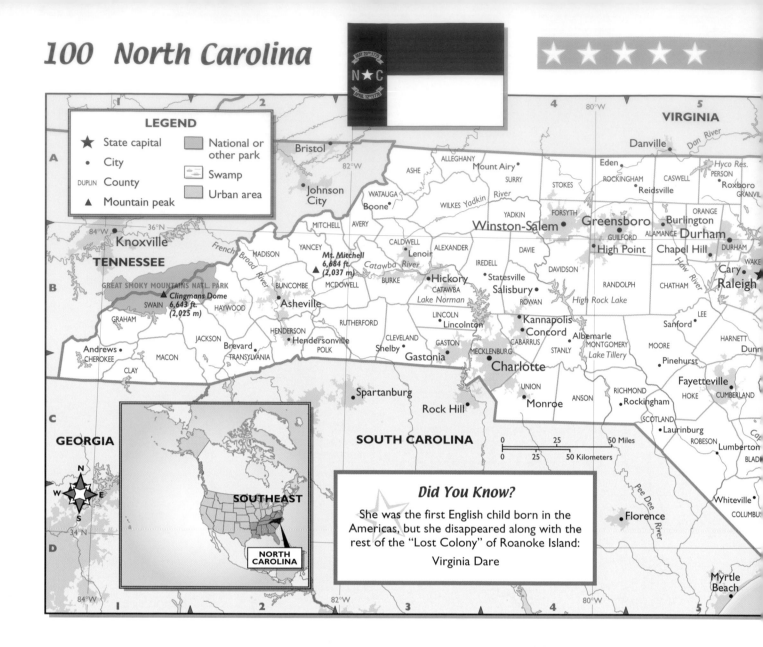

LEGEND
- ★ State capital
- • City
- DUPLIN County
- ▲ Mountain peak
- National or other park
- Swamp
- Urban area

VIRGINIA

TENNESSEE

GEORGIA

SOUTHEAST

NORTH CAROLINA

SOUTH CAROLINA

Did You Know?

She was the first English child born in the Americas, but she disappeared along with the rest of the "Lost Colony" of Roanoke Island:

Virginia Dare

North Carolina Almanac

Nicknames	Tar Heel State, Old North State		**Lowest elevation**	sea level
State capital	Raleigh		**Land area & rank**	48,711 sq. miles (126,161 sq. km); 29th
Date of statehood	Nov. 21, 1789; 12th state		**Average January temperature**	40°F (4°C)
State bird	Cardinal			
State flower	Dogwood		**Average July temperature**	77°F (25°C)
State tree	Pine			
State motto	Esse Quam Videri (To Be Rather Than to Seem)		**Average yearly precipitation**	50 inches (127 cm)
Total population & rank	8,186,268 (in 2001); 11th		**Major industries**	manufacturing, agriculture, tourism
Population density	168 per sq. mile (65 per sq. km)			
Population distribution	60% urban, 40% rural		**Places to visit**	Great Smoky Mountains National Park, Cape Hatteras National Seashore, Wright Brothers National Memorial
Largest cities	Charlotte, Raleigh, Greensboro, Durham, Winston-Salem			
Highest elevation	Mt. Mitchell, 6,684 ft. (2,037 m)		**Web site**	www.ncgov.com

North Carolina is one of the widest states, stretching for 500 miles (800 km) from the wave-lapped beaches of the Atlantic Ocean to its mountainous western tip. As in all large states, the geographical variety is remarkable. Delicate barrier islands are dangerous to ships but protect the bays where pirates once roamed and fishermen still work. The cool and green mountains feature the most-visited national park, Great Smoky Mountains, and the highest point east of the Mississippi River. Its cities are concentrated in the Piedmont among gently rolling hills. For years and years, North Carolina has been associated with three products—tobacco, textiles, and furniture. Recently, the state has become known for fast-growing, high-tech businesses involved with medicine, electronics, and research. With its attractive environment and appealing cities, North Carolina has been one of the fastest growing states.

Physical

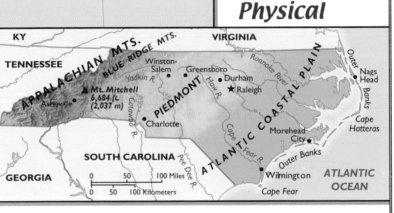

LEGEND

- Glacier
- 15,000 ft. / 4,572.1 m
- 5,000 ft. / 1,524 m
- 3,000 ft. / 914.4 m
- 1,500 ft. / 457.2 m
- 500 ft. / 152.4 m
- 250 ft. / 76.2 m
- Sea Level

Economy – Chief Products

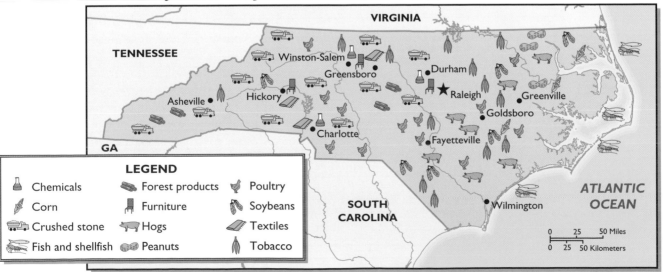

LEGEND

- Chemicals
- Corn
- Crushed stone
- Fish and shellfish
- Forest products
- Furniture
- Hogs
- Peanuts
- Poultry
- Soybeans
- Textiles
- Tobacco

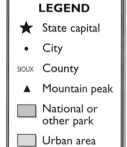

LEGEND

★ State capital
• City
SIOUX County
▲ Mountain peak
▨ National or other park
▨ Urban area

NORTH DAKOTA

MIDWEST

North Dakota is the nearly rectangular, top and center state of the lower 48 states. Only the eastern boundary, established by the Red River, is a natural feature. Immigration to the United States was at its peak during the years that North Dakota was being settled. Many of the state's first residents came from Europe, especially Scandinavia and Germany. Their descendants still live there. In the last ten years, however, the population has grown very little, and many of the rural counties are losing people. The gently rolling land may lack spectacular scenery, but a closer look reveals details like the prairie potholes, small lakes and ponds that are important for waterfowl. North Dakota's soil, formed under a vast carpet of grass, is perfect for growing grains. Only one other state produces more wheat, and North Dakota harvests the most of the special wheat used for spaghetti and noodles. Colorful fields of sunflowers are also common.

North Dakota Almanac

Nickname	Peace Garden State	**Land area & rank**	68,976 sq. miles (178,648 sq. km); 17th
State capital	Bismarck	**Average January temperature**	7°F (−14°C)
Date of statehood	Nov. 2, 1889; 39th state		
State bird	Western meadowlark	**Average July temperature**	69°F (21°C)
State flower	Wild prairie rose		
State tree	American elm	**Average yearly precipitation**	17 inches (36 cm)
State motto	Liberty and Union, Now and Forever, One and Inseparable	**Major industries**	agriculture, mining, tourism, manufacturing, telecommunications, energy, food processing,
Total population & rank	634,448 (in 2001); 48th		
Population density	9 per sq. mile (3.5 per sq. km)	**Places to visit**	Theodore Roosevelt National Park, Bonanzaville (Fargo), North Dakota Heritage Center (Bismarck), Dakota Dinosaur Museum (Dickinson)
Population distribution	56% urban, 44% rural		
Largest cities	Fargo, Bismarck, Grand Forks, Minot		
Highest elevation	White Butte, 3,506 ft. (1,069 m)		
Lowest elevation	Red River in Pembina Co., 750 ft. (229 m)	**Web site**	www.discovernd.com

Physical

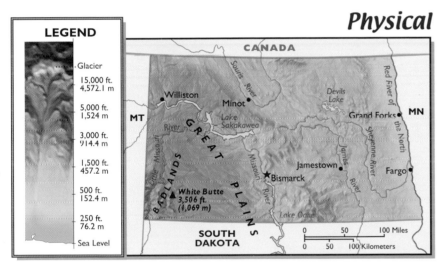

Did You Know?

Theodore Roosevelt wrote about a North Dakota phenomenon that has slowly and steadily endured for more than 80 years:

Underground fire in beds of lignite coal

Economy – Chief Products

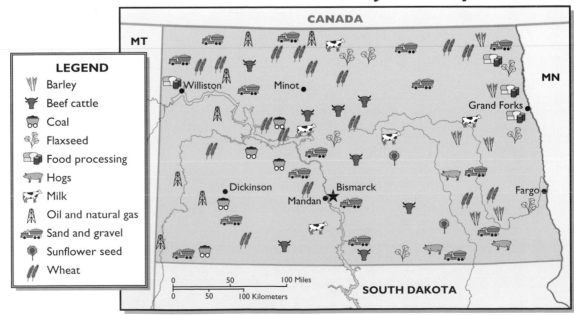

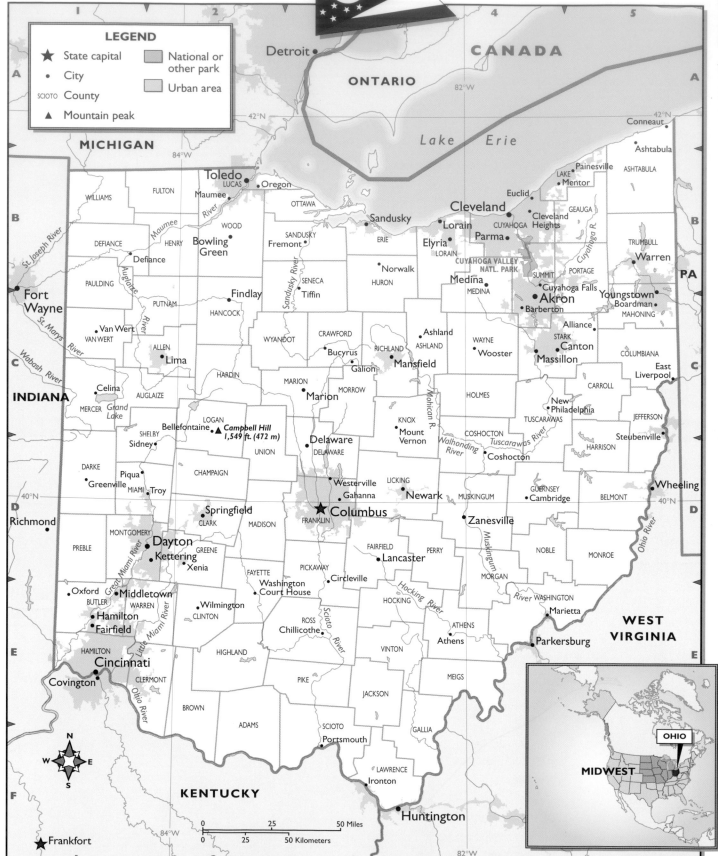

LEGEND
★ State capital
• City
SCIOTO County
▲ Mountain peak
National or other park
Urban area

MICHIGAN

CANADA

ONTARIO

84°W

82°W

42°N

Lake Erie

Detroit

Conneaut

Ashtabula

WILLIAMS

FULTON

LUCAS

Toledo

Oregon

Maumee

Maumee River

OTTAWA

WOOD

Bowling Green

SANDUSKY

Fremont

Sandusky

ERIE

Norwalk

HURON

Painesville

Mentor

LAKE

Euclid

Cleveland

Lorain

CUYAHOGA

Cleveland Heights

Parma

GEAUGA

Elyria

LORAIN

CUYAHOGA VALLEY NATL. PARK

Medina

MEDINA

SUMMIT

Akron

Barberton

Cuyahoga Falls

PORTAGE

TRUMBULL

Warren

Youngstown

Boardman

MAHONING

DEFIANCE

Defiance

HENRY

PAULDING

PUTNAM

HANCOCK

Findlay

SENECA

Tiffin

Sandusky River

WYANDOT

CRAWFORD

Bucyrus

RICHLAND

Ashland

ASHLAND

WAYNE

Wooster

HOLMES

Mansfield

Galion

STARK

Canton

Massillon

Alliance

COLUMBIANA

East Liverpool

CARROLL

ST. JOSEPH RIVER

Fort Wayne

Wabash River

St. Marys River

INDIANA

Van Wert

VAN WERT

ALLEN

Lima

HARDIN

Celina

MERCER

Grand Lake

AUGLAIZE

LOGAN

Bellefontaine

▲ Campbell Hill 1,549 ft. (472 m)

SHELBY

Sidney

UNION

CHAMPAIGN

MARION

Marion

MORROW

DELAWARE

Delaware

KNOX

Mount Vernon

Mohican R.

COSHOCTON

Coshocton

TUSCARAWAS

New Philadelphia

Tuscarawas River

HARRISON

JEFFERSON

Steubenville

Walhonding River

PA

DARKE

Greenville

Piqua

MIAMI

Troy

MONTGOMERY

Dayton

Kettering

Xenia

GREENE

Springfield

CLARK

MADISON

FAYETTE

Washington Court House

Westerville

Gahanna

FRANKLIN

Columbus

LICKING

Newark

MUSKINGUM

Zanesville

GUERNSEY

Cambridge

BELMONT

Wheeling

40°N

Richmond

PREBLE

Great Miami River

Oxford

BUTLER

Middletown

WARREN

Hamilton

Fairfield

Little Miami River

HAMILTON

Cincinnati

Covington

CLERMONT

Ohio River

Wilmington

CLINTON

HIGHLAND

ROSS

Chillicothe

Scioto River

PICKAWAY

Circleville

FAIRFIELD

Lancaster

PERRY

HOCKING

Hocking River

VINTON

NOBLE

MORGAN

Muskingum River

MONROE

WASHINGTON

Marietta

Parkersburg

WEST VIRGINIA

Ohio River

ATHENS

Athens

BROWN

ADAMS

PIKE

SCIOTO

Portsmouth

JACKSON

MEIGS

GALLIA

LAWRENCE

Ironton

KENTUCKY

Huntington

84°W

82°W

N
W E
S

0   25   50 Miles
0 25 50 Kilometers

OHIO

MIDWEST

The outline of Ohio comes close to being a square, although this square is missing its lower corners. The irregular southern boundary of the state is formed by the Ohio River as it twists and turns on its way to the Mississippi River. Most of the state's rivers flow south and do not enter Lake Erie. Ohio's many urban areas are one reason the state has the seventh-largest population. However, the very largest cities, historic centers of heavy industry, have actually had shrinking populations in the last 30 years. Despite its modest size, Ohio features geographic variety. The southeastern quarter of the state is hilly and wooded. The rest of the state, once covered by unbroken forest, is now primarily farmland producing a typical Midwestern mix of corn, soybeans, and livestock. Continuing to follow their traditional way of life, more Amish live in Ohio than any other state. Their communities are now popular tourist attractions.

Did You Know?

In 1967, Cleveland elected the first African-American mayor of a major U.S. city: Carl B. Stokes

Economy – Chief Products

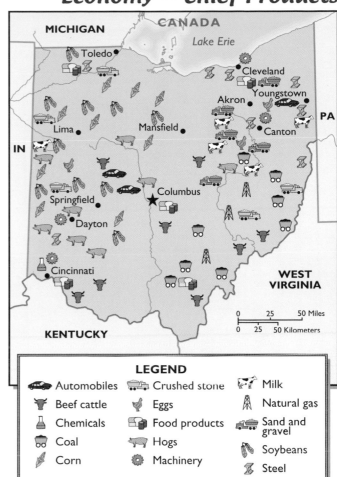

LEGEND

Automobiles	Crushed stone	Milk
Beef cattle	Eggs	Natural gas
Chemicals	Food products	Sand and gravel
Coal	Hogs	Soybeans
Corn	Machinery	Steel

Ohio Almanac

Nickname	Buckeye State
State capital	Columbus
Date of statehood	March 1, 1803; 17th state
State bird	Cardinal
State flower	Scarlet carnation
State tree	Buckeye
State motto	With God, All Things Are Possible
Total population & rank	11,373,541 (in 2001); 7th
Population density	278 per sq. mile (107 per sq. km)
Population distribution	77% urban, 23% rural
Largest cities	Columbus, Cleveland, Cincinnati, Toledo, Akron, Dayton
Highest elevation	Campbell Hill, 1,549 ft. (472 m)
Lowest elevation	Ohio River in Hamilton Co., 455 ft. (139 m)
Land area & rank	40,948 sq. miles (106,055 sq. km); 35th
Average January temperature	27°F (−3°C)
Average July temperature	73°F (23°C)
Average yearly precipitation	38 inches (97 cm)
Major industries	manufacturing, trade, services
Places to visit	Mound City Group (Chillicothe), Pro Football Hall of Fame (Canton), Rock and Roll Hall of Fame and Museum (Cleveland), Air Force Museum (Dayton)
Web site	www.state.oh.us

Physical

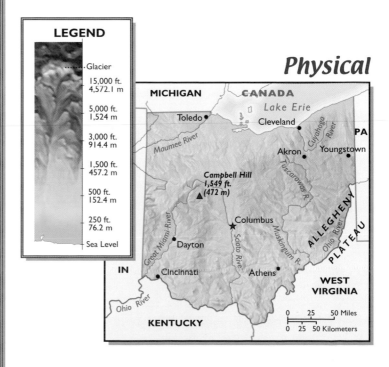

LEGEND

- Glacier
- 15,000 ft. / 4,572.1 m
- 5,000 ft. / 1,524 m
- 3,000 ft. / 914.4 m
- 1,500 ft. / 457.2 m
- 500 ft. / 152.4 m
- 250 ft. / 76.2 m
- Sea Level

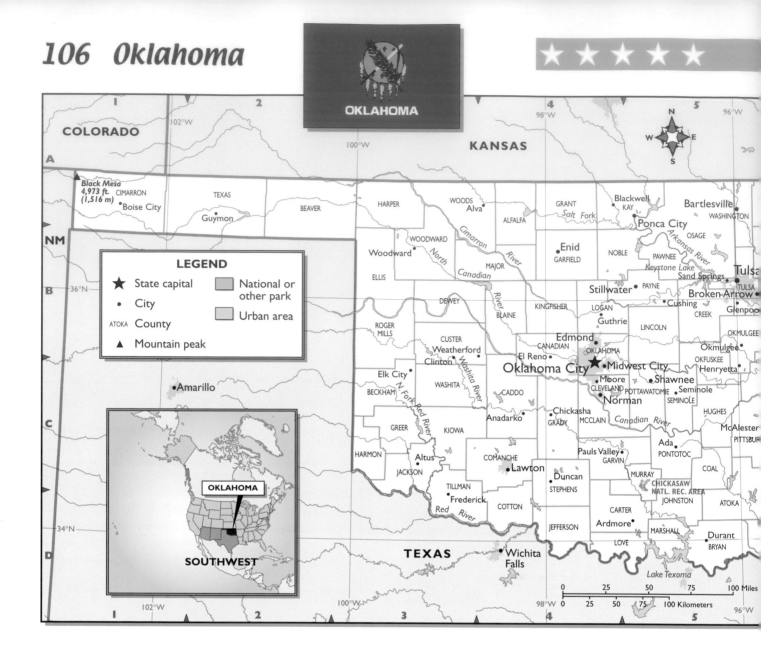

OKLAHOMA

LEGEND

★ State capital

• City

ATOKA County

▲ Mountain peak

National or other park

Urban area

Black Mesa
4,973 ft.
(1,516 m)

OKLAHOMA

SOUTHWEST

Oklahoma Almanac

Nickname	Sooner State	**Lowest elevation**	Little River in McCurtain Co., 289 ft. (88 m)
State capital	Oklahoma City		
Date of statehood	Nov. 16, 1907; 46th state	**Land area & rank**	68,667 sq. miles (177,848 sq. km); 19th
State bird	Scissor-tailed flycatcher		
State flower	Mistletoe	**Average January temperature**	37°F (3°C)
State tree	Redbud		
State motto	Labor Omnia Vincit (Labor Conquers All Things)	**Average July temperature**	82°F (28°C)
Total population & rank	3,460,097 (in 2001); 28th	**Average yearly precipitation**	34 inches (86 cm)
Population density	50 per sq. mile (19 per sq. km)	**Major industries**	manufacturing, mineral and energy exploration and production, agriculture, services
Population distribution	65% urban, 35% rural		
Largest cities	Oklahoma City, Tulsa, Norman, Lawton	**Places to visit**	Indian City U.S.A. (Anadarko), Cherokee Heritage Center (Tahlequah), National Cowboy Hall of Fame (Oklahoma City), Oklahoma City National Memorial
Highest elevation	Black Mesa, 4,973 ft. (1,516 m)		
		Web site	www.state.ok.us

Like an upside-down baseball cap, Oklahoma sits on the northern shoulder of Texas. The "bill" of the baseball cap is a narrow, western extension called the Panhandle. The Red River separates most of Texas and Oklahoma, but the Arkansas River is more important. Using it, ocean-going ships can reach port facilities near Tulsa. Many residents of Oklahoma are Native American. The percentage is nearly ten times the U.S. average. More than 60 tribal groups live in the state, but few of those lived there 200 years ago. Most were moved to Oklahoma by the U.S. government after 1830. Oklahoma grows wheat and raises cattle, and the eastern hills contain more forestland than states to its north, but Oklahoma's most valuable resources are oil and natural gas. There are even oil wells on the grounds of the state capitol. Many businesses are involved with oil and natural gas production. Tourists come to Oklahoma to visit museums and places associated with the Native American cultures and with its Old West heritage.

Physical

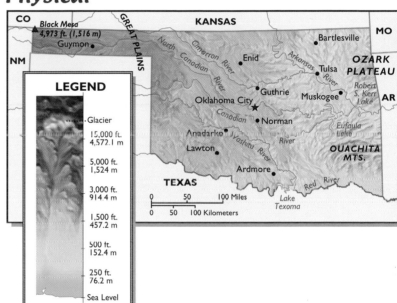

Did You Know?

In just one day, Oklahoma City grew from zero residents to more than 10,000 residents:

April 22, 1889

LEGEND

- Glacier
- 15,000 ft. / 4,572.1 m
- 5,000 ft. / 1,524 m
- 3,000 ft. / 914.4 m
- 1,500 ft. / 457.2 m
- 500 ft. / 152.4 m
- 250 ft. / 76.2 m
- Sea Level

Economy – Chief Products

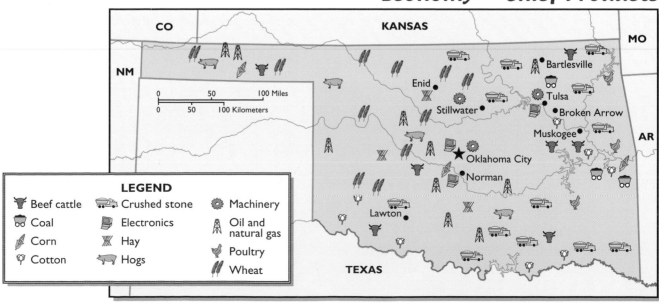

LEGEND

- Beef cattle
- Coal
- Corn
- Cotton
- Crushed stone
- Electronics
- Hay
- Hogs
- Machinery
- Oil and natural gas
- Poultry
- Wheat

STATE OF OREGON

1859

WASHINGTON

PACIFIC OCEAN

Cape Disappointment
FORT CLATSOP NATL. MEMORIAL
Seaside
Astoria
CLATSOP
Longview
COLUMBIA
St. Helens
WASHINGTON
Hillsboro
Tillamook
TILLAMOOK
Beaverton
Vancouver
Portland
Gresham
MULTNOMAH
Oregon City
CLACKAMAS
YAMHILL
McMinnville
Woodburn
Silverton
POLK
Dallas
Salem
Monmouth
Stayton
MARION
Newport
LINCOLN
Corvallis
Albany
LINN
Lebanon
BENTON
Sweet Home
Eugene
Springfield
LANE
Florence
OREGON DUNES NATL. REC. AREA
Reedsport
Umpqua River
North Bend
Coos Bay
COOS
Coquille
Sutherlin
North Umpqua River
Roseburg
DOUGLAS
South Umpqua River
CRATER LAKE NATL. PARK
Crater Lake
Rogue River
CURRY
Gold Beach
Grants Pass
JOSEPHINE
OREGON CAVES NATL. MON.
Mt. McLoughlin 9,495 ft. (2,894 m)
JACKSON
Medford
Ashland
CASCADE-SISKIYOU NATL. MON.
Brookings
Crescent City
Klamath River

Hood River
HOOD RIVER
The Dalles
Mt. Hood 11,239 ft. (3,426 m)
SHERMAN
WASCO
Madras
JEFFERSON
Mt. Jefferson 10,497 ft. (3,199 m)
Deschutes River
Prineville
Redmond
Crooked River
Bend
CROOK
DESCHUTES
Klamath Falls
Upper Klamath Lake
Sprague R.
KLAMATH
Lost River
Summer Lake
LAKE
Lake Abert
Goose Lake
Lakeview

Columbia River
Richland
Pasco
Kennewick
Lake Umatilla
Lake Wallula
Hermiston
Milton-Freewater
Umatilla River
Pendleton
UMATILLA
MORROW
Heppner
GILLIAM
John Day River
JOHN DAY FOSSIL BEDS NATL. MON.
WHEELER
GRANT
John Day
Silver Creek
Silvies River
Burns
Harney Lake
Malheur Lake
HARNEY

Lewiston
Grande Ronde River
WALLOWA
HELLS CANYON NATL. REC. AREA
Enterprise
La Grande
UNION
Sacajawea Pk. 9,839 ft. (2,999 m)
Powder River
Baker City
BAKER
Snake River
IDAHO
Weiser
Ontario
Vale
Malheur River
MALHEUR
Lake Owyhee
Boise
Nampa
Jordan Valley
Owyhee River

NEVADA
CALIFORNIA

0 25 50 75 100 Miles
0 25 50 75 100 Kilometers

N E S W

LEGEND

★ State capital

• City

YAMHILL County

▲ Mountain peak

National or other park

Urban area

OREGON

WEST

Oregon is a Pacific Coast state that treasures its 296-mile (476-km) coastline. All of the beaches are public property, and the unique sand dunes of the central coast are protected within a national scenic area. Although its population is only one-tenth that of its southern neighbor California, the state is well known for its residents' involvement in social causes. Sometimes this involves the way the government works, but often it involves environmental issues. Some people think Oregon is entirely made up of misty forests, rich and fertile farmland, and solitary, snow-capped volcanic peaks — like Mt. Hood — but this describes only the western third of the state. The rest of Oregon is a mix of mountains, hills, and plateaus where water is too valuable to waste, and the scattered communities depend on lumber, cattle, and sheep. The southeastern corner is a desert. Many people who live in Portland and the other cities along the banks of the Willamette River work in high-tech businesses.

Oregon Almanac

Nickname	Beaver State	**Land area & rank**	95,997 sq. miles (248,632 sq. km); 10th
State capital	Salem	**Average January temperature**	33°F (1°C)
Date of statehood	Feb. 14, 1859; 33rd state	**Average July temperature**	66°F (19°C)
State bird	Western meadowlark	**Average yearly precipitation**	27 inches (69 cm)
State flower	Oregon grape	**Major industries**	manufacturing, services, trade, finance, insurance, real estate, government, construction
State tree	Douglas fir		
State motto	She Flies with Her Own Wings		
Total population & rank	3,472,867 (in 2001); 27th		
Population density	36 per sq. mile (14 per sq. km)	**Places to visit**	Crater Lake National Park, Oregon Caves National Monument, Fort Clatsop National Memorial
Population distribution	79% urban, 21% rural		
Largest cities	Portland, Eugene, Salem		
Highest elevation	Mt. Hood, 11,239 ft. (3,426 m)		
Lowest elevation	sea level	**Web site**	www.oregon.gov

Physical

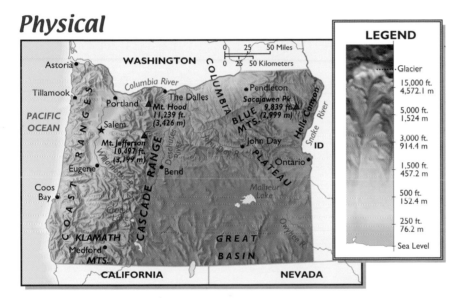

Did You Know?

The deepest lake in the United States is found in the bowl-shaped depression atop an extinct Oregon volcano: Crater Lake

Economy – Chief Products

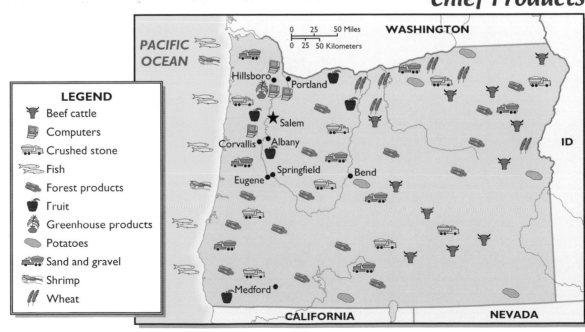

Lake Erie

Erie
ERIE

Edinboro
Corry
ALLEGHENY NATL. REC. AREA
Bradford
Warren
Allegheny Reservoir
WARREN
MCKEAN

NEW YORK
Elmira
Binghamton
Sayre
BRADFORD
SUSQUEHANNA

Pymatuning Res.
CRAWFORD
Meadville
Titusville
FOREST
Ridgway
ELK
St. Marys
CAMERON
POTTER
Wellsboro
TIOGA
Allegheny River

OHIO
Oil City
Franklin
VENANGO
CLARION
Clarion
Clarion River
JEFFERSON
DuBois
CLEARFIELD
Clearfield
West Branch Susquehanna River
CLINTON
Lock Haven
LYCOMING
Williamsport
SULLIVAN
WYOMING
LACKAWANNA
STEAMTOWN NATL. HISTORIC SITE
Scranton
Pittston
Nanticoke
LUZERNE
Wilkes Barre

Sharon
MERCER
Youngstown
New Castle
LAWRENCE
BUTLER
Butler
ARMSTRONG
Kittanning
INDIANA
Indiana
Punxsutawney
CENTRE
Bellefonte
State College
UNION
Lewisburg
MONTOUR
Sunbury
NORTHUMBERLAND
Shamokin
COLUMBIA
Bloomsburg
Berwick
Hazleton
CARBON
Tamaqua
LEHIGH

Beaver Falls
BEAVER
Aliquippa
Ohio River
Allegheny River
ALLEGHENY
Pittsburgh
Monroeville
MIFFLIN
Lewistown
JUNIATA
Juniata River
SNYDER
SCHUYLKILL
Pottsville
Weirton
Conemaugh R.
CAMBRIA
Altoona
BLAIR
Huntingdon
HUNTINGDON
Raystown Lake
PERRY
DAUPHIN
LEBANON
Lebanon
Hershey
BERKS
Reading

WESTMORELAND
Johnstown
Greensburg
WASHINGTON
Washington
Monessen
Youghiogheny R.
Connellsville
Somerset
SOMERSET
BEDFORD
FULTON
FRANKLIN
Chambersburg
ADAMS
Gettysburg
GETTYSBURG NATL. MILITARY PARK
Hanover
Harrisburg
Carlisle
CUMBERLAND
Middletown
LANCASTER
Lancaster
York
YORK
Ephrata
Pottstow
CHES
Susquehanna River

Monongahela River
Waynesburg
GREENE
FAYETTE
Uniontown
Mt. Davis 3,213 ft. (979 m)

WEST VIRGINIA
MARYLAND
Chesapeake Bay

Waynesboro

0   25   50 Miles
0   25   50 Kilometers

LEGEND

★ State capital
• City
CENTRE County
▲ Mountain peak

National or other park
Urban area

MIDATLANTIC

PENNSYLVANIA

Physical

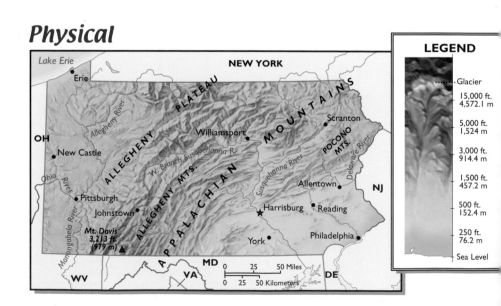

Lake Erie
Erie
NEW YORK
OH
New Castle
Ohio River
Allegheny River
ALLEGHENY PLATEAU
Williamsport
W. Br. Susquehanna R.
ALLEGHENY MTS.
APPALACHIAN MOUNTAINS
POCONO MTS.
Scranton
Delaware River
Pittsburgh
Johnstown
Mt. Davis 3,213 ft. (979 m)
Monongahela River
Allentown
Harrisburg
Reading
NJ
York
Philadelphia
WV
APPALACHIAN
VA
MD
DE

0   25   50 Miles
0   25   50 Kilometers

LEGEND

Glacier

15,000 ft. 4,572.1 m
5,000 ft. 1,524 m
3,000 ft. 914.4 m
1,500 ft. 457.2 m
500 ft. 152.4 m
250 ft. 76.2 m
Sea Level

Pennsylvania's nickname, the Keystone State, is appropriate for both its geographic location at the center of the original 13 colonies and its position as a key state in U.S. history. Both the Declaration of Independence and the U.S. Constitution were written, debated, and signed in Philadelphia. There are hundreds of museums and historic sites, including the Philadelphia Art Museum, Independence Hall, the Liberty Bell, Valley Forge, and Gettysburg. The state's abundant forests, lakes, rivers, and recreational parks are sandwiched between its two largest financial, business, and manufacturing centers: Philadelphia and Pittsburgh. Pennsylvania is also known for some of the richest farmland in the United States, and it has the largest rural population in the United States. Because Pennsylvania was founded in the Quaker tradition of tolerance and religious freedom, many plain sects such as the Mennonites and Amish settled in the state and continue to thrive here.

Pennsylvania Almanac

Nickname	Keystone State
State capital	Harrisburg
Date of statehood	Dec. 12, 1787; 2nd state
State bird	Ruffed grouse
State flower	Mountain laurel
State tree	Hemlock
State motto	Virtue, Liberty and Independence
Total population & rank	12,287,150 (in 2001); 6th
Population density	274 per sq. mile (106 per sq. km)
Population distribution	77% urban, 23% rural
Largest cities	Philadelphia, Pittsburgh, Allentown, Erie
Highest elevation	Mt. Davis, 3,213 ft. (979 m)
Lowest elevation	sea level
Land area & rank	44,817 sq. miles (116,076 sq. km); 32nd
Average January temperature	27°F (−3°C)
Average July temperature	71°F (22°C)
Average yearly precipitation	41 inches (104 cm)
Major industries	agribusiness, manufacturing, health care, tourism, biotechnology, printing and publishing, research and consulting
Places to visit	Gettysburg National Military Park, Independence Hall (Philadelphia), Pennsylvania Dutch country (Lancaster Co.), Steamtown National Historic Site, Hershey
Web site	www.pennsylvania.gov

Did You Know?

This bloody Civil War battle broke the strength of the Confederate army, which would no longer be able to mount an offensive against the North:

Gettysburg

Economy – Chief Products

LEGEND

- Beef cattle
- Chemicals
- Coal
- Corn
- Crushed stone
- Electronics
- Food products
- Milk
- Mushrooms
- Natural gas
- Poultry
- Textiles

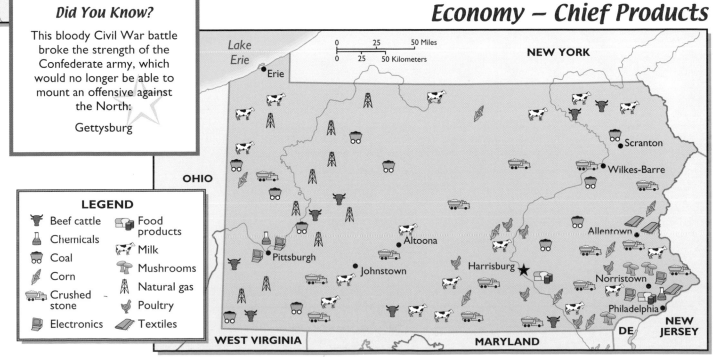

LEGEND
⭐ State capital
• City
KENT County
▲ Mountain peak
⬜ Urban area

MASSACHUSETTS

CONNECTICUT

Blackstone River

71°30'W

Woonsocket

Manville

Pawtucket Reservoir

Pascoag
Harrisville

Chepachet River

42°N

Greenville

North Providence

Central Falls

Pawtucket

Jerimoth Hill
812 ft.
(247 m)
▲

PROVIDENCE

Woonasquatucket R.

Providence ⭐

East Providence

Cranston

Ponaganset R.

Scituate Reservoir

Barrington

Warren

Taunton River

Flat River Res.
West Warwick

Pawtuxet River

Warwick

BRISTOL

Bristol

Mount Hope Bay

Fall River

KENT

East Greenwich

Greenwich Bay

Tiverton
Stafford Pond

Prudence Island

Narragansett Bay

Portsmouth

NEWPORT

Sakonnet River

Wood River

Queen River

Wickford

Rhode Island

Middletown

41°30'N

Hope Valley

Chipuxet R.

Jamestown

Newport

WASHINGTON

Kingston

Sakonnet Point

Wood River

Ashaway

Worden Pond

Wakefield

Narragansett Pier

River

Pawcatuck River

Bradford
Watchaug Pond

Charlestown

Westerly

Pawcatuck

Ninigret Pond

Point Judith

Rhode Island Sound

NEW YORK

Block Island Sound

ATLANTIC OCEAN

Block Island

0   5   10 Miles
0   5   10 Kilometers

71°30'W

71°W

NEW ENGLAND

RHODE ISLAND

Rhode Island is the smallest state in the United States, yet it is also one of the most densely populated. In 1776, it became the first colony to declare independence from Great Britain and has contributed significantly to the history of the United States ever since. Situated on the scenic Narragansett Bay, it attracts many tourists who delight in boating, fishing, and viewing the great beauty of the state's beaches and resort islands. Narragansett Bay is also home to Rhode Island's fishing industry. Rhode Island is famous for the immense Victorian mansions in the Newport area, such as Cornelius Vanderbilt's "Breakers." Newport is known as the "sailing capital of America" and is the historic site of the America's Cup yacht race. Providence, Rhode Island's capital and home to most of Rhode Island's residents, is also a center for the arts, jewelry trade, tourism, and service industries. Metal products and scientific instruments are manufactured in Rhode Island as well.

Economy – Chief Products

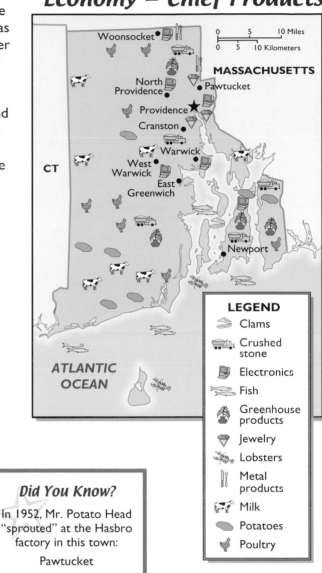

LEGEND

- 🦪 Clams
- 🚛 Crushed stone
- 💻 Electronics
- 🐟 Fish
- 🌱 Greenhouse products
- 💎 Jewelry
- 🦞 Lobsters
- 🍴 Metal products
- 🐄 Milk
- 🥔 Potatoes
- 🐓 Poultry

Physical

LEGEND

- .... Glacier
- 15,000 ft. / 4,572.1 m
- 5,000 ft. / 1,524 m
- 3,000 ft. / 914.4 m
- 1,500 ft. / 457.2 m
- 500 ft. / 152.4 m
- 250 ft. / 76.2 m
- Sea Level

Did You Know?

In 1952, Mr. Potato Head "sprouted" at the Hasbro factory in this town:

Pawtucket

Rhode Island Almanac

Nicknames	Little Rhody, Ocean State	**Lowest elevation**	sea level
State capital	Providence	**Land area & rank**	1,045 sq. miles (2,707 sq. km); 50th
Date of statehood	May 29, 1790; 13th state		
State bird	Rhode Island red	**Average January temperature**	29°F (–2°C)
State flower	Violet		
State tree	Red maple	**Average July temperature**	71°F (22°C)
State motto	Hope		
Total population & rank	1,058,920 (in 2001); 43rd	**Average yearly precipitation**	45 inches (114 cm)
Population density	1,013 per sq. mile (391 per sq. km)	**Major industries**	services, manufacturing
Population distribution	91% urban, 9% rural	**Places to visit**	Newport mansions and Cliff Walk, Block Island, Touro Synagogue (Newport)
Largest cities	Providence, Warwick, Cranston, Pawtucket		
Highest elevation	Jerimoth Hill, 812 ft. (247 m)	**Web site**	www.state.ri.us

114 South Carolina

NORTH CAROLINA

Asheville
Charlotte
Fayetteville

▲ Sassafras Mtn. 3,560 ft. (1,085 m)

Gaffney
CHEROKEE
York
YORK
Lake Wylie
Rock Hill
LANCASTER
Lancaster
Cheraw
CHESTERFIELD
Bennettsville
MARLBORO

Greer
Spartanburg
SPARTANBURG
PICKENS
GREENVILLE
Greenville

OCONEE
Easley
Clemson
Seneca
ANDERSON
Anderson
Laurens
LAURENS
Simpsonville
Union
UNION
Clinton
Chester
CHESTER

Catawba River
Broad River

Hartwell Lake

Russell Lake
ABBEVILLE
Abbeville
GREENWOOD
Greenwood
NEWBERRY
Newberry
FAIRFIELD
Winnsboro
Lake Wateree
KERSHAW
Camden
LEE
DARLINGTON
Hartsville
Darlington
Florence
FLORENCE
Dillon
DILLON
Mullins
Marion
MARION

Lake Greenwood
Lake Murray
Irmo
RICHLAND
Columbia
SUMTER
Sumter
Lake City
HORRY
Conway
Myrtle Beach
North Myrtle Beach

Athens
MCCORMICK
SALUDA
Lexington
LEXINGTON
Batesburg-Leesville
CONGAREE SWAMP NATL. MON.
Manning
CLARENDON
Kingstree
WILLIAMSBURG
Grand Strand
Long Bay

J. Strom Thurmond Lake
EDGEFIELD
AIKEN
Aiken
North Augusta
Congaree River
CALHOUN
Black R.
Santee River
GEORGETOWN
Georgetown

Augusta
GEORGIA
Orangeburg
ORANGEBURG
Lake Marion
BERKELEY
Lake Moultrie
Moncks Corner

Denmark
BARNWELL
Barnwell
Bamberg
BAMBERG
Edisto River
DORCHESTER
Summerville
Goose Creek
CHARLESTON
Bulls Bay

Savannah River
Allendale
ALLENDALE
Walterboro
COLLETON
North Charleston
Mount Pleasant

HAMPTON
Charleston
CHARLESTON
FORT SUMTER NATL. MONUMENT
Kiawah Island

JASPER
Edisto Island
St. Helena Sound

BEAUFORT
Beaufort
ATLANTIC OCEAN
Savannah
Port Royal Sound
Hilton Head Island
Hinesville

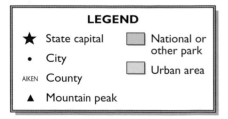

SOUTHEAST
SOUTH CAROLINA

0   25   50 Miles
0   25   50 Kilometers

LEGEND

★ State capital
• City
AIKEN County
▲ Mountain peak

National or other park
Urban area

Did You Know?

In the Revolutionary War, two battles in South Carolina helped to turn the tide of war in the south:

Kings Mountain and Cowpens

It's easy to pick out the triangular shape of South Carolina with its nearly straight Atlantic Ocean edge. Look more closely to see that the coastline is actually pierced with bays and dotted with islands. With its population almost equally divided between urban and rural residents and with many small towns, South Carolina has been able to preserve a way of life that is disappearing in other southern states. A fascinating community of African Americans is the Gullah, descendants of slaves who lived in isolation for many years on the coastal islands. Mountains are limited to the northwestern corner, and a large part of the state is good for farming. A wide variety of crops are grown. The manufacture of fabrics and clothing remains an important industry, but tourism has become even more valuable. Many visitors vacation at the sandy beaches of the northern coast or at the coastal islands devoted to golf and tennis. Others come to Charleston to enjoy its gardens, architecture, and culture.

Economy – Chief Products

LEGEND

Automobiles		Greenhouse products	
Beef cattle		Poultry	
Cement		Shellfish	
Chemicals		Soybeans	
Cotton		Clothing and textiles	
Crushed stone		Tobacco	
Forest products			

Physical

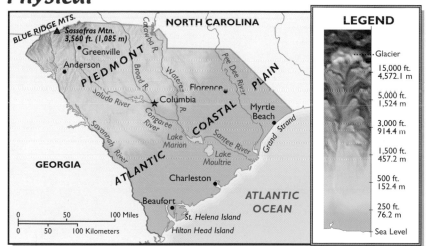

LEGEND

Glacier
15,000 ft. 4,572.1 m
5,000 ft. 1,524 m
3,000 ft. 914.4 m
1,500 ft. 457.2 m
500 ft. 152.4 m
250 ft. 76.2 m
Sea Level

South Carolina Almanac

Nickname	Palmetto State	**Lowest elevation**	sea level
State capital	Columbia	**Land area & rank**	30,109 sq. miles (77,982 sq. km); 40th
Date of statehood	May 23, 1788; 8th state		
State bird	Carolina wren	**Average January temperature**	44°F (7°C)
State flower	Yellow jessamine		
State tree	Palmetto	**Average July temperature**	79°F (26°C)
State motto	Dum Spiro Spero (While I Breathe, I Hope)	**Average yearly precipitation**	48 inches (122 cm)
Total population & rank	4,063,011 (in 2001); 26th	**Major industries**	tourism, agriculture, manufacturing
Population density	135 per sq. mile (52 per sq. km)	**Places to visit**	Fort Sumter National Monument, Charleston Museum, Historic Charleston, Grand Strand and Hilton Head beaches
Population distribution	60% urban, 40% rural		
Largest cities	Columbia, Charleston, North Charleston, Greenville		
Highest elevation	Sassafras Mountain, 3,560 ft. (1,085 m)	**Web site**	www.myscgov.com

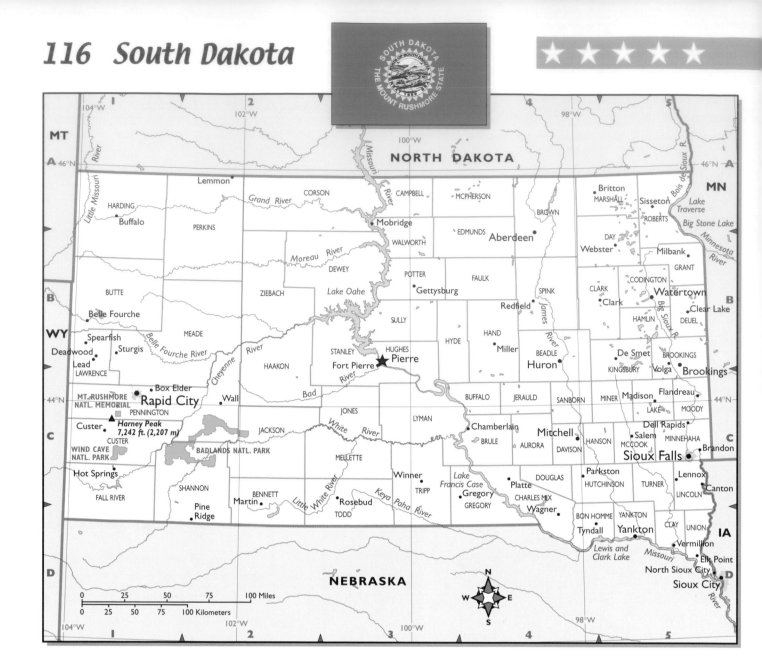

NORTH DAKOTA

MT

MN

WY

WYOMING

NEBRASKA

IA

Lemmon
HARDING
Buffalo
PERKINS
Belle Fourche
BUTTE
Spearfish
Deadwood
Lead
Sturgis
LAWRENCE
MEADE
Box Elder
MT. RUSHMORE NATL. MEMORIAL
Rapid City
Wall
PENNINGTON
Custer
Harney Peak 7,242 ft. (2,207 m)
CUSTER
WIND CAVE NATL. PARK
Hot Springs
FALL RIVER
SHANNON
Pine Ridge
TODD
BENNETT
Martin
JACKSON
BADLANDS NATL. PARK
MELLETTE
JONES
LYMAN
Winner
TRIPP
Rosebud
CORSON
Grand River
Moreau River
DEWEY
ZIEBACH
HAAKON
STANLEY
Fort Pierre
Bad River
White River
Little White River
Keya Paha River
CAMPBELL
Mobridge
WALWORTH
Lake Oahe
POTTER
Gettysburg
SULLY
HUGHES
Pierre
HYDE
BUFFALO
BRULE
Chamberlain
Lake Francis Case
Platte
Gregory
CHARLES MIX
GREGORY
Wagner
BON HOMME
Tyndall
MCPHERSON
EDMUNDS
Aberdeen
FAULK
SPINK
Redfield
HAND
Miller
HYDE
BEADLE
Huron
JERAULD
SANBORN
AURORA
DAVISON
Mitchell
DOUGLAS
HUTCHINSON
TURNER
YANKTON
Yankton
CLAY
Lewis and Clark Lake
BROWN
Britton
MARSHALL
Sisseton
ROBERTS
Lake Traverse
Big Stone Lake
DAY
Webster
Milbank
GRANT
CODINGTON
CLARK
Clark
Watertown
HAMLIN
DEUEL
Clear Lake
KINGSBURY
De Smet
BROOKINGS
Volga
Brookings
LAKE
Madison
MINER
Flandreau
MOODY
Dell Rapids
MCCOOK
Salem
MINNEHAHA
Sioux Falls
Brandon
Parkston
LINCOLN
Lennox
Canton
UNION
Vermillion
Elk Point
North Sioux City
Sioux City
James River
Big Sioux R.
Bois de Sioux R.
Minnesota River
Cheyenne River
Belle Fourche River
Little Missouri River
Missouri River

104°W 102°W 100°W 98°W
46°N 44°N

0 25 50 75 100 Miles
0 25 50 75 100 Kilometers

N W E S

LEGEND

★ State capital
• City
BRULE County
▲ Mountain peak
█ National or other park
░ Urban area

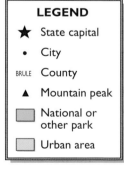

SOUTH DAKOTA

MIDWEST

South Dakota is second from the top in the column of nearly rectangular states that rises above Texas like a stack of Legos. The Missouri River wiggles up through the center of South Dakota, creating a distinct eastern half and western half. Most of the residents live in the eastern half, but many Native Americans live on reservations in the western half. The southwestern corner contains the most obvious geographical feature of the entire state, the Black Hills. Native Americans consider the Black Hills to be sacred land, and an immense sculpture of the Sioux warrior Crazy Horse is slowly being carved in the rock. Another famous mountain sculpture is nearby—the faces of four U.S. presidents carved in Mount Rushmore. Rich soils in the eastern half of the state support agriculture, but more people work in manufacturing and services. Businesses related to banking and insurance are the most important.

South Dakota Almanac

Nicknames	Mount Rushmore State, Coyote State	**Land area & rank**	75,885 sq. miles (196,542 sq. km); 16th
State capital	Pierre	**Average January temperature**	16°F (–9°C)
Date of statehood	Nov. 2, 1889; 40th state		
State bird	Chinese ring-necked pheasant	**Average July temperature**	73°F (23°C)
State flower	Pasqueflower		
State tree	Black Hills spruce	**Average yearly precipitation**	19 inches (48 cm)
State motto	Under God the People Rule		
Total population & rank	756,600 (in 2001); 46th	**Major industries**	agriculture, services, manufacturing
Population density	10 per sq. mile (3.9 per sq. km)	**Places to visit**	Mount Rushmore National Memorial, Badlands National Park, Wind Cave National Park, Deadwood
Population distribution	52% urban, 48% rural		
Largest cities	Sioux Falls, Rapid City		
Highest elevation	Harney Peak, 7,242 ft. (2,207 m)	**Web site**	www.state.sd.us
Lowest elevation	Big Stone Lake in Roberts Co., 966 ft. (294 m)		

Physical

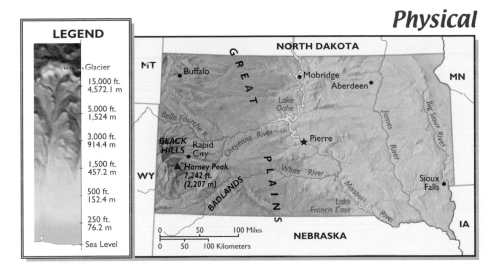

Did You Know?

The outside of an exhibition building in Mitchell is decorated every year with murals made of multicolored corn, barley, and other grains:

The Corn Palace

Economy – Chief Products

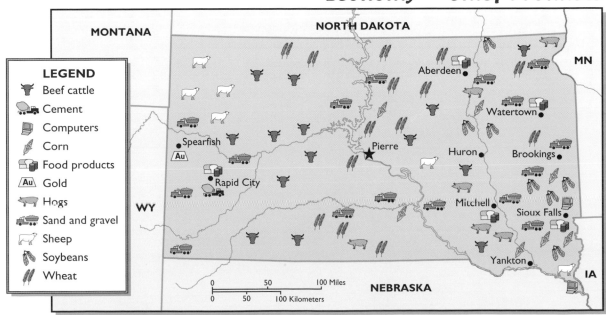

LEGEND

- Beef cattle
- Cement
- Computers
- Corn
- Food products
- Au Gold
- Hogs
- Sand and gravel
- Sheep
- Soybeans
- Wheat

Looking a bit like a sharpened pencil lying on its side, Tennessee has the flattest shape of all the states. Spanning hundreds of miles from the crest of the Appalachian Mountains to the Mississippi River, Tennessee boasts three distinct geographical regions. The Tennessee River generally forms their boundaries as it flows south from the mountains, makes a detour through Alabama, and turns north to cross the western part of the state. Tennessee was one of the first areas across the Appalachians to be settled, and it is one of the oldest non-colonial states. The first settlements were made in the mountains, and examples of traditional ways of life have been preserved in Great Smoky Mountains National Park. Western Tennessee, flat and fertile, is the most important farming area. Many tourists visit Memphis and Nashville to appreciate music. Memphis is famous for the blues, while Nashville is the capital of country and western.

Nickname	Volunteer State
State capital	Nashville
Date of statehood	June 1, 1796; 16th state
State bird	Mockingbird
State flower	Iris
State tree	Tulip poplar
State motto	Agriculture and Commerce
Total population & rank	5,740,021 (in 2001); 16th

Physical

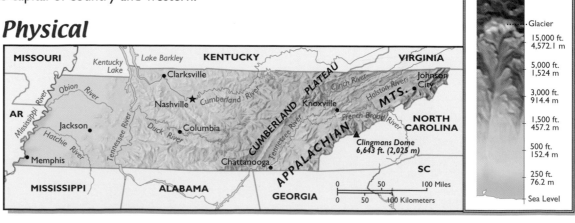

LEGEND

Glacier

15,000 ft.
4,572.1 m

5,000 ft.
1,524 m

3,000 ft.
914.4 m

1,500 ft.
457.2 m

500 ft.
152.4 m

250 ft.
76.2 m

Sea Level

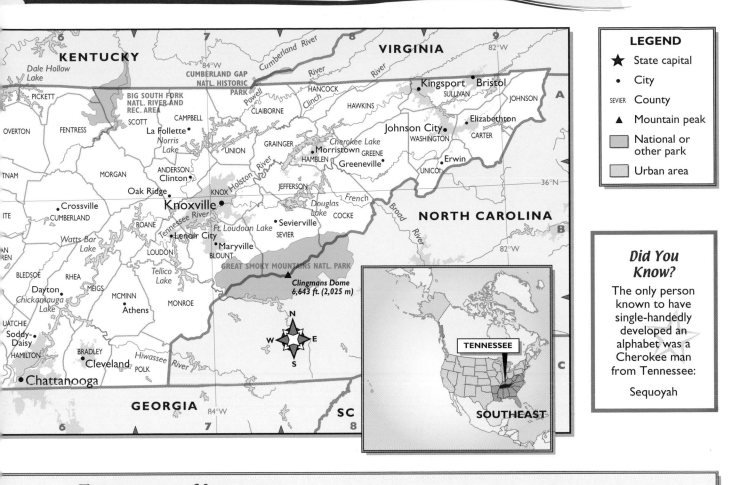

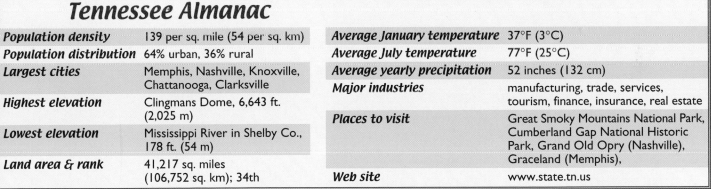

LEGEND

★ State capital
• City
SEVIER County
▲ Mountain peak
National or other park
Urban area

Clingmans Dome 6,643 ft. (2,025 m)

TENNESSEE

SOUTHEAST

Did You Know?

The only person known to have single-handedly developed an alphabet was a Cherokee man from Tennessee:

Sequoyah

Tennessee Almanac

Population density	139 per sq. mile (54 per sq. km)	**Average January temperature**	37°F (3°C)
Population distribution	64% urban, 36% rural	**Average July temperature**	77°F (25°C)
Largest cities	Memphis, Nashville, Knoxville, Chattanooga, Clarksville	**Average yearly precipitation**	52 inches (132 cm)
		Major industries	manufacturing, trade, services, tourism, finance, insurance, real estate
Highest elevation	Clingmans Dome, 6,643 ft. (2,025 m)	**Places to visit**	Great Smoky Mountains National Park, Cumberland Gap National Historic Park, Grand Old Opry (Nashville), Graceland (Memphis),
Lowest elevation	Mississippi River in Shelby Co., 178 ft. (54 m)		
Land area & rank	41,217 sq. miles (106,752 sq. km); 34th	**Web site**	www.state.tn.us

LEGEND

🚗 Automobiles
🐂 Beef cattle
🧪 Chemicals
⛏ Coal
❀ Cotton
🚚 Crushed stone
🐄 Milk
🐔 Poultry
🌿 Soybeans
🌱 Tobacco
Zn Zinc

Economy – Chief Products

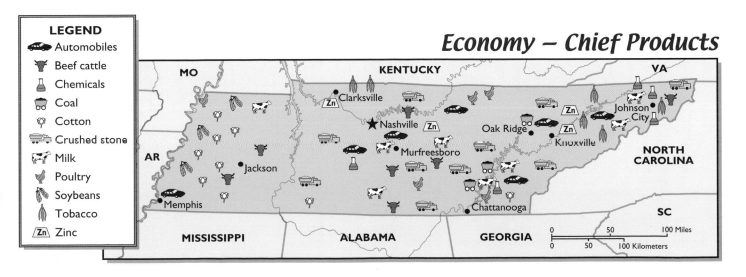

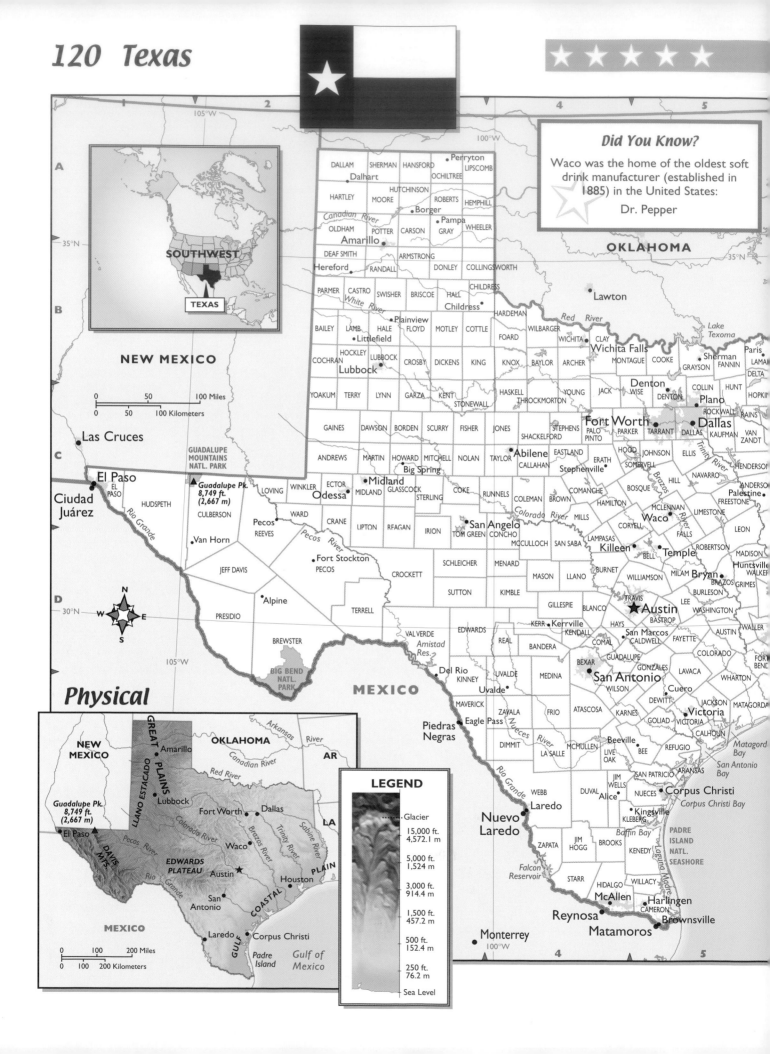

Did You Know?

Waco was the home of the oldest soft drink manufacturer (established in 1885) in the United States: Dr. Pepper

SOUTHWEST

TEXAS

NEW MEXICO

OKLAHOMA

0   50   100 Miles
0   50   100 Kilometers

Las Cruces

El Paso
EL PASO

Ciudad Juárez

GUADALUPE MOUNTAINS NATL. PARK

▲ Guadalupe Pk. 8,749 ft. (2,667 m)

DALLAM   SHERMAN   HANSFORD   OCHILTREE   LIPSCOMB
Dalhart
HARTLEY   MOORE   HUTCHINSON   ROBERTS   HEMPHILL
Borger
OLDHAM   POTTER   CARSON   GRAY   WHEELER
Amarillo   Pampa
DEAF SMITH   ARMSTRONG
Hereford   RANDALL   DONLEY   COLLINGSWORTH
PARMER   CASTRO   SWISHER   BRISCOE   HALL   CHILDRESS
Childress
White River   HARDEMAN
BAILEY   LAMB   HALE   FLOYD   MOTLEY   COTTLE   FOARD   WILBARGER
Plainview   Littlefield
COCHRAN   HOCKLEY   LUBBOCK   CROSBY   DICKENS   KING   KNOX   BAYLOR   ARCHER
Lubbock
YOAKUM   TERRY   LYNN   GARZA   KENT   STONEWALL   HASKELL   THROCKMORTON   YOUNG   JACK
GAINES   DAWSON   BORDEN   SCURRY   FISHER   JONES   SHACKELFORD   STEPHENS
ANDREWS   MARTIN   HOWARD   MITCHELL   NOLAN   TAYLOR   CALLAHAN   EASTLAND
Big Spring   Abilene
Midland
LOVING   WINKLER   ECTOR   MIDLAND   GLASSCOCK   STERLING   COKE   RUNNELS   COLEMAN   BROWN
Odessa
CULBERSON   Pecos   WARD   CRANE   UPTON   RFAGAN   IRION   TOM GREEN   CONCHO   McCULLOCH   SAN SABA
REEVES   San Angelo
Van Horn   Pecos River
JEFF DAVIS   Fort Stockton   PECOS   SCHLEICHER   MENARD   MASON   LLANO
CROCKETT
Alpine   SUTTON   KIMBLE
PRESIDIO   TERRELL   EDWARDS
BREWSTER   VAL VERDE   REAL   BANDERA
Amistad Res.   KERR   KENDALL
BIG BEND NATL. PARK   Del Rio   KINNEY   UVALDE   MEDINA   BEXAR
MEXICO   Uvalde   San Antonio
MAVERICK   ZAVALA   FRIO   ATASCOSA   WILSON
Piedras Negras   Eagle Pass   Nueces River   KARNES
DIMMIT   LA SALLE   McMULLEN   LIVE OAK   BEE
Rio Grande   WEBB   DUVAL   JIM WELLS
Nuevo Laredo   Laredo   Alice   NUECES
ZAPATA   JIM HOGG   BROOKS   KLEBERG
Falcon Reservoir   STARR   HIDALGO   WILLACY   KENEDY
Monterrey   McAllen   Harlingen   CAMERON
Reynosa   Matamoros   Brownsville

OKLAHOMA
Lawton
Red River   Lake Texoma
Wichita Falls   Paris
WICHITA   CLAY   MONTAGUE   COOKE   GRAYSON   FANNIN   LAMAR   DELTA
Denton   Sherman   HOPKIN
WISE   DENTON   COLLIN   HUNT
Plano   ROCKWALL   RAINS
Fort Worth   Dallas
PALO PINTO   PARKER   TARRANT   DALLAS   KAUFMAN   VAN ZANDT
HOOD   JOHNSON   ELLIS   HENDERSON
ERATH   SOMERVELL   HILL   NAVARRO
Stephenville   Trinity River   ANDERSON
COMANCHE   HAMILTON   BOSQUE   McLENNAN   LIMESTONE   FREESTONE
Brazos River   Waco   Palestine
CORYELL   FALLS   LEON
LAMPASAS   BELL   ROBERTSON   MADISON
Killeen   Temple   MILAM   Bryan   Huntsville
BURNET   WILLIAMSON   BRAZOS   GRIMES   WALKER
TRAVIS   LEE   BURLESON
BLANCO   ★ Austin   WASHINGTON
HAYS   BASTROP   AUSTIN   WALLER
Kerrville   San Marcos   CALDWELL   FAYETTE
COMAL   COLORADO   FORT BEND
GUADALUPE   GONZALES   LAVACA   WHARTON
DEWITT   Cuero   JACKSON   MATAGORDA
Victoria   VICTORIA
GOLIAD   CALHOUN   Matagord Bay
REFUGIO   San Antonio Bay
Beeville   SAN PATRICIO   ARANSAS
Corpus Christi
Corpus Christi Bay
Kingsville   PADRE ISLAND NATL. SEASHORE
Baffin Bay   Laguna Madre

Physical

NEW MEXICO   OKLAHOMA   Arkansas River   AR
GREAT PLAINS   Amarillo   Red River   Canadian River
LLANO ESTACADO   Lubbock
Guadalupe Pk. 8,749 ft. (2,667 m)
El Paso   Fort Worth   Dallas   LA
Colorado River   Brazos River   Trinity River   Sabine River
DAVIS MTS.   Pecos River   Waco   COASTAL PLAIN
EDWARDS PLATEAU   Austin   Houston
Rio   San Antonio
MEXICO   Laredo   GULF   Corpus Christi
Padre Island   Gulf of Mexico

0   100   200 Miles
0   100   200 Kilometers

LEGEND

.... Glacier
15,000 ft. 4,572.1 m
5,000 ft. 1,524 m
3,000 ft. 914.4 m
1,500 ft. 457.2 m
500 ft. 152.4 m
250 ft. 76.2 m
Sea Level

Just like the biggest and strongest cheerleader holding up his partners in formation, Texas, at the bottom center of the United States, looks like it is supporting a stack of states upon its arms and shoulders. In many ways, Texas is a state that is big. Its borders enclose a tremendous geographical variety, from the damp and thick forests of the east across the mixed prairies and woodlands of the midlands to the dry and barren mesas of the west. Texas is the second most populated state, and its people are as varied as its landscape. Texas claims more than half of the entire U.S. border with Mexico, a border formed by the curving Rio Grande, and Mexican immigration has influenced the food, music, and language of Texas. The state is famous for its struggle for independence from Mexico, for cities that have grown rapidly in the last 25 years, and for a 100-year-old oil and natural gas industry. Sometimes forgotten is the contribution of agriculture. Texas is a leading producer of cattle and cotton, as well as fruits and vegetables.

Economy – Chief Products

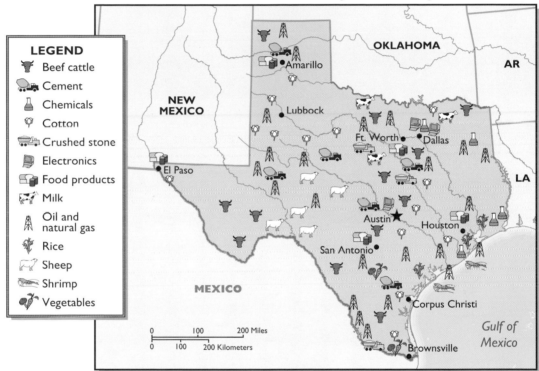

LEGEND
- Beef cattle
- Cement
- Chemicals
- Cotton
- Crushed stone
- Electronics
- Food products
- Milk
- Oil and natural gas
- Rice
- Sheep
- Shrimp
- Vegetables

Texas Almanac

Nickname	Lone Star State	Lowest elevation	sea level
State capital	Austin	Land area & rank	261,797 sq. miles (678,054 sq. km); 2nd
Date of statehood	Dec. 29, 1845; 28th state	Average January temperature	48°F (9°C)
State bird	Mockingbird		
State flower	Bluebonnet	Average July temperature	83°F (28°C)
State tree	Pecan		
State motto	Friendship	Average yearly precipitation	28 inches (71 cm)
Total population & rank	21,325,018 (in 2001); 2nd		
Population density	81 per sq. mile (31 per sq. km)	Major industries	manufacturing, trade, oil and gas extraction, services
Population distribution	82% urban, 18% rural		
Largest cities	Houston, Dallas, San Antonio, Austin, El Paso, Fort Worth	Places to visit	The Alamo (San Antonio), Big Bend National Park, Guadalupe Mountains National Park, Lyndon B. Johnson Space Center (Houston), Padre Island National Seashore
Highest elevation	Guadalupe Peak, 8,749 ft. (2,667 m)	Web site	www.state.tx.us

1896

IDAHO

WYOMING

LEGEND

★ State capital
• City
JUAB County
▲ Mountain peak
National or other park
Urban area

WEST

UTAH

Smithfield
Logan
Tremonton
CACHE
RICH
Bear Lake
BOX ELDER
Brigham City
WEBER
Great Salt Lake
Roy
Ogden
MORGAN
Layton
DAVIS
Farmington
Antelope I.
Bountiful
Weber River
SUMMIT
FLAMING GORGE NATL. REC. AREA
Green River
DAGGETT
Salt Lake City
Jordan R.
SALT LAKE
Park City
Wendover
West Valley City
Sandy
Tooele
TOOELE
Heber City
WASATCH
Lehi
Orem
Utah Lake
Provo
Spanish Fork
Payson
UTAH
Kings Pk. 13,528 ft. (4,123 m)
DINOSAUR NATL. MON.
Yampa River
Vernal
DUCHESNE
Roosevelt
Duchesne River
Strawberry River
UINTAH
White River
40°N
COLORADO

NV

Ibapah Pk. 12,087 ft. (3,684 m)
JUAB
Nephi
Helper
CARBON
Price
Green River
Sevier River
SANPETE
Ephraim
Manti
Price River
MILLARD
Delta
Sevier Lake (dry lake)
Castle Dale
San Rafael River
Green River
EMERY
GRAND
Colorado River
River
Grand Junction
Fillmore
Salina
SEVIER
Beaver River
Richfield
Muddy Creek
CANYONLANDS NATL. PARK (HORSESHOE CANYON UNIT)
ARCHES NATL. PARK
Moab
Delano Pk. 12,169 ft. (3,709 m)
Milford
Loa
Fremont R.
Dirty Devil River
WAYNE
CAPITOL REEF NATL. PARK
Mt. Peale 12,721 ft. (3,877 m)
CANYONLANDS NATL. PARK
BEAVER
Beaver
PIUTE
38°N
Mt. Pennell 11,371 ft. (3,466 m)
GARFIELD
Monticello
IRON
Parowan
Panguitch
Sevier River
Escalante
SAN JUAN
Cedar City
CEDAR BREAKS NATL. MON.
BRYCE CANYON NATL. PARK
Escalante River
Colorado River
GLEN CANYON NATL. REC. AREA
NATURAL BRIDGES NATL. MON.
Blanding
Enterprise
GRAND STAIRCASE-ESCALANTE NATL. MON.
WASHINGTON
ZION NATL. PARK
Paria River
KANE
San Juan River
Bluff
St. George
Virgin River
Washington
Kanab
Lake Powell
Page
ARIZONA
NM

Dolores River

N
W E
S

0 25 50 75 100 Miles
0 25 50 75 100 Kilometers

114°W 112°W 110°W

42°N 40°N 38°N

Utah burst onto the international scene during the 2002 Winter Olympics, when visitors from around the world saw a Utah that was both natural and sophisticated. High, snow-capped mountains lend a magnificent backdrop to the towns and cities. In the more arid southern half of the state, mountains give way to a rugged landscape full of awe-inspiring national parks like Zion and Arches, broken by the long, meandering man-made Lake Powell. The Great Salt Lake is the largest saltwater lake in the Western Hemisphere. The Mormons settled the Utah territory in 1847, and the state remains heavily influenced by their beliefs. World War I and World War II saw a large influx of outsiders as the wartime economy boomed, resulting in a more diverse mix of people. The economy now relies strongly on the services industry, joined by tourism, mining, and ranching. The state boasts that its powder snow is the best on earth, and many skiers visit the mountain resorts to test that statement personally.

Economy – Chief Products

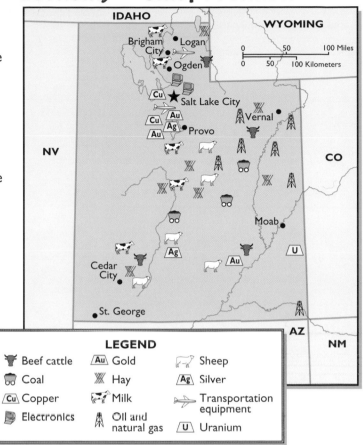

LEGEND

🐂 Beef cattle	Au Gold	🐑 Sheep	
Coal	Hay	Ag Silver	
Cu Copper	Milk	✈ Transportation equipment	
Electronics	Oil and natural gas	U Uranium	

Utah Almanac

Nickname	Beehive State
State capital	Salt Lake City
Date of statehood	Jan. 4, 1896; 45th state
State bird	Seagull
State flower	Sego lily
State tree	Blue spruce
State motto	Industry
Total population & rank	2,269,789 (in 2001); 34th
Population density	28 per sq. mile (11 per sq. km)
Population distribution	88% urban, 12% rural
Largest cities	Salt Lake City, West Valley City, Provo
Highest elevation	Kings Peak, 13,528 ft. (4,123 m)
Lowest elevation	Beaver Dam Wash, 2,000 ft. (610 m)
Land area & rank	82,144 sq. miles (212,753 sq. km); 12th
Average January temperature	26°F (−3°C)
Average July temperature	73°F (23°C)
Average yearly precipitation	12 inches (30 cm)
Major industries	services, trade, manufacturing, government, transportation, utilities
Places to visit	Bryce Canyon National Park, Zion National Park, Arches National Park, Great Salt Lake, Temple Square (Salt Lake City)
Web site	www.utah.gov

Did You Know?

Salt Lake City has the highest per captita consumption, and it's the official state snack food: Jell-O™

Physical

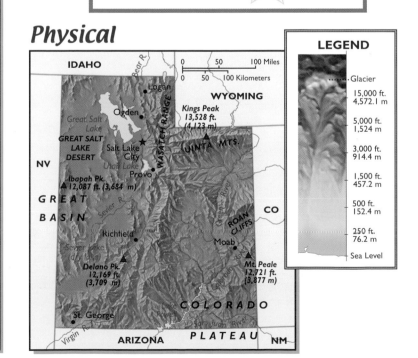

LEGEND

Glacier
15,000 ft. 4,572.1 m
5,000 ft. 1,524 m
3,000 ft. 914.4 m
1,500 ft. 457.2 m
500 ft. 152.4 m
250 ft. 76.2 m
Sea Level

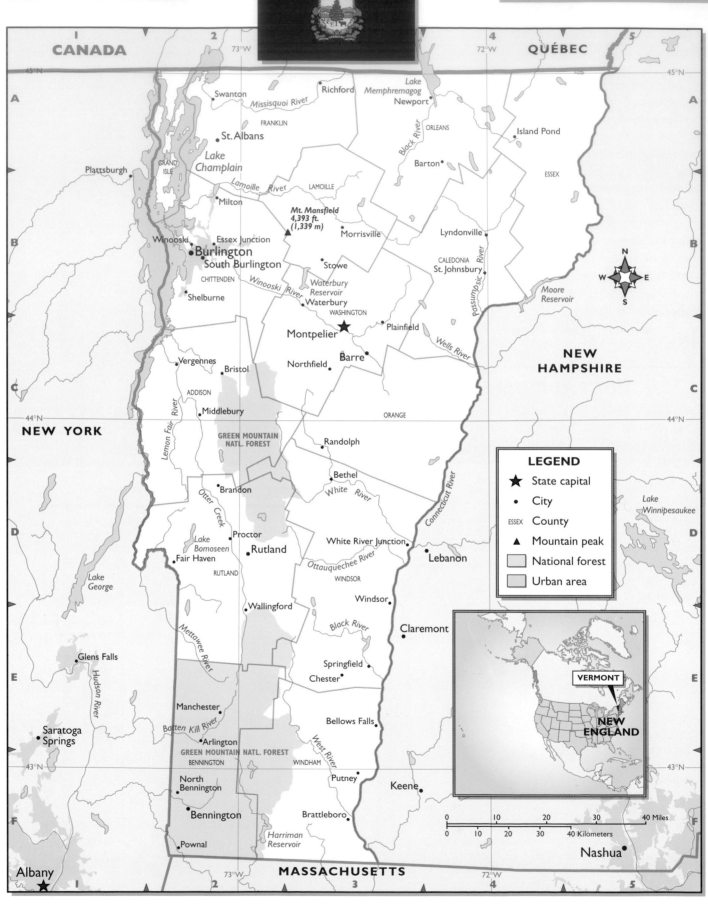

CANADA

QUÉBEC

73°W

72°W

45°N

45°N

Swanton

Richford

Lake Memphremagog

Newport

Missisquoi River

FRANKLIN

ORLEANS

Island Pond

St. Albans

Barton

ESSEX

GRAND ISLE

Lake Champlain

Plattsburgh

Lamoille River

LAMOILLE

Black River

Milton

Mt. Mansfield 4,393 ft. (1,339 m)

Morrisville

Lyndonville

Stowe

CALEDONIA

St. Johnsbury

Winooski

Essex Junction

Burlington

South Burlington

Passumpsic River

Moore Reservoir

CHITTENDEN

Winooski River

Waterbury Reservoir

Waterbury

Shelburne

WASHINGTON

NEW HAMPSHIRE

Montpelier

Plainfield

N

W   E

S

Vergennes

Barre

Wells River

Northfield

Bristol

ADDISON

Middlebury

44°N

44°N

ORANGE

Lemon Fair River

GREEN MOUNTAIN NATL. FOREST

Randolph

NEW YORK

LEGEND

★ State capital

Bethel

• City

Brandon

White River

ESSEX County

Otter Creek

Lake Bomoseen

Proctor

Rutland

▲ Mountain peak

National forest

Fair Haven

RUTLAND

White River Junction

Urban area

Ottauquechee River

Lake Winnipesaukee

WINDSOR

Lebanon

Wallingford

Lake George

Windsor

Black River

Claremont

Glens Falls

Springfield

Mettawee River

Chester

Hudson River

Manchester

Bellows Falls

Batten Kill River

Saratoga Springs

West River

Arlington

GREEN MOUNTAIN NATL. FOREST

BENNINGTON

WINDHAM

43°N

43°N

North Bennington

Putney

Keene

Bennington

Brattleboro

Harriman Reservoir

Pownal

0   10   20   30   40 Miles

Albany

0   10   20   30   40 Kilometers

Nashua

MASSACHUSETTS

73°W

72°W

VERMONT

NEW ENGLAND

Vermont's most spectacular geographic feature is the Green Mountains area that runs like a spine down the center of the state. Forests cover much of the state. While Vermont is the only New England state without an Atlantic coastline, it is bounded by water on two sides. On the east is the Connecticut River, and on the west is Lake Champlain. Vermont has a small population, the smallest east of the Mississippi River, and the lowest percentage of urban residents in the United States. Most of the people live in picturesque New England towns that become ski resorts during Vermont's long, snowy winters. This happy coexistence of mountains, trees, lakes, rivers, wilderness trails, and charming small towns makes Vermont an exceptionally scenic state and one of the most popular tourist destinations in the nation. Vermont's delicious maple syrup is famous. The lumber industry and paper products, along with marble and granite, are also important in Vermont's economy.

Economy – Chief Products

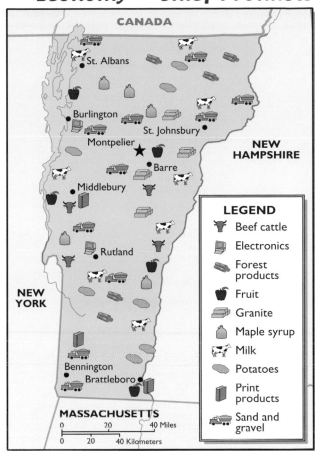

Physical

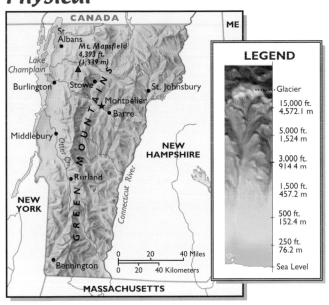

Did You Know?

In 1978, Ben and Jerry started making ice cream in a renovated garage in this northern town:

Burlington

Vermont Almanac

Nickname	Green Mountain State	**Land area & rank**	9,250 sq. miles (23,958 sq. km); 43rd
State capital	Montpelier	**Average January temperature**	17°F (–8°C)
Date of statehood	March 4, 1791; 14th state		
State bird	Hermit thrush	**Average July temperature**	68°F (20°C)
State flower	Red clover		
State tree	Sugar maple	**Average yearly precipitation**	40 inches (102 cm)
State motto	Freedom and Unity		
Total population & rank	613,090 (in 2001); 49th	**Major industries**	manufacturing, tourism, agriculture, trade, finance, insurance, real estate, government
Population density	66 per sq. mile (25 per sq. km)		
Population distribution	38% urban, 62% rural		
Largest cities	Burlington, Essex	**Places to visit**	Green Mountain National Forest, Vermont Marble Exhibit (Proctor), Maple Grove Maple Museum (St. Johnsbury)
Highest elevation	Mt. Mansfield, 4,393 ft. (1,339 m)		
Lowest elevation	Lake Champlain, 95 ft. (29 m)	**Web site**	www.state.vt.us

126 Virginia

LEGEND

★ State capital
• City
WYTHE County
▲ Mountain peak

National or other park
Swamp
Urban area

VIRGINIA

SOUTHEAST

Did You Know?

In 1619, Virginia had the first law-making body with elected representatives in the United States: The House of Burgesses

OHIO

PENNSYLVANIA

WEST VIRGINIA

KENTUCKY

TENNESSEE

NORTH CAROLINA

Mt. Rogers 5,729 ft (1,746 m)

MOUNT ROGERS NATL. REC. AREA

CUMBERLAND GAP NATL. HISTORIC PARK

Bristol, Abingdon, Marion, Norton, Wytheville, Galax, Bluefield, Blacksburg, Radford, Pulaski, Christiansburg, Salem, Roanoke, Bedford, Lynchburg, Martinsville, Danville, South Boston, Covington, Lexington, Buena Vista, Waynesboro, Staunton, Charlottesville, Harrisonburg, Luray, Front Royal, Warrenton, Winchester, Leesburg, Fredericksburg

Counties: BUCHANAN, DICKENSON, WISE, RUSSELL, SCOTT, WASHINGTON, LEE, SMYTH, TAZEWELL, BLAND, GILES, GRAYSON, CARROLL, WYTHE, PULASKI, MONTGOMERY, FLOYD, PATRICK, HENRY, FRANKLIN, ROANOKE, CRAIG, ALLEGHANY, BOTETOURT, BEDFORD, CAMPBELL, PITTSYLVANIA, HALIFAX, MECKLENBURG, BRUNSWICK, CHARLOTTE, LUNENBURG, NOTTOWAY, PRINCE EDWARD, APPOMATTOX, AMELIA, CHESTERFIELD, POWHATAN, CUMBERLAND, BUCKINGHAM, AMHERST, NELSON, ROCKBRIDGE, BATH, HIGHLAND, AUGUSTA, ROCKINGHAM, SHENANDOAH, PAGE, GREENE, ORANGE, ALBEMARLE, FLUVANNA, GOOCHLAND, LOUISA, SPOTSYLVANIA, MADISON, CULPEPER, RAPPAHANNOCK, FAUQUIER, WARREN, FREDERICK, CLARKE, LOUDOUN, DINWIDDIE, GREENSVILLE, EMPORIA

Rivers and lakes: Potomac River, Shenandoah River, Rappahannock River, James River, Appomattox River, Roanoke River, New River, Clinch River, Holston River, Powell River, S. Holston Lake, Smith Mountain Lake, John H. Kerr Reservoir, Lake Gaston, Roanoke Rapids Lake, Nottoway River, Meherrin River

---

Virginia Almanac

Nickname	Old Dominion
State capital	Richmond
Date of statehood	June 25, 1788; 10th state
State bird	Cardinal
State flower	Dogwood
State tree	Dogwood
State motto	Sic Semper Tyrannis (Thus Always to Tyrants)
Total population & rank	7,187,734 (in 2001); 12th
Population density	182 per sq. mile (70 per sq. km)
Population distribution	73% urban, 27% rural
Largest cities	Virginia Beach, Norfolk, Chesapeake, Richmond, Newport News
Highest elevation	Mt. Rogers, 5,729 ft. (1,746 m)
Lowest elevation	sea level
Land area & rank	39,594 sq. miles (102,548 sq. km); 37th
Average January temperature	35°F (3°C)
Average July temperature	75°F (24°C)
Average yearly precipitation	43 inches (109 cm)
Major industries	services, trade, government, manufacturing, tourism, agriculture
Places to visit	Shenandoah National Park, Colonial Williamsburg, Arlington National Cemetery, George Washington's Home (Mount Vernon), Thomas Jefferson's Home—Monticello (Charlottesville),
Web site	www.myvirginia.org

Virginia is the site of Jamestown, the first permanent English settlement in North America. From colonial sites like Williamsburg to Revolutionary and Civil War battlefields, historic plantations like Thomas Jefferson's Monticello and George Washington's Mount Vernon to Arlington National Cemetery—the burial place of President John F. Kennedy and honored U.S. soldiers—Virginia's historic sites span the history of the United States. It is the birthplace of eight presidents—more than any other state. Virginia is also a place of great natural beauty. The Blue Ridge Mountains, the Shenandoah Valley, Luray Caverns and Virginia's beaches are all major tourist attractions. The economy of Virginia started strong with the establishment of tobacco farming in colonial times. Virginia is thriving today because many diverse industries like shipbuilding, tobacco processing, tourism, government, and financial businesses make their home here. All of these industries create good jobs for Virginia's residents, so population growth is consistently higher here than in the rest of the United States. Most of the people live in the urban areas along Chesapeake Bay and the Atlantic coast.

LEGEND

Glacier

15,000 ft.
4,572.1 m

5,000 ft.
1,524 m

3,000 ft.
914.4 m

1,500 ft.
457.2 m

500 ft.
152.4 m

250 ft.
76.2 m

Sea Level

Physical

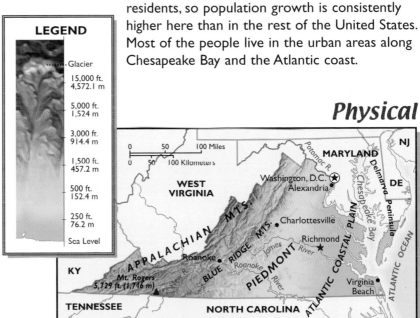

Economy – Chief Products

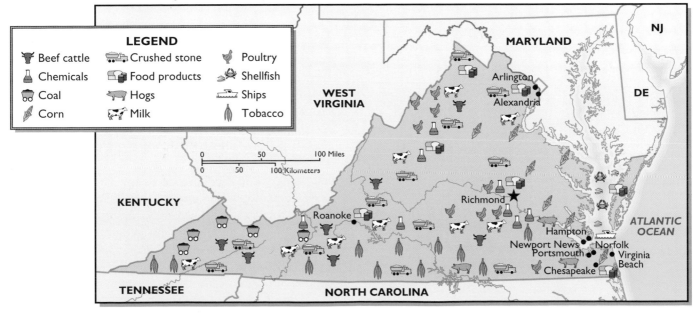

LEGEND

- 🐂 Beef cattle
- 🍶 Chemicals
- Coal
- 🌽 Corn
- 🚚 Crushed stone
- Food products
- 🐖 Hogs
- 🐄 Milk
- 🐓 Poultry
- 🦀 Shellfish
- 🚢 Ships
- Tobacco

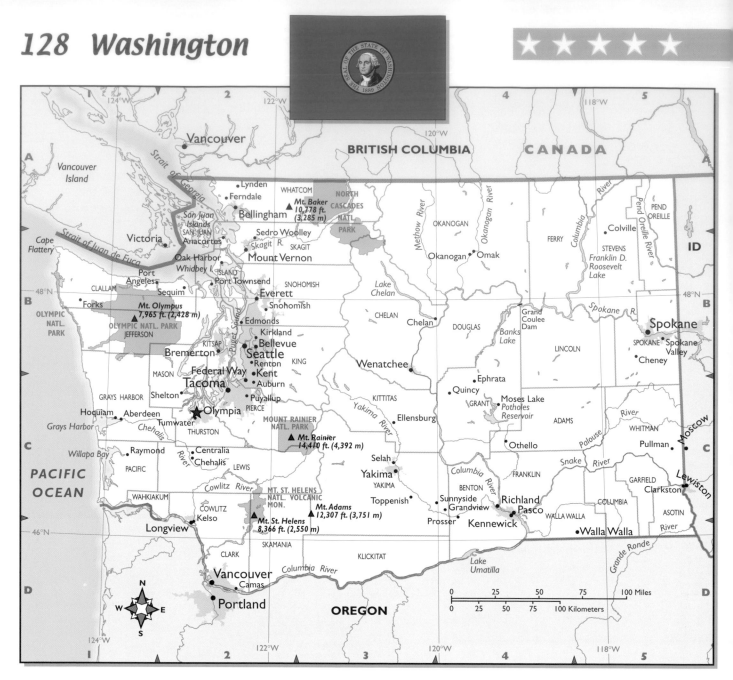

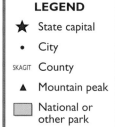

LEGEND

★ State capital

• City

SKAGIT County

▲ Mountain peak

National or other park

Urban area

WASHINGTON

WEST

Located in the upper-left corner of the lower 48 states, Washington has many important connections to Alaska, Canada, and countries across the Pacific Ocean. A number of people who live in Washington and many who visit as tourists come from Asia. Most of the state's residents live next to or very close to Puget Sound. Seattle is often selected as one of the most comfortable and appealing cities in the United States. The mountains of western Washington are famous for receiving much rain and snow and for having forests filled with tall trees. Mount Rainier is a 14,410-foot (4,392-m) active volcano and site of a popular national park in the Cascade Range. The eastern half of the state is quite dry. Fortunately, the Columbia River makes a large S-curve through central Washington and provides water for cities and farms. This geographical variety allows the state to produce many different agricultural products, especially wheat, apples, and grapes. The most important industrial products are airplanes and computer software.

Washington Almanac

Nickname	Evergreen State
State capital	Olympia
Date of statehood	Nov. 11, 1889; 42nd state
State bird	Willow goldfinch
State flower	Western rhododendron
State tree	Western hemlock
State motto	*Alki* (By and By)
Total population & rank	5,987,973 (in 2001); 15th
Population density	90 per sq. mile (35 per sq. km)
Population distribution	82% urban, 18% rural
Largest cities	Seattle, Spokane, Tacoma, Vancouver
Highest elevation	Mount Rainier, 14,410 ft. (4,392 m)
Lowest elevation	sea level

Land area & rank	66,544 sq. miles (172,349 sq. km); 20th
Average January temperature	32°F (0°C)
Average July temperature	65°F (18°C)
Average yearly precipitation	38 inches (97 cm)
Major industries	advanced technology, aerospace, biotechnology, international trade, forestry, tourism, recycling, agriculture
Places to visit	Mount Rainier National Park, Olympic National Park, Mount St. Helens National Volcanic Monument, Grand Coulee Dam, Seattle Center
Web site	www.access.wa.gov

Physical

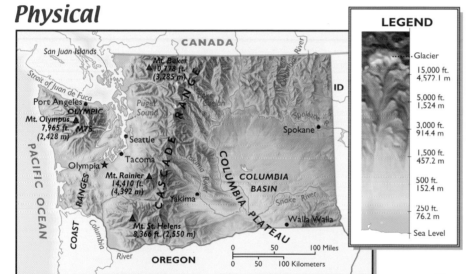

LEGEND

Glacier

15,000 ft.
4,572.1 m

5,000 ft.
1,524 m

3,000 ft.
914.4 m

1,500 ft.
457.2 m

500 ft.
152.4 m

250 ft.
76.2 m

Sea Level

Did You Know?

On May 18, 1980, a powerful and violent eruption lowered a volcano's elevation by more than 1,000 feet (305 m) and killed 57 people:

Mount St. Helens

Economy – Chief Products

LEGEND

- ✈ Aircraft
- 🐂 Beef cattle
- 🧬 Biotechnology products
- 🚚 Cement
- Coal
- 💻 Computers
- 🐟 Fish
- Forest products
- 🍎 Fruit
- 🐄 Milk
- Potatoes
- 🚛 Sand and gravel
- 🚢 Ships
- 🌾 Wheat

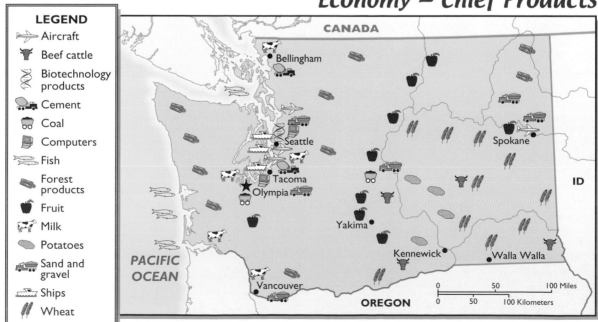

OHIO

Mansfield • I 82°W Canton •

Ohio River

Pittsburgh •

PENNSYLVANIA

Altoona •

Johnstown •

Newark •

40°N

Weirton

HANCOCK

BROOKE

Wheeling • OHIO

Moundsville •

MARSHALL

MARYLAND

Cumberland •

Berkeley Springs

Hagerstown

New Martinsville •

WETZEL

MONONGALIA

Morgantown •

Cheat River

MORGAN

BERKELEY

Martinsburg

Paden City

TYLER

Marietta • St. Marys •

PLEASANTS

MARION

Fairmont •

PRESTON

Grafton •

HARPERS FERRY NATL. HIST. PARK

JEFFERSON

Vienna •

Parkersburg •

Clarksburg

DODDRIDGE

TAYLOR

Bridgeport •

N. Br. Potomac River

Keyser •

MINERAL

HAMPSHIRE

Charles Town •

Winchester •

WOOD

Harrisville •

RITCHIE

HARRISON

Philippi •

BARBOUR

TUCKER

GRANT

S. Br. Potomac River

Moorefield •

WIRT

Little Kanawha R.

GILMER

LEWIS

Weston •

Buckhannon •

HARDY

Petersburg •

Ravenswood •

CALHOUN

UPSHUR

RANDOLPH

Elkins •

SPRUCE KNOB-SENECA ROCKS NATL. REC. AREA

Point Pleasant

Ripley •

Spencer •

ROANE

BRAXTON

Sutton

Spruce Knob 4,861 ft. (1,482 m)

MASON

JACKSON

Sutton Lake

WEBSTER

Franklin •

PENDLETON

Harrisonburg •

PUTNAM

Elk River

CLAY

Ohio River

CABELL

KANAWHA

Charleston ★

NICHOLAS

POCAHONTAS

VIRGINIA

Huntington

St. Albans •

Summersville •

Gauley River

Big Sandy R.

WAYNE

LINCOLN

GAULEY RIVER NATL. REC. AREA

38°N

Madison •

BOONE

Fayetteville •

FAYETTE

NEW RIVER GORGE NATL. REC. AREA

GREENBRIER

White Sulphur Springs •

Tug Fork

Guyandotte River

Logan •

LOGAN

Oak Hill •

RALEIGH

Beckley •

Lewisburg •

Greenbrier River

MINGO

Williamson •

WYOMING

Hinton •

SUMMERS

Bluestone Lake

MONROE

KENTUCKY

Welch •

MCDOWELL

MERCER

Princeton •

Bluefield

Bluefield •

Roanoke •

Blacksburg •

0 25 50 Miles
0 25 50 Kilometers

WEST VIRGINIA

SOUTHEAST

Did You Know?

Long frequented by Native Americans, and later surveyed by George Washington, this site became the first public spa in the United States:

Berkeley Springs

West Virginia is called the mountain state for good reason—there is hardly any flat land in the entire state. Made up of the Appalachian Mountains, rolling hills, and steep river valleys, West Virginia is the highest state east of the Mississippi River. Valuable hardwood forests cover four-fifths of the state. Because of the rugged terrain, large-scale farming is difficult. As a result, the wild character of the land has been maintained, attracting many visitors to the wilderness areas and whitewater rivers. West Virginia's mountains also contain another of its most important natural resources—coal and other mineral deposits. Before the Civil War, the state was part of Virginia. However, since West Virginia was not part of the slave plantation economy in the rest of Virginia, it sided with the Northern states in the war and became a state in 1863. This independent spirit is reflected in West Virginia's people, who are justly proud of their lovely state with its Appalachian music and dance as well as traditional crafts like pottery, quilting, and glassmaking.

West Virginia Almanac

Nickname	Mountain State
State capital	Charleston
Date of statehood	June 20, 1863; 35th state
State bird	Cardinal
State flower	Big rhododendron
State tree	Sugar maple
State motto	Montani Semper Liberi (Mountaineers Are Always Free)
Total population & rank	1,801,916 (in 2001); 37th
Population density	75 per sq. mile (29 per sq. km)
Population distribution	46% urban, 54% rural
Largest cities	Charleston, Huntington, Parkersburg, Wheeling
Highest elevation	Spruce Knob, 4,861 ft. (1,482 m)
Lowest elevation	Potomac River in Jefferson Co., 240 ft. (73 m)
Land area & rank	24,078 sq. miles (62,362 sq. km); 41st
Average January temperature	31°F (−1°C)
Average July temperature	73°F (23°C)
Average yearly precipitation	44 inches (112 cm)
Major industries	manufacturing, services, mining, tourism
Places to visit	Exhibition Coal Mine (Beckley), Harpers Ferry National Historic Park, New River Gorge Bridge (Fayetteville)
Web site	www.state.wv.us

Economy— Chief Products

LEGEND

- 🐂 Beef cattle
- ⚗ Chemicals
- Coal
- Forest products
- 🍎 Fruit
- 🥛 Glass
- ✖ Hay
- Oil and natural gas
- 🦃 Poultry
- Steel
- Tobacco

Physical

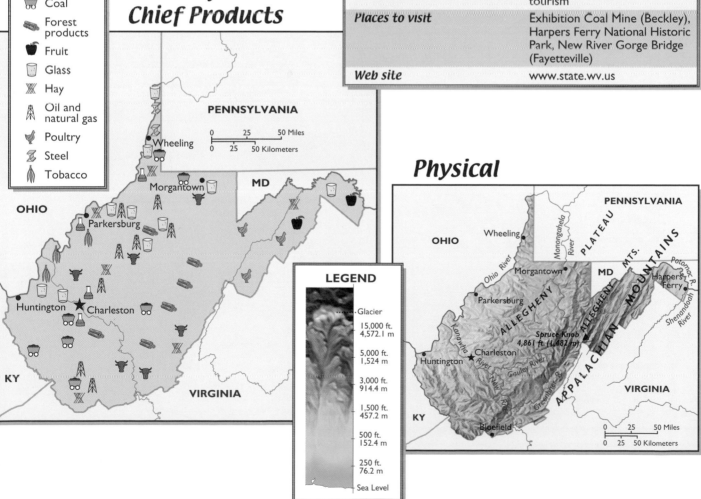

LEGEND

- Glacier
- 15,000 ft. 4,572.1 m
- 5,000 ft. 1,524 m
- 3,000 ft. 914.4 m
- 1,500 ft. 457.2 m
- 500 ft. 152.4 m
- 250 ft. 76.2 m
- Sea Level

WISCONSIN
1848

WISCONSIN

MIDWEST

Lake Superior

APOSTLE ISLANDS
NATL. LAKESHORE

Duluth
Superior

MINNESOTA

BAYFIELD

Ashland

Ironwood

MICHIGAN

DOUGLAS

ASHLAND

IRON

VILAS

FLORENCE

Iron Mountain

Hayward

BURNETT

WASHBURN

Lake
Chippewa

SAWYER

PRICE

ONEIDA

Rhinelander

FOREST

MARINETTE

Namekagon River

St. Croix River

46°N

Rice
Lake

BARRON

POLK

RUSK

Flambeau

Thornapple River

River

Timms Hill
1,951 ft.
(595 m) ▲

Wisconsin R.

LINCOLN

Merrill

LANGLADE

Antigo

MENOMINEE

Wolf River

Menominee R.

Peshtigo R.

Menominee
Marinette

DOOR

Sturgeon Bay

ST. CROIX

Hudson

DUNN

CHIPPEWA

TAYLOR

MARATHON

Wausau

SHAWANO

Shawano

OCONTO

Oconto River

Green Bay

St.
Paul

River Falls

PIERCE

Menomonie

Chippewa Falls

Eau Claire

EAU CLAIRE

CLARK

Marshfield

Stevens Point

WAUPACA

De Pere

BROWN

Green Bay

KEWAUNEE

Red Cedar R.

PEPIN

Chippewa River

Black River

WOOD

Wisconsin
Rapids

PORTAGE

OUTAGAMIE

Appleton

Fox R.

BUFFALO

JACKSON

Neenah

Lake
Poygan

CALUMET

MANITOWOC

Two Rivers

Manitowoc

TREMPEALEAU

Rochester

Winona

44°N

WAUSHARA

WINNEBAGO

Lake
Winnebago

Petenwell
Lake

Oshkosh

Mississippi River

LA CROSSE

Sparta

MONROE

JUNEAU

ADAMS

Castle Rock
Lake

MARQUETTE

GREEN
LAKE

Fox R.

Ripon

Fond du Lac

FOND DU LAC

SHEBOYGAN

Sheboygan

La Crosse

VERNON

Wisconsin Dells

Baraboo

SAUK

Portage

COLUMBIA

Beaver Dam

DODGE

WASHINGTON

OZAUKEE

Lake
Michigan

RICHLAND

CRAWFORD

Wisconsin River

Watertown

Menomonee Falls

West Bend

Prairie du Chien

Blue Mounds

IOWA

Madison

DANE

JEFFERSON

Waukesha

WAUKESHA

Milwaukee

West Allis

MILWAUKEE

Eagle

GRANT

Platteville

LAFAYETTE

Pecatonica River

GREEN

Monroe

ROCK

Janesville

Beloit

Rock River

WALWORTH

Whitewater

RACINE

KENOSHA

Racine

Kenosha

Dubuque

Mississippi River

IOWA

Fox River

Waukegan

Rockford

ILLINOIS

Cedar Rapids

Chicago

92°W

90°W

88°W

42°N

LEGEND
★ State capital
• City
DOOR County
▲ Mountain peak
National or
other park
Urban area

0   30   60 Miles
0   30   60 Kilometers

Wisconsin is a land of rolling hills and fertile farmlands. The extreme southwestern corner was somehow spared the effects of continental glaciation, and here many of the state's prettiest valleys and ridges can be found. About half of the state is farmland, and dairying is the most prevalent agricultural activity. Situated in the upper Midwest, Wisconsin has warm summers and winters that can be both long and severe. The presence of Lakes Superior and Michigan helps moderate the temperatures near the shore, but they can also provide more moisture for snow. These two lakes and the many smaller interior ones provide recreational activities for residents and tourists alike. Wisconsin's early settlers were immigrants from Germany, Poland, and Ireland. In the early 1900s, Wisconsin instituted many social, educational, political, and economic policies for the betterment of the people, and for decades Milwaukee, in the heavily populated southeast, elected socialists to political office. Today, Wisconsin remains one of the most socially conscious states.

Economy – Chief Products

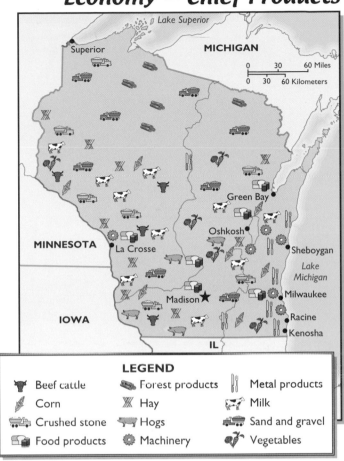

LEGEND

Beef cattle	Forest products	Metal products
Corn	Hay	Milk
Crushed stone	Hogs	Sand and gravel
Food products	Machinery	Vegetables

Wisconsin Almanac

Nickname	Badger State
State capital	Madison
Date of statehood	May 29, 1848; 30th state
State bird	Robin
State flower	Wood violet
State tree	Sugar maple
State motto	Forward
Total population & rank	5,401,906 (in 2001); 18th
Population density	99 per sq. mile (39 per sq. km)
Population distribution	68% urban, 32% rural
Largest cities	Milwaukee, Madison, Green Bay, Kenosha, Racine
Highest elevation	Timms Hill, 1,951 ft. (595 m)
Lowest elevation	Lake Michigan, 579 ft. (176 m)
Land area & rank	54,310 sq. miles (140,663 sq. km); 25th
Average January temperature	15°F (–9°C)
Average July temperature	70°F (21°C)
Average yearly precipitation	31 inches (79 cm)
Major industries	services, manufacturing, trade, government, agriculture, tourism
Places to visit	Circus World Museum (Baraboo), Old World Wisconsin (Eagle), Cave of the Mounds (Blue Mounds), Wisconsin Dells
Web site	www.wisconsin.gov

Did You Know?

This town on the shore of Lake Michigan claims to have invented the ice cream sundae in 1881:

Two Rivers

Physical

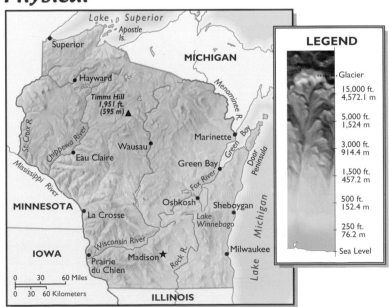

LEGEND

- Glacier
- 15,000 ft. 4,572.1 m
- 5,000 ft. 1,524 m
- 3,000 ft. 914.4 m
- 1,500 ft. 457.2 m
- 500 ft. 152.4 m
- 250 ft. 76.2 m
- Sea Level

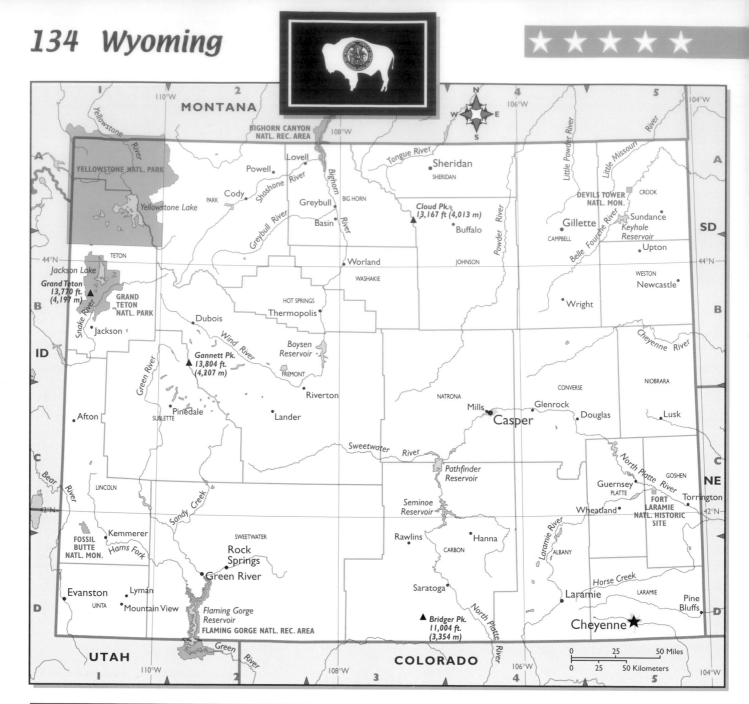

MONTANA

YELLOWSTONE NATL. PARK

Yellowstone Lake

BIGHORN CANYON
NATL. REC. AREA

Lovell
Powell
Cody
PARK
Greybull
Basin
Sheridan
SHERIDAN

Cloud Pk.
13,167 ft (4,013 m)
Buffalo
JOHNSON

DEVILS TOWER
NATL. MON.
CROOK
Gillette
CAMPBELL
Sundance
Keyhole
Reservoir
Upton

TETON
Jackson Lake
Grand Teton
13,770 ft.
(4,197 m)
GRAND
TETON
NATL. PARK
Jackson

Dubois

Thermopolis
HOT SPRINGS

Worland
WASHAKIE

Boysen
Reservoir
FREMONT

Gannett Pk.
13,804 ft.
(4,207 m)

Wind River

WESTON
Newcastle

Wright

ID

Afton
Pinedale
SUBLETTE
Lander
Riverton

Green River

NATRONA
Mills
Casper
Glenrock
Douglas
CONVERSE

NIOBRARA

Lusk

Cheyenne River

LINCOLN
Bear River

Sweetwater River

Pathfinder
Reservoir

Seminoe
Reservoir

North Platte River
GOSHEN
Guernsey
PLATTE
Torrington
FORT
LARAMIE
NATL. HISTORIC
SITE
Wheatland
NE

FOSSIL
BUTTE
NATL. MON.
Kemmerer
Hams Fork
Sandy Creek
SWEETWATER
Rock
Springs
Green River
Rawlins
CARBON
Hanna
Laramie River
ALBANY

Evanston
UINTA
Lyman
Mountain View
Flaming Gorge
Reservoir
FLAMING GORGE NATL. REC. AREA
Saratoga
Bridger Pk.
11,004 ft.
(3,354 m)
North Platte River
Horse Creek
Laramie
LARAMIE
Pine
Bluffs
Cheyenne

UTAH
Green River
COLORADO

0   25   50 Miles
0   25   50 Kilometers

Wyoming is the ninth largest state in size but has the smallest population of any state, with less than half a million people. Like Colorado, its neighbor to the south, Wyoming has a rectangular shape. Within its boundaries are wide arid plains, high snow-capped mountains, refreshing evergreen forests, and spectacular parklands. Yellowstone National Park with its Old Faithful geyser and hot springs, Grand Teton National Park, and Devil's Tower National Monument are all located here. Known as the Equality State, Wyoming Territory was the first to grant women the right to vote in 1869. The population is concentrated in a number of small cities, leaving vast expanses of open land used for cattle and sheep ranching and recreation. This shared environment draws the people of Wyoming together. It results in a friendly and open attitude toward each other and toward visitors. This is important, since tourism is slowly replacing the traditional economic foundations of coal and trona (soda ash) mining and ranching.

LEGEND

★ State capital
• City
TETON County
▲ Mountain peak
National or other park
Urban area

WYOMING

WEST

Wyoming Almanac

Nicknames	Equality State, Cowboy State	**Land area & rank**	97,100 sq. miles (251,489 sq. km); 9th
State capital	Cheyenne	**Average January temperature**	19°F (−7°C)
Date of statehood	July 10, 1890; 44th state	**Average July temperature**	67°F (19°C)
State bird	Western meadowlark	**Average yearly precipitation**	13 inches (33 cm)
State flower	Indian paintbrush		
State tree	Plains cottonwood	**Major industries**	mineral extraction, oil, natural gas, tourism and recreation, agriculture
State motto	Equal Rights		
Total population & rank	494,423 (in 2001); 50th	**Places to visit**	Yellowstone National Park, Grand Teton National Park, Fort Laramie National Historic Site
Population density	5 per sq. mile (2 per sq. km)		
Population distribution	65% urban, 35% rural		
Largest cities	Cheyenne, Casper, Laramie	**Web site**	www.state.wy.us
Highest elevation	Gannett Peak, 13,804 ft. (4,207 m)		
Lowest elevation	Belle Fourche River in Crook Co., 3,099 ft. (945 m)		

Physical

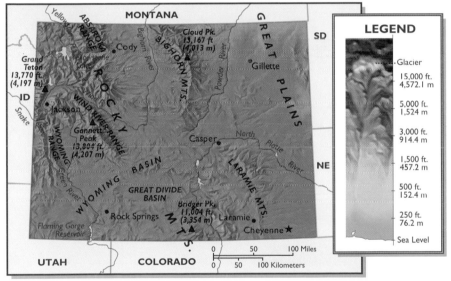

Did You Know?

The fastest animal in the Western Hemisphere is a Wyoming native:

Pronghorn antelope

Economy— Chief Products

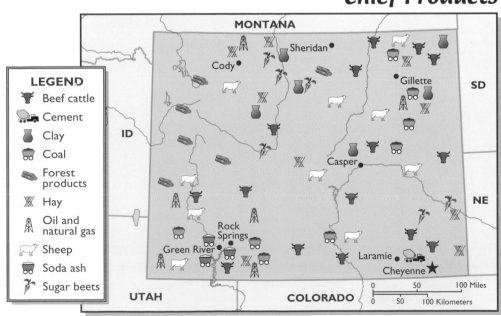

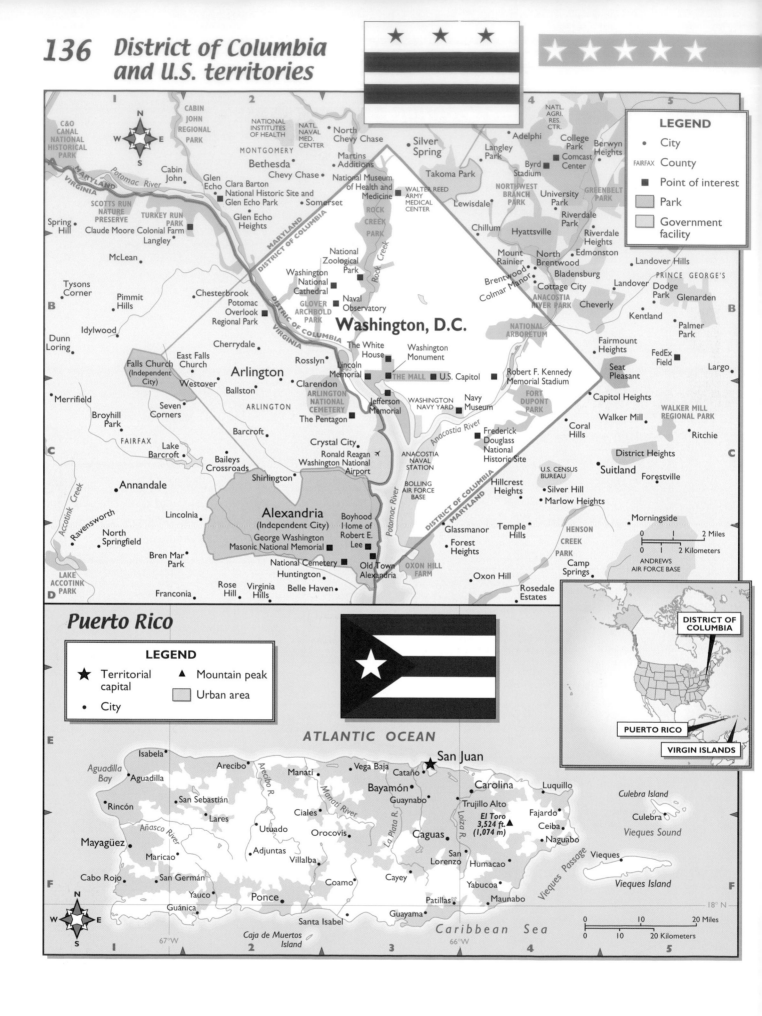

District of Columbia

C&O CANAL NATIONAL HISTORICAL PARK
CABIN JOHN REGIONAL PARK
NATIONAL INSTITUTES OF HEALTH
NATL. NAVAL MED. CENTER
North Chevy Chase
Silver Spring
Adelphi
College Park
Berwyn Heights
NATL. AGRI. RES. CTR.

MARYLAND
VIRGINIA
Potomac River
MONTGOMERY
Bethesda
Martins Additions
Chevy Chase
Takoma Park
Langley Park
Byrd Stadium
Comcast Center

SCOTTS RUN NATURE PRESERVE
Cabin John
Glen Echo
Clara Barton National Historic Site and Glen Echo Park
Somerset
National Museum of Health and Medicine
WALTER REED ARMY MEDICAL CENTER
NORTHWEST BRANCH PARK
University Park
GREENBELT PARK

Spring Hill
TURKEY RUN PARK
Claude Moore Colonial Farm
Langley
Glen Echo Heights
Lewisdale
Chillum
Hyattsville
Riverdale Park
Riverdale Heights
Landover Hills

McLean
MARYLAND
DISTRICT OF COLUMBIA
ROCK CREEK PARK
Mount Rainier
North Brentwood
Edmonston
PRINCE GEORGE'S

Tysons Corner
Pimmit Hills
Chesterbrook
Potomac Overlook Regional Park
National Zoological Park
Washington National Cathedral
GLOVER ARCHBOLD PARK
Rock Creek
Brentwood
Colmar Manor
Bladensburg
Cottage City
ANACOSTIA RIVER PARK
Landover
Dodge Park
Glenarden

Idylwood
Naval Observatory
Cheverly
Kentland
Palmer Park

Dunn Loring
Cherrydale
Washington, D.C.
NATIONAL ARBORETUM
Fairmount Heights
FedEx Field
Largo

East Falls Church
Rosslyn
The White House
Washington Monument
Seat Pleasant

Falls Church (Independent City)
Westover
Arlington
Ballston
Lincoln Memorial
THE MALL
U.S. Capitol
Robert F. Kennedy Memorial Stadium
Capitol Heights
WALKER MILL REGIONAL PARK

Merrifield
Seven Corners
Clarendon
ARLINGTON NATIONAL CEMETERY
Jefferson Memorial
WASHINGTON NAVY YARD
Navy Museum
Walker Mill
Ritchie

Broyhill Park
Barcroft
ARLINGTON
The Pentagon
FORT DUPONT PARK
Coral Hills

FAIRFAX
Lake Barcroft
Crystal City
Frederick Douglass National Historic Site
District Heights

Annandale
Baileys Crossroads
Ronald Reagan Washington National Airport
ANACOSTIA NAVAL STATION
U.S. CENSUS BUREAU
Suitland
Forestville

Shirlington
BOLLING AIR FORCE BASE
Hillcrest Heights
Silver Hill
Marlow Heights

Lincolnia
Alexandria (Independent City)
Boyhood Home of Robert E. Lee
Glassmanor
Temple Hills
Morningside

Ravensworth
North Springfield
George Washington Masonic National Memorial
MARYLAND
Forest Heights
HENSON CREEK PARK
Camp Springs
ANDREWS AIR FORCE BASE

Bren Mar Park
National Cemetery
Huntington
Old Town Alexandria
OXON HILL FARM
Oxon Hill
Rosedale Estates

Franconia
Rose Hill
Virginia Hills
Belle Haven

ANDREWS AIR FORCE BASE

0   1   2 Miles
0   1   2 Kilometers

Puerto Rico

ATLANTIC OCEAN

Isabela
Arecibo
Vega Baja
Cataño
★ San Juan
Aguadilla Bay
Aguadilla
Manatí
Bayamón
Carolina
Luquillo
Culebra Island

Rincón
San Sebastián
Ciales
Guaynabo
Trujillo Alto
Fajardo
Culebra

Mayagüez
Lares
Utuado
Orocovis
El Toro 3,524 ft. (1,074 m) ▲
Ceiba
Naguabo
Vieques Sound

Maricao
Adjuntas
Villalba
Caguas
San Lorenzo
Humacao
Vieques

Cabo Rojo
San Germán
Coamo
Cayey
Yabucoa
Vieques Island

Yauco
Ponce
Santa Isabel
Guayama
Maunabo
Vieques Passage

Guánica
Caja de Muertos Island
Caribbean Sea

67°W   66°W   18°N

0   10   20 Miles
0   10   20 Kilometers

DISTRICT OF COLUMBIA
PUERTO RICO
VIRGIN ISLANDS

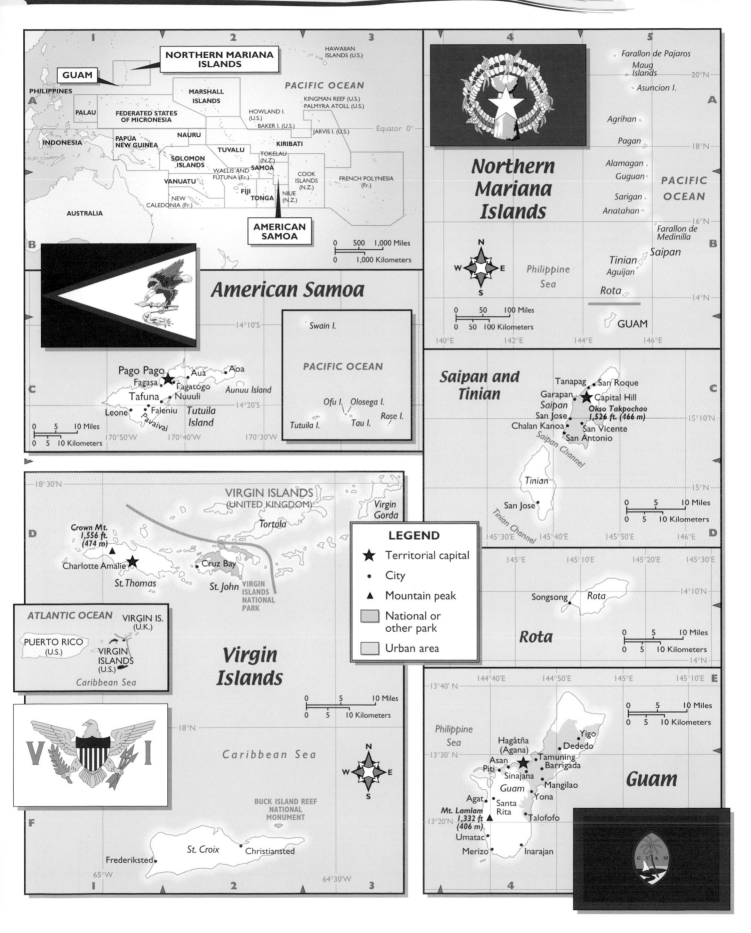

NORTHERN MARIANA ISLANDS

GUAM

PHILIPPINES

PALAU

INDONESIA

PAPUA NEW GUINEA

NAURU

TUVALU

SOLOMON ISLANDS

VANUATU

NEW CALEDONIA (Fr.)

AUSTRALIA

MARSHALL ISLANDS

FEDERATED STATES OF MICRONESIA

HAWAIIAN ISLANDS (U.S.)

PACIFIC OCEAN

KINGMAN REEF (U.S.)
PALMYRA ATOLL (U.S.)

HOWLAND I. (U.S.)
BAKER I. (U.S.)

JARVIS I. (U.S.)

Equator 0°

KIRIBATI

TOKELAU (N.Z.)

WALLIS AND FUTUNA (Fr.)

SAMOA

COOK ISLANDS (N.Z.)

FRENCH POLYNESIA (Fr.)

FIJI

TONGA

NIUE (N.Z.)

AMERICAN SAMOA

0   500   1,000 Miles
0   1,000 Kilometers

American Samoa

Swain I.

PACIFIC OCEAN

Pago Pago
Fagasa
Aua
Aoa

Fagatogo
Tafuna
Nuuuli
Aunuu Island

Leone
Faleniu
Tutuila Island

Pavaiavai

Ofu I.   Olosega I.

Tutuila I.   Tau I.   Rose I.

0   5   10 Miles
0   5   10 Kilometers

14°10'S
14°20'S

170°50'W   170°40'W   170°30'W

Northern Mariana Islands

Farallon de Pajaros
Maug Islands

Asuncion I.

Agrihan

Pagan

Alamagan
Guguan

Sarigan

Anatahan

Philippine Sea

Farallon de Medinilla

Tinian
Aguijan
Saipan

Rota

GUAM

PACIFIC OCEAN

N W E S

0   50   100 Miles
0   50   100 Kilometers

20°N
18°N
16°N
14°N

140°E   142°E   144°E   146°E

Saipan and Tinian

Tanapag   San Roque
Garapan   Capital Hill
Saipan
San Jose   Okso Takpochao
1,526 ft. (166 m)
Chalan Kanoa   San Vicente
San Antonio

Saipan Channel

Tinian

San Jose

Tinian Channel

15°10'N

15°N

0   5   10 Miles
0   5   10 Kilometers

145°30'E   145°40'E   145°50'E   146°E

Rota

Songsong   Rota

14°10'N

14°N

0   5   10 Miles
0   5   10 Kilometers

145°E   145°10'E   145°20'E   145°30'E

Virgin Islands

VIRGIN ISLANDS (UNITED KINGDOM)

Virgin Gorda

Tortola

Crown Mt.
1,556 ft.
(474 m)

Charlotte Amalie

St. Thomas

Cruz Bay

St. John

VIRGIN ISLANDS NATIONAL PARK

18°30'N

18°N

ATLANTIC OCEAN

PUERTO RICO (U.S.)

VIRGIN IS. (U.K.)

VIRGIN ISLANDS (U.S.)

Caribbean Sea

Caribbean Sea

BUCK ISLAND REEF NATIONAL MONUMENT

Frederiksted   St. Croix   Christiansted

N W E S

65°W   64°30'W

1   2   3

LEGEND

★ Territorial capital

• City

▲ Mountain peak

National or other park

Urban area

Guam

Philippine Sea

Yigo
Dededo
Hagåtña (Agana)
Asan   Tamuning
Piti   Barrigada
Sinajana
Guam   Mangilao
Agat   Yona
Santa Rita
Mt. Lamlam   Talofofo
1,332 ft
(406 m)
Umatac
Merizo   Inarajan

13°40'N
13°30'N
13°20'N

144°40'E   144°50'E   145°E   145°10'E

0   5   10 Miles
0   5   10 Kilometers

138 Index

Figures after entries indicate population, page number, and grid reference.

Figures after entries indicate population,
page number, and grid reference.

142 Index

Figures after entries indicate population, page number, and grid reference.

Figures after entries indicate population, page number, and grid reference.

Abbreviations

AS................American Samoa
GU................Guam
MP............Northern Mariana Islands
PR................Puerto Rico
VI................Virgin Islands